# Witchcraft and Magic

# Witchcraft and Magic
## Contemporary North America

*Edited by* HELEN A. BERGER

**PENN**

University of Pennsylvania Press
Philadelphia

The indexing of this book was underwritten by the deans of the College of Arts and Sciences at West Chester University through the College of Arts and Sciences Support and Development Awards.

10   9   8   7   6   5   4   3   2   1

Published by
University of Pennsylvania Press
Philadelphia, Pennsylvania 19104–4011

Library of Congress Cataloging-in-Publication Data

Witchcraft and magic : contemporary North America / edited by Helen A. Berger.
    p. cm.
Includes bibliographical references and index.
ISBN 0-8122-3877-X (alk. paper)
1. Witchcraft—North America.   2. Magic—North America.   3. Neopaganism—North America.   I. Berger, Helen A., 1949–

BF1584.N58W57 2005
133.4′3′0973—dc22                                                    2004065106

*To my brother*
*Jeff Berger*
*For a lifetime of support*

# Contents

Introduction    1
  *Helen A. Berger*

1. New Age and Magic    8
  *Michael York*

2. Witchcraft and Neopaganism    28
  *Helen A. Berger*

3. Webs of Women: Feminist Spiritualities    55
  *Wendy Griffin*

4. Shamanism and Magic    81
  *Michael York*

5. Lucumí: The Second Diaspora    102
  *Ysamur M. Flores-Peña*

6. Satanic Cults, Ritual Abuse, and Moral Panic:
   Deconstructing a Modern Witch-Hunt    120
  *Stuart A. Wright*

7. The Commodification of Witchcraft    137
  *Tanice G. Foltz*

*Notes*    169

*Works Cited*    177

*List of Contributors*    197

*Index*    199

# Introduction

## Helen A. Berger

Magic, always part of the occult underground in North America, has experienced a resurgence since the 1960s. Religions such as Witchcraft, Neopaganism, Goddess Worship, the New Age, and Yoruba (also known as Santería), which incorporate magic or mystical beliefs, have gained adherents, particularly among well-educated middle-class individuals.[1] Some of these religions, such as Witchcraft and Neopaganism, openly embrace magic. Others, most notably Yoruba, do not define their practices as magical, although outsiders have viewed the religion as incorporating and using magic. For example, healing within the Yoruba tradition involves both herbal remedies and divination to determine and address the underlying spiritual cause of the illness.

Magic and religion have traditionally been conceptualized as two separate entities (Malinowski 1954; Durkheim 1965). Religion is viewed as more complex than magic, involving the worship of and prayer to the divine, who can choose either to answer or deny those prayers. Magic, to the contrary, has been perceived as a series of techniques to control or manipulate the spirit world. The distinction is flawed, as magic neither in traditional societies nor in contemporary magical religions is solely a matter of manipulation. Shamans in traditional societies have always practiced their techniques within a larger spiritual framework. Similarly, contemporary magical religions define their practices within a religious or spiritual cosmology, not separate from it. There are some exceptions to this. Most notably, some non-Native American Shamans and some branches of the New Age believe their techniques can be separated from a larger spiritual cosmology. For these groups, magical techniques form an alternative technology that relies on tapping into natural sources that have been overlooked by science. The distinction between magic and religion is further blurred by the fact that mainline religions often have magical components—such as the belief in miracles or angels. For magical religions, the interweaving of magic and religion is stronger than it is in more mainline religions. Most of the religions discussed in this volume openly embrace magic as an important element of their spiritual path that empowers the

individual and puts him or her in touch with the forces of nature and/or
the divine.

The terms *magic* and *occult* are often used interchangeably by contemporary practitioners of magical religions. Magic has traditionally been seen as
distinct from the occult, which literally means "hidden knowledge." The
occult defines a series of beliefs and practices that are outside standard scientific reasoning. The purpose of occult practices, like magic, is to influence
the normal course of events through nonordinary means. Occultists, however, view their practice as either the forerunners of new scientific paradigms or as consistent with present scientific theory but misunderstood or
overlooked by traditional scientists. Books such as *The Tao of Physics* (Capra
1984) help to justify the view that today's occult or magical practices can
ultimately be explained by the new physics.

Contemporary magical religions, which developed and grew in the second half of the twentieth century, initially seemed to be an enigma as they
came on the heels of a period in which science appeared to be replacing
religion, at least among the educated. In most instances contemporary magical religions have come from abroad, but they have found fertile ground
in which to develop in North America. Witchcraft traveled to the United
States from the United Kingdom in the 1960s and attracted men and
women who were influenced by the counterculture. Once on American
soil, the antiauthoritarianism, environmentalism, and feminism that were
part of the social movements of that era transformed the religion, which
spread quickly across the United States and into Canada. As there is no
central authority in Witchcraft that determines orthodoxy or even membership, a number of sects have developed directly or indirectly from
Witchcraft that now fall under the umbrella of Neopaganism. Some of
these forms of Neopaganism differ only subtly from Witchcraft. Others,
such as Odinism and Druidism, are distinct forms that have their own history. Possibly the most important sect is feminist Witchcraft—or women-
only groups that venerate the goddess or goddesses to the exclusion of gods
(Eller 1993).

The emphasis on the Goddess in her three aspects—maid, mother, and
crone—as a symbol of women's empowerment in feminist Witchcraft has
subsequently influenced the larger Witchcraft and Neopagan movement
to, on the whole, become more openly feminist. Witchcraft, because of
the veneration of the Goddess, as well as the god force was always attractive
to women. Feminist Witchcraft, however, radicalized this image and made
groups that are inclusive of women and men think about inherent sexism
and heterosexism in their practices and rituals. Feminist Witchcraft has also
influenced the larger women's spirituality movement, which is a diverse
group incorporating those who explore goddess images as the main part of
the spiritual quest and those who incorporate it into more mainline reli-

gions. In some instances, the women's spirituality movement has fought for and won more inclusive God language, female images of the divine, and greater inclusion of women in leadership roles in mainline churches and synagogues. At other times, divisions have developed in religious organizations because of women's quest for the inclusion of goddess imagery and language in rituals and liturgy.

Although movements in their own right. New Age spirituality and "urban" shamans—that is, non-Native Americans who define themselves as Shamans—are influenced by the Witchcraft movement as well as by Native American spirituality. Interest in Native American spiritual traditions has blossomed in the past thirty years and has resulted in the growth of a pan-American concept of Native American spirituality, which focuses on the similarities and ignores the differences among Native American peoples. A division has developed among Native Americans between those who teach their religious and magical wisdom to outsiders and those who view the practice as a form of cultural imperialism. While the debates continue among Native Americans and those who are sympathetic to their cause, religious synchrony remains unabated (Rose 1992).

The New Age tends to be a catchall for those people who practice a series of techniques taken from Native Americans, Eastern philosophies, and the Western occult tradition that are aimed at enhancing the individual's consciousness. Many of the same techniques that are practiced by members of the New Age, such as astral projection, meditation, sending healing energy, are also practiced by Witches, Neopagans, and Shamans. Although there are important overlaps, there are, nonetheless, differences among these groups. The most important difference lies in how each group defines its activities. For most Neopagans and Witches, the focus of their practices is on the celebration of nature. Magic is viewed as part of that celebration and as a form of self-empowerment. Non-Native American Shamans are more concerned with techniques of power and control, and less with the larger spiritual system from which these techniques are taken. The New Age is in some ways the most diverse group. Some members are minimally involved; others view their practices as part of a larger spiritual path and lifestyle.

The New Age, Witchcraft, Neopaganism, non–Native American Shamanism, and women's spirituality have mostly attracted white middle-class individuals. Afro-Caribbean religions, such as Yoruba, Palo, Curanderismo, and Voodoo, have primarily attracted immigrants from the Caribbean and African Americans. Yoruba in particular is appealing to African Americans in search of a spiritual expression that has its roots in Africa. Yoruba came to North America from the Caribbean. The religion, which was developed by slaves, combines elements of West African spiritual traditions and Catholicism. Tensions have developed in the United States between African

American and Latino/Latina practitioners, each of whom focuses on a different aspect of the religion's history—emphasizing respectively the religion's African or Hispanic background.

All magical religions that have come to North America have been modified—sometimes in subtle, but sometimes in more dramatic ways—by their emigration. This is true as well for Afro-Caribbean religion. These religions in some instances have greater interaction with one another in North America than they did in their countries of origin. Practitioners of many different forms of Afro-Caribbean religion, as well as Witches, Neopagans, non–Native American Shamans, often shop at the same *botánicas* for herbs, candles, and other ritual materials, resulting in individuals learning about and at time incorporating elements of others' religious practice. Neopagans have attempted to engage in a dialogue and integration with Afro-Caribbean religions. Some Neopagans have studied with Afro-Caribbean spiritual teachers, and members of Afro-Caribbean religions have been invited to participate on Neopagan panels and in Neopagan study groups. However, the two traditions continue to be largely separate.

## SATANISM AND NEO-NAZIS

The terms *witchcraft, magic,* and *occult* are loaded words that for many conjure a set of images derived largely from popular culture. Witchcraft has traditionally been associated with evil. Contemporary Witches and practitioners of the New Age, Yoruba, and Voodoo have all been accused at some point of being Satanists or in league with the devil. All of these groups note that they are not Satanists. The Church of Satan in California, however, does take the label *Satanist.* Members of this group participate in magical acts and curses, but not in the worship of the devil, whom they see as within, not without. Their practices are largely an inversion of Christianity and a celebration of self-interest. For example, they celebrate the seven deadly sins as virtues and extol an extreme form of individualism. Although the group has received attention for its open avowal of Satanism, it does not advocate or participate in ritual murders, stealing, or any other illegal acts. The group is mostly of interest because it accepts the label of *Satanist,* a label rejected by most other groups (Moody 1974).

The belief in a satanic underground that participates in stealing babies, raping children, and murdering innocent people became widespread in the 1980s in the United States, Canada, and the United Kingdom. Although no longer taken as seriously, there continues to be outbreaks of communities worried about an organized satanic underground. The movement has been fueled by the religious right and one wing of radical feminism. The Federal Bureau of Investigation has concluded, after a thorough search for evidence of a satanic underground, that none exists. Nonetheless, the religious right, which believes that Lucifer's influence can be seen in daily life, continues to argue that powerful satanic groups exist nationwide and are involved in immoral and illegal acts. The satanic scare is also fueled by some radical feminists who have been influenced by the recovered-memory movement in psychology. This movement contends that all so-called recovered memories of childhood sexual and physical abuse are literally true. Some women, with the help of specialists in recovered memory, have claimed that their parents, their parents' friends, and prominent members of their community raped them in their childhood and murdered infants as part of satanic rituals. To date, no such case has been confirmed by evidence, such as records of missing babies or corpses in the areas where these women claim the rituals were performed. Some recovered-memory specialists have such a high proportion of clients who develop recovered memories that other psychologists have raised the concern that vulnerable individuals are being manipulated into creating memories. Nonetheless, throughout the United States and Canada, local police continue to receive reports of satanic groups (Victor 1993).

Although there is no evidence for a satanic underground, and those who do claim to be Satanists embrace only self-centeredness and not evil, another group—Neo-Nazi Pagans—is more problematic, as they have incorporated Nazi racism into their religious practice. Neo-Nazi Neopagans are distinct from other Neopagan groups, which emphasize the celebration of diversity in nature and among people and which tend to be politically liberal (Berger et al. 2003). White male prisoners and other disenfranchised men populate Neo-Nazi Neopagan groups.

Presently, although there are very few of these groups in North America (Kaplan 1996), they have gained the attention of the FBI which included them in their Megiddo report about potentially dangerous doomsday groups as the new millennium was arriving. The very existence of these groups raises questions for the Neopagan movement, which has traditionally avoided setting clear boundaries of who is and is not a member of the group. If Neo-Nazi Neopagans grow either in number or in notoriety, they may ultimately force the larger Neopagan movement to rethink their own openness as these right-wing groups may tarnish the image of the larger movement. This would be particularly irksome to those groups and individuals who have been working to have Witchcraft and Neopaganism recognized as a legitimate religion by participating in the Parliament of World Religions and other interfaith councils.

## COMMERCIALIZATION AND GROWTH

Although it is almost impossible to prove, there is a sense among researchers that all forms of magical religion are becoming more popular. The lack of bureaucratic structure of many of these religions makes it impossible to know the number of participants they each have today and whether or not there were fewer in the past. Nonetheless, both participants and those researching these groups have noted an increasing interest in them. There is a growing number of books, movies, television shows, and news stories about Witchcraft and other magical religions. These are indications of both increased interest in these religions and a growing commercialization.

The commercialization is most clearly seen in Salem, Massachusetts. Contemporary Salem has developed a tourist industry which capitalizes on the trials that occurred there in the seventeenth century. Salem calls itself "Witch City," and the local high school's football team is named the Salem Witches. There are shops selling T-shirts, witch dolls, and magical potions. This commercialization is symbolic of the larger process of selling the mystique of witchcraft and magic that may be seen in popular movies and television shows, which have increased interest in the occult among some segments of the population. For example, tarot cards are available at Barnes and Noble and other mainstream bookstores, as are books on horoscopes, love magic, and reading runes. There is an increasing belief in paranormal events in the general population (Berger et al. 2003). But there has also been a backlash. The most recent example of this is the response of the religious right to the *Harry Potter* books. In some communities, particularly in the more religiously conservative areas of the United States, there has been an attempt to ban these popular children's books from school and public libraries because they are viewed as presenting too positive a view of magic and witchcraft—even though the books do not advocate contemporary Witchcraft, Satanism, or evil. Magical religions, commercialization of magic, and a fear of magical religions have all been growing since the 1960s in North America.

## CONTEMPORARY MAGICAL RELIGIONS

The growing interest in magical religions and the occult in the second half of the twentieth and early twenty-first centuries has many sources. The social movements of the late 1960s and 1970s resulted in the questioning of all authority, including that of science and traditional religions. Changes in employment have resulted in individuals repeatedly transforming themselves to fit into new communities, new jobs, and new careers. Magical religions, which tend to focus on self-transformation, provide rituals and a worldview for their adherents that make this process central. Furthermore, these new religions speak to the social and political concerns of the current generation (Beckford 1984, 1992). Religions that have come most immediately from the Caribbean but have African roots appeal to African Americans interested in reclaiming their African heritage. For women, all forms of goddess worship potentially provide a feminist form of spirituality, which creates empowering metaphors and images. All of these religions call for a renegotiation of our relationship with nature, in which people come to view nature as sacred. Contemporary magical religions, are bringing into question Weber's prediction that rationalization and bureaucratization would result in the disenchantment of the world. For practitioners of magical religions the world is enchanted, the earth is alive, and magic is real. These magical religions look to the past for inspiration, but their practices and beliefs are clearly shaped by contemporary concerns and worldviews.

There are variations among contemporary magical religions. Those of Afro-Caribbean origin differentiate themselves to the greatest degree from the other religions that are discussed in this volume. Like the other religions, Afro-Caribbean religions view the world as enchanted and venerate multiple deities. The use of herbal healing and rituals to invoke power and to change the world are used by Afro-Caribbean religions, Neopagans, New Age practitioners, urban Shamans, and Goddess Worshipers alike. Within Afro-Caribbean religions, neophytes must be trained by elders in the community. Other forms of magical religions can be practiced alone or with others. A growing industry that supplies books and spiritual paraphernalia has developed that helps to create and maintain these solitary practitioners. The non Afro-Caribbean magical religions emphasize individual religious expression. The way in which magic is practiced, the spirits worshiped, or nature celebrated is viewed as a matter of individual choice. Nonetheless, for all these religions, a community of practitioners exists that influences their practice and to which even solitary practitioners belong. This community may no longer be a face-to-face community but one that is realized on the Internet, through reading the same books, and by occasionally interacting at open rituals and other gatherings. Although these religions share some similarities with earlier movements, such as Theosophy and Spiritualism, they provide a religious form that is consistent with the social and cultural trends at the end of the twentieth and beginning of the twenty-first centuries.

1

# New Age and Magic

## Michael York

The New Age movement emerged in the West during the closing decades of the twentieth century as a popular and alternate form or forms of spiritual practice. However, in Rothstein (2001:59), Masimo Introvigne already raises the issue of the demise of New Age spirituality—at least " 'classic' New Age [as] a movement dating back to the 1960s in the English-speaking world [and] based on the utopic, millenarian expectation of a golden age." Predictions of the failure of New Age are, of course, nothing new and have occurred regularly since at least Basil 1988 in which various scholars saw the New Age movement as fatally handicapped with its incorporation of false, scientistic principles. Gordon Melton (Basil 1988:51), in particular, foresaw the imminent self-destruction of the New Age movement through the pseudoscientization characteristic of much of its metaphysics. Ten years later, Melton (Barker and Warberg 1998) presented empirical evidence of the New Age crisis in reference to the bankruptcy of New Age bookstores, publishers, and journals. The commercialism of New Age was also cited as a destructive counterforce undermining from within the movement as a whole. Introvigne, however, takes the New Age crisis even further and claims that "[w]hen a millennial group announces a golden age, and fails to deliver, crisis is to be expected" (Rothstein 2001:60). In other words, it is conjectured that the movement's pending conclusion follows the established trajectory of any optimistic or progressive form of millennialism (Wessinger 1997, 2000). With no golden age occurring, this theory suggests, the movement invariably collapses—as Introvigne feels has already happened with the New Age.

The Introvigne-Melton evaluation and analysis, however, raise a series of questions. Foremost, while Melton (1986) originally understood New Age as a vision of radical mystical transformation for both the individual and the human collective—heralding the birth of a new millennium and entering the Western lingua franca through the celebratory affirmation of the 1960s rock musical *Hair*, namely, "This is the dawning of the Age of Aquarius," what exactly is the millennial vision of New Age, and how soon is it expected to occur? This question alone necessitates gaining some understanding of what New Age spirituality is for its adherents—not only how it is sociologically structured, but, more important, how does it relate to the paranormal? Additional questions concern how new or innovative is the New Age, how different is it from its recognized predecessors, where does it fit within the distribution of the world's theological thought, and how much is it essentially a North American phenomenon and export? All these questions relate to New Age's understanding of magic and its role in the human endeavor.

As the Rothstein (2001) volume makes clear through its focus, New Age religion is intimately connected with the emergence of "globalization"—particularly as a transnational and transocietal collective network of meaning. For globalization itself, Rothstein (2001:145) sees it as "a process of communication of public representations." Melton (Rothstein 2001:75), likewise, comprehends globalization primarily as the communication advances that, as far as innovative religious communities are concerned, grant them instant worldwide audiences. Consequently, the essential distinguishing feature of globalization is the rapidity of communication throughout the global arena—a rapidity on an unprecedented scale and one by which is fostered "the creation of a new global culture, one that increasingly becomes the broader social context of all particular cultures of the world" (Frisk in Rothstein 2001:38).

The various presenters to the Research Network of New Religions' 1999 Copenhagen conference on New Age religion and globalization basically agree that "the New Age is indeed a globalized phenomenon" (Introvigne in Rothstein 2001:66). While "[t]he majority of New Age books seem to be produced in USA, . . . American New Age books may not be very different from British, Danish, or Norwegian counterparts" (Mikaelsson in Rothstein 2001:97). Such countries as those of Scandinavia are rich, modern societies oriented toward the materialism, individualism and privatization that are themselves characteristic of the United States. But if Gilhus (Rothstein 2001:114) can assert that a "significant part of the European experience with new religions is the consummation of American New Age books," this is even more the case with regard to Canada.

Apart from the Francophone areas north of the U.S. border, North America has historically functioned as a single cultural pool—represented by two political states and with the Canadian voice manifesting essentially the more moderate and less chauvinistic of the two. While globalization itself dissolves and disrespects boundaries, it is balanced in the process of glocalization, that is—the customization of products or services intended for the global market to suit the local culture. Indeed, within Canada, these glocalized aspects of New Age have allowed more localized expression. Nevertheless, by and large Canadian and American versions of New Age represent if not a single spiritual community at least a single congeries of overlapping spiritual traditions that can be identified as New Age. The border between the two countries has not precluded the movement of spiritual ideas and practices freely across it. For instance, in the second half of the 1960s, Fritz Perls, the Jewish-German expatriate who had established group gestalt theory at the Esalen Center of Big Sur, California, and thereby helped to launch the Human Potential Movement, left the United States and founded his own disseminating center in Victoria, British Columbia. In general, there appears little to distinguish Canadian New Age from its American version. Since a detectable imbalance is to be witnessed in the direction of flow of New Age books and leaders from the United States— leading Wouter Hanegraaff (Rothstein 2001:16) to claim that "the global-ization of New Age spirituality is more appropriately seen as an aspect of global Americanization," a case can equally be made that the Canadian New Age spiritual scene simply represents a most successful instance of U.S. American cultural imperialism.

## WHAT IS THE NEW AGE?

Apart from the chiefly astrologically inspired metaphor of a new age—in other words, the Age of Aquarius, the contemporary New Age movement represents essentially a fusion of the American New Thought and Anglo-American Theosophical movements. Theosophy, as recognized by Melton (1986:87), is itself an offshoot development of American Spiritualism. All three together, along with such groups as the Arcane School of Alice Bailey, Earlyne Chaney's Astara Foundation, Mary Baker Eddy's Christian Science, and Edgar Cayce's Association for Research and Enlightenment as well as the Spiritual Frontiers Fellowship that coalesced around the seminars of Arthur Ford constitute what J. Stillson Judah (1967) identified as the American metaphysical movement—with its original impetus springing from the New England Transcendentalism of Emerson, Thoreau, Alcott, Fuller et al. Common to most if not all American metaphysical thought is the understanding that evil and negativity are illusions of the mind. Jesus Christ, rather than the Supreme Redeemer of a fallen humanity, functions here as the most achieved exemplar of one who discovered and realized the divine inner self.

Thanks to the oscillating shenanigans of the Fox sisters in 1848, the séance-centered Spiritualist craze quickly swept North American salons as a popular and innovative form of spirituality—extending to Great Britain and the European continent as well.[1] In many respects, the receptive em-brace of Spiritualism had already been prepared by the writings and teach-ings of the Swedish visionary Emanuel Swedenborg (1688–1772) and the Paris-based Austrian physician Anton Mesmer (1734–1815), who pro-moted the notion of animal magnetism. Spiritualism teaches that contact with transcendental beings and powers is possible for anyone. Mediumistic possession became, accordingly, an early means by which to challenge established authority. In this questioning and even rejecting of authoritative fiat, Spiritualism launched the democratization of religion in North America. Allegedly through our departed loved ones and deceased family members who have preceded us to the next world of Summerland and have gained consequently a new perspective on the divine, the godhead can speak to all of us—either mediumistically or directly from within our individual being. This more direct access to the spiritual counters institutionalizations that have traditionally enshrined hierarchical legitimacy. This "opening" to greater spiritual-vernacular equality is the Spiritualist legacy that has emerged in the late twentieth/early twenty-first centuries and of which the New Age movement is among several heirs.

But while the mission of Spiritualism was primarily "to prove" demonstrable forms of the paranormal, the theosophical creation of Helena Petrowna Blavatsky (1831–91) "elevated" itself into a more intense transcendental mode.[2] Theosophists are less interested in establishing their understanding to the scientific community and more desirous of gaining the reputed wisdom of discarnate beings. In a sense, Theosophy is the augmentation of Spiritualist ideas with Dharmic theology and metaphysics. Through theosophical thought, such Hindu and Buddhist notions as karma, reincarnation, bodhisattvas or ascended masters, a divine hierarchy, a divine plan for the world, akashic records, auras, *chakras*, and astral projection entered the American or Western metaphysical tradition (York 1995b:33). But with such Eastern understandings of the illusory nature of the phenomenal world and the divine spark of each individual that seeks reunion with God, Theosophy is to be seen as a recurrence of ancient Gnosticism, an early rival to Orthodox Christianity in its formative stages. This is, however, a Gnosticism that stresses the unifying essence of Eastern and Western religion and employs the symbolism and terminology of both spiritualities. But Theosophy's gnostic denial or devaluing of the tangible world has provided one of the chief streams of thought that infuses its New Age descendent—at least implicitly if not occasionally explicitly as well. From the New Age perspective, this gnostic-hermetic-theosophical continuum forms a timeless "Ancient Wisdom Tradition"—one that includes the Hermetic tradition of the magical, alchemical, and occult sciences attributed to Hermes Trismegistus (the ancient Egyptian god Thoth). But what becomes new and different with New Age is its insistence that esoteric knowledge is no longer the possession of a spiritual elite or the labor of prolonged and austere initiation but now belongs in the public domain.

The literary critic Harold Bloom (1996:221) argues for the recognition of a Gnostic American religion that focuses on angelology, the near-death experience and the approach of the millennium.[3] It is this religion, an

American form of Christianity that focuses more on the resurrected Jesus than on the crucified Christ, that Bloom (1996:2) argues is being exported worldwide. It seeks the divine as something within and contrasts with the European God of biblical history and doctrine. But its more popular, de-based, and commercialized forms Bloom recognizes as the panoply of New Age. Replacing outward belief with an "inward knowledge," Bloom's American Gnosticism and its crass New Age extension stress direct knowledge of God to be found within the self. At the core of both, there is an incessant predisposition "to focus on self, to see the human being as spiritual, and to interpret the processional and material side of the human condition more like an outer covering or a shell, not to be mistaken for the real person" (Gilhus in Rothstein 2001:118).

The real link between Bloom's gnostic New Age and its predecessor in Theosophy is the presupposition of an intermediate realm existing between the sensory and intellectual worlds—the dimension of angels and ascended masters. Whether considered *devas*, extraterrestrials, mahatmas, discarnates, or angelic beings, this panoply of the extrahuman or superhuman becomes a central locus for the magical in New Age thought. It is akin to the animism of paganism and shamanism but becomes more focused on the evolution of consciousness per se—whether in assuming the form of nature spirits, embodied in dolphins, solidified as crystals or transcendentalized as seraphim. The New Age always understands this magical conscious dimension as complementary to human consciousness—especially as a property of an emerging collective self. It becomes the source of spiritual assistance that leads to increased awareness. In New Age, life itself is equated to consciousness. It is considered inherent in everything and constitutes, accordingly, New Age's neosacral, neotranscendental vision (York 1995b:164). Vitality as consciousness allows a mystical-magical (re-)enchantment of the world but, in the New Age case, not a world that simply brims with life but one that is ever poised for the liberation that comes through ascending enlightenment. It is cosmic world forever on the move.

But if the New Age may be seen as a legacy of the gnostic and theosophical traditions, it is no less a culmination of New Thought spirituality.[4] This last may be traced essentially through a lineage that begins with Anton Mesmer and continues through Phineas Parkhurst Quimby, Mary Baker Eddy, and Emma Curtis Hopkins. But once again, in drawing as well from the school of New England's Transcendentalism emphasizing intuition and idealism, New Thought evolves a metaphysics that in all essentials is Eastern and Gnostic. While Mesmer's original notion of animal magnetism became steadily drained of any tangible etheric element by his American disciples, it was Christian Science founder, Eddy, who first clearly articulated the formulation that matter is a mental illusion. But whereas Eddy firmly anchored her transcendental reality on a relatively canonical understanding of the Christ of Christianity, Curtis and her students developed a less Christo-centric form of belief in a worldview comprising the mental-spiritual as the sole reality. New Thought stresses that evil is an aberrational product of the mind alone. This fictional negativity includes illness and poverty as well. The underlying reality is affirmed as one of pure goodness and light. Our failure to know this stems from enculturated and incorrect thinking that has lost an original understanding of the illusory nature of the physical world. In short, though the terminology is different, this is the Hindu concept of maya. Once again, with its Western manifestation, we are dealing with an expression of Gnosticism. As Peter Berger (1954:479), in his typology of sectarian movements, finds, in gnostic movements, "there is always indifference to the world"—at one level or another.

Bryan Wilson (1959:6) likewise delineates a gnostic or manipulationist response as a sectarian type and, for what is fully expressive of the New Thought–New Age continuum, is one for which "conventional Christian eschatology is replaced by a more optimistic and esoteric eschatology; Christ is a wayshower, an exemplar of truth, rather than a savior." In an understanding of sin and evil as illusions, there is no need for the salvational redeemer of the Crucifixion. If Berger's perception of indifference to the world may be indicative of an underlying and largely unarticulated tenor of New Age spirituality—as it certainly is of Bloom's American Gnosticism, Wilson captures the dominant and prevailing emphasis of the Western metaphysical tradition centered on an esoteric teaching or wishful mysticism that, all things being considered, appears to emphasize attainment rather than rejection of the worldly goals of success, health, wealth, happiness, and self-realization (York 1995b:30).

At the heart of New Thought and, consequently, New Age is the affirmation of positive reality. The many different Human Potential techniques that grow out of this affirmation and its welding of both psychology and/or physical therapy represent various technical means for putting this affirmation to effect (Drury 1989). Whether reiki, Silva Mind Control, Neuro-Linguistic Programming, Psychosynthesis or any of countless additional techniques, all are variations of the principle of "positive thinking" and psychotherapeutic practices that seek to hone the mental faculties into this self-disciplinary construct and way of viewing reality. Consequently, each "New Age" undertaking searches for its own means, its particular expression or lineage, in providing the alchemist's golden key or philosopher's stone that can foster the sought-after transformation. While Theosophy, coupled with various contemporary psychophysiological developments, provides much of the outer tools of New Age expression, it is the New Thought insistence on the power and reality of mind alone that constitutes the core of New Age spirituality *qua* spirituality.

THE ASTROLOGICAL CONTEXT OF NEW AGE MILLENNIALISM

The new age of New Age itself is a metaphor taken from the astrological register that informs much if not most of the North American metaphysical community. Astrology itself has since the beginnings of human civilization been a means for humanity to divine its place in the cosmic scheme and its navigation through the vagaries of terrestrial existence. Condemned by Christianity, it has nevertheless remained central to an atavistic core of humanity's fascination and dialogue with the cosmos. Its perennial persistence has also not been ultimately threatened by the rise of Western rationalism and scientific methodology. Beginning with the emergence of popular horoscope columns in newspapers from the late 1930s, astrology has steadily entered the vernacular idiom. In the counterculture of the 1960s, it formed the general lingua franca of subcultural exchange.

Consequently, following the astronomical principle known as the precession of the equinoxes, the New Age is recognized as the coming Age of Aquarius—a new era that follows the present age of Pisces lasting roughly two millennia. Much of this imagery follows a recasting of twelfth-century Joachim de Fiore's "Three Ages of History" theory, namely, the patriarchal age of God the Father, the present age of Jesus the Savior, and the coming age of the Holy Spirit (Melton et al. 1990:30). The first of these, the age of Aries, is understood as that which lasted up to the birth of Christ. It represents the period of the Old Testament. The present age has been the New Testament "Age of the Son"—as different from its predecessor as its successor is to be from it. De Fiore understood the Age of Pisces as embodied in the Roman Catholic Church. And according to New Age astrological interpretation, the future age will be a time of great and millennial changes. In the understanding of New Age's Church Universal and Triumphant, as Jesus Christ has been the pivotal figure of the now concluding Piscean age, the equivalent for the new era will be the Ascended Master, Comte de Saint-Germain, a legendary eighteenth-century occultist and magician (York 1995a:72). From this perspective, Saint-Germain is an exemplar of spiritual ascendancy who serves as the chief model for human endeavor in the Age of Aquarius.

But any expectation of a future golden age in the Western context almost by default must navigate the doomsday prophecies of the Book of Revelation. The New Age scenarios vary significantly and tend to conform according to the particular emphasis of New Age practice: occult, spiritual, or social (York 1995b:36f). While scholars frequently insist on the "demise" of New Age concomitant with the nature of progressive millenarianism (for example, Introvigne in Rothstein 2001), such predictions may in fact be "jumping the gun." True enough, at the time the coming of the new Age of Aquarius was first heralded in the musical *Hair*, it was often couched in terms of an imminent quantum leap of collective consciousness. Increasingly since the late 1990s, however, there has been less emphasis on this "imminence." While catastrophic millennianism as outlined by Wessinger (2000) has a more built-in safety valve in that it can always consider upheaval events (such as the September 11 World Trade Center attack) as "signs" of what is to come, progressive millennialism is presumed to be handicapped when its supporters proclaim a golden age but fail to deliver. Nevertheless, and despite Introvigne's assessment that ultimately "the New Age *went* the same way as many other forms of progressive millennianism before it" (Rothstein 2001:60),[5] the contended crisis for New Age is not as clear-cut as it might seem. For one, there are competing expectations of the form of the Aquarian age and even how it will arrive. But even more important, work by British astrologer Nicholas Campion has uncovered the wide discrepancy that exists even among the astrological predictions of the Age of Aquarius. In the precession of the equinoxes, the zodiacal constellations shift in relation to the fixed point of the vernal equinox. While this springtime event of the equal day–equal night occurs against the astrological sign of the fish, we are said to be in the Age of Pisces. A complete rotation occurs approximately every 26,000 years, and this means that the sun shifts one degree every 72 years relative to the fixed stars of the zodiac. To complete a full zodiacal sign, it requires 2,160 years. The confusion arises, however, due not only to competing systems of astrology (for example, the tropical Western zodiac defined by the equinoxes and solstices, the Indian sidereal system in which the astrological signs correspond to the actual constellations rather than simply to 30 degrees of the sky) but, more important, over confusion when an age supposedly begins. Campion has been able to collect 95 published dates from astrological literature. The span between the various dates range from 1457 to 3599 c.e. (Campion 2000:10–16). Consequently, any impending start of the Age of Aquarius is not necessarily supported by astrological considerations. The New Age may yet be sometime off, though—as a spirituality—it seeks to prepare the way for whenever the golden age is to come.

DIFFERENT UNDERSTANDINGS OF NEW AGE EXPECTATION

But if New Age is a concern with preparing for the millennium, there are different understandings of how that "quantum leap" is to occur. Apart from the diverse range of tools and products associated with New Age, some of the sharpest differences between the movement's various components are to be found precisely on this point. The millennium is not only differently conceived, but it is also expected differently.

The more Christian wing of New Age can often entertain a belief that the New Age will be preceded by apocalyptic earth changes and upheavals. For those of this persuasion, the New Age is to be a literal, historical passage of time rather than simply a metaphor for mystical change. Adopting a premillennial form of Christian millenarialism, the period of terrestrial catastrophes is expected to culminate with the Second Coming of Christ, who will inaugurate the New Age millennium. Apocalyptic millennianism clearly takes this seminal inspiration from the biblical Revelation to John. Among its chief expressions within New Age literature are the works of Edgar Cayce and Ruth Montgomery. But whether the New Age is to be preceded by physical and social upheaval or not, catastrophic millenarianism is part of a broader view that recognizes the new epoch as somehow triggered by supernatural intervention. The onus of change lies beyond human control.

In contrast to this more magical arrival of the new era of peace, harmony, and collective consciousness, the more prevailing New Age position is "postmillennial." Whether there is to be a literal "Second Coming" at the conclusion of a "thousand years" of righteousness or not, the New Age is to be essentially the product of human effort rather than something engineered through a deus ex machina principle. But again there are contrasting views on the form human effort is to take. Social New Agers argue for collective and environmental reform, canceling world debt for undeveloped nations, redistribution of the world's wealth on a more equitable basis: in short, it is to be brought about literally through worldly activism—much if not most of it beginning at grassroots levels. Spiritual New Agers, by contrast, stress personal, individual development through, chiefly, meditation and yogic discipline. The argument claims that when a critical mass of enlightened people is reached, the New Age will come about through spiritual catalysis. The foremost person for the social position is Marilyn Ferguson, editor of the *Brain/Mind Bulletin* and *Leading Edge Bulletin* and author of *The Aquarian Conspiracy* (1987). The spiritual argument, on the other hand, has been most clearly articulated by the Maharishi Mahesh Yogi, but others whose position essentially supports this approach range from Baba Ram Dass to Deepak Chopra. Much of the spiritual expectation of the New Age coincides with the Human Potential Movement. In addition to this last's founding technique of meditation, the Human Potential spiritual arsenal includes yoga, ritual dance, chanting, visualization, gestalt, encounter, analysis, body cleansing, bodywork, rolfing, reflexology, reiki, and shiatsu among a host of others. In preparing for the new millennium, spiritual New Agers seek self-improvement and inner personal harmony. Among the many practitioners we can associate with this spiritual approach to the New Age, we consider Louise Hay, Shakti Gawain, Shirley MacLaine, Matthew Fox, Meher Baba, Bhagawan Rajneesh/Osho, Adidam, and John-Roger Hinkins. The underlying theme behind the medita-

tive and self-help techniques is expected to be exponential—culminating
in what Thomas Kuhn refers to as "paradigm shift" (Ferguson 1987:28).
The Maharishi identifies the threshold for achieving collective consciousness as involving the square root of 1 percent of the population. When a
sufficient number of people achieve a "higher state of being," they serve as
the catalyst for the "spiritual leap" of their community and, ultimately, of
the world at large. We find a similar understanding in the Triangle meditations of Alice Bailey's World Goodwill, Lucis Trust, and Arcane School
practices.[6]

This same concept is held by the social reformers as well. Ferguson
speaks of the growing "Aquarian conspiracy" as part of the process of
breaking the established "cultural trance" of the status quo. Following in
the spiritual-meditative tradition of Neem Karoli Baba, both Ram Dass and
Ma Jaya Bhagavati additionally stress the central notion of *sewa* (service),
and this brings them no less into the social approach as well. For Matthew
Fox (1999:127, 156), the purpose of "creation spirituality" is, through education and celebration, to develop compassion and the values of heart and
soul. While much of the purely spiritual focus on self appears to be narcis-
sistic and egoistic, for those of the reformist persuasion, the self and society
are inseparable. Consequently, and in line with Bryan Wilson's expectation
that utopianism in its millennialist form tends "towards the establishment
of a more rational order" as people count less on the supernatural and more
upon themselves in the construction of a new social order (1973:494), both
the spiritual and social approaches to the new age of New Age are postmillennial, nonapocalyptic and metaphorically visionary. While the magical is
still present—especially in much of the seminal ideology of the gnostic-
theosophical/New Thought–New Age continuum, it becomes increasingly less apparent inasmuch as the New Age comes to involve pragmatic
and sustainable efforts for institutional change.

## CRITICISMS OF THE NEW AGE

But as laudable as some of the New Age aims are, the movement as a
whole—disparate and at best a loosely coordinated confederation of contrasting beliefs, techniques, and practices—is frequently lampooned as self-
indulgent, superficial, naïve, and childish. At its worst, New Age is considered not only insipid but directly dangerous—whether psychologically and
regressively (Faber 1996) or socially and fascistically (Sjoo 1989). Less
sweeping than these extremist opinions, the New Age is nevertheless generally condemned for its introspective indulgence as well as elitism and
irrationality. Charges of narcissism (as a "me religion") have been leveled
against the movement from the start. Coupling rampant self-interest with

the consumerism that has become characteristic of late modern–postmodern society in the West, New Age consumption often appears as shallow and ephemeral—the complaint of Harold Bloom (1996:74) who wishes instead for a literary gnosticism based on the kabbalah, hermeticism, Christian Gnosticism and Shiite Sufism "that can serve as a spiritual standard of measurement." Aldous Huxley's "perennial philosophy" has, in New Age hands, been transformed into something that often seems to be little more than a license to contemporary religious commercialism.

It is precisely this pastiche element of New Age that is attacked by traditionalists as appalling eclecticism. With no coordinating authority, New Age adopts on an ad hoc and willy-nilly basis. Whatever works to provide a spokesperson a disseminating stage and ready-made audience appears to become the latest New Age incorporation. Superficial consumption—based on "what works for me now"—tends to render New Age in the eyes of many, let alone its critics, a worst-case scenario of spiritual faddism. The bricolage that continues to augment the New Age repertoire can seem like an ever-growing bag of gimmicks and clever tricks.

The adoption of ready-made spirituality is increasingly the kind of religious consumerism that is itself identified as New Age. While the "Wisdom Tradition" might be considered by Bloom as the esoteric and hermetic tradition of ancient Gnosticism, New Age spirituality contends—even insists—that the formerly exclusive and private areas of occult knowledge are now part of the public domain. This complete democratization of religion that New Age espouses challenges any and all private ownership of spirituality. New Age identifies itself as the Age of Information—one that is increasingly accelerated by electronic and technical invention (Davis 1998:239). The rapid exchange of information that has become the hallmark of the transition into the twenty-first century is by the New Age insistence unrestricted by the former boundaries demarcating private possession. New Age claims its rightful use of any and all the world's religious and spiritual traditions (York 1997:414).

But how this collective ownership of all spirituality translates for those who do not share the same open access views of New Age is a different matter. Many condemn as cultural appropriation what New Agers see as freedom. While all religions have and do appropriate selected elements from each other, New Age has pursued this process with unbridled abandon. For those people whose cultural identity is particularly under threat—people such as the American Indian or Australian Aborigine, New Age appropriation of their traditions, practices, and institutions is perceived as an appropriation of their very existence. While the Native American community of North America divides on this issue of sharing spiritual teachings with Euro-Americans, the Lakota have spearheaded the movement that seeks to reclaim what has been taken by "New Agers and Neopaganists."

Attempts to draft a "Declaration of War" on this issue of appropriation by the American Indian community during the Chicago Parliament of World Religions in 1993 failed, but the Lakota have proceeded subsequently to ratify the declaration on their own (York 1994).

The issue of spiritual rights and cultural ownership is one that a world undergoing a process of steady globalization must confront. It is, however, an issue that calls forth no clear answer. From the New Age perspective, everything is available. There are no forbidden frontiers. But from the perspective of those unwilling victims or recipients of New Age acquisition, New Age appropriation represents simply the latest stage of Western imperialism. Whatever else they may also be, the September 11 attacks in New York and Washington spring from the same animosity that arises in a world of unequal exchange. Whether the global pool of spiritual truth belongs to no one but to everyone or not, it is perhaps the key issue that New Agers must themselves confront if indeed theirs is a religiosity that does indeed respect the integrity of all peoples. The question relates to whether the New Age is simply another name for Westernization if not Americanization—one that reduces all to the same—rather than an augmentation of a truly pluralistic world of diversity.

## NEW AGE THEOLOGY

William Sims Bainbridge (1997:386) sees that the "forms of religious movement most closely associated with the New Age are occult, Neopagan, and Asian," and he is joined by many other scholars who argue the same: Paul Heelas (1996), M. D. Faber (1996), Lowell Streiker (1990), Peter Spink (1996), even Harold Bloom (1992, 1996). Nevertheless, it is important to recognize the Theosophical and New Thought origins of the predominant and essential thrust of New Age. While contemporary Western Paganism has likewise been strongly influenced by similar Freemasonic and perhaps Rosicrucian lodges it harkens much more toward the ancient paganisms that preceded Christianity. It is true that the overt practices often found within present-day Paganism that are concerned with ceremonial, or "high," magic owe much to the hermeticism that developed from the likes of Orphism, Neo-Pythagoreanism, and Neo-Platonism. Nevertheless, these last must be understood as nominally but not generically pagan. The decisive factor is theological, and the decisive point here is that to understand New Age theology, it must be understood in contrast to the theology of its emerging rival—namely, contemporary Western paganism.[7]

It is, of course, not to be denied that New Age and Neopaganism are natural allies vis-à-vis canonical, mainstream forms of religion. Both place exegetical stress on the individual him- or herself. Both represent democratizations of religion. Both are from the traditional perspective outsider heresies. Both also strongly fuse the religious and the psychological. And both draw their adherents chiefly from the broader religious consumer market. But it is not this market that itself is New Age. The market is the array of choice within what Colin Campbell (1972) identifies as the "cultic milieu." But within that range of choice exists two radically different theologies: paganism and gnosticism.

As to be seen in its largely Theosophical and New Thought heritage, New Age is in its fuller development a contemporary form of Gnosticism—perhaps not the esoteric and intellectual expression of Bloom's American Gnosticism, but a transcendental positing nonetheless. With no overall or coordinating authority that can speak for the movement as a whole, the dialogue between its New Age emphasis and any residual pagan elements remains to date largely unarticulated. But in the increasing divergence between the New Age and Neopagan movements, the theological divide becomes ever clearer.

For paganism, the physical world is considered sacred in and of itself. Divinity is recognized as immanent in the tangible reality of existence—not as something fundamentally transcendental or "wholly other." Unlike the gnostic orientation that either denies the reality of the corporeal or at least any intrinsic value to it, paganism celebrates the material as mother or at least as the sacred *primus inter pares*. There is no desire to "escape" from the tangible or be free from it.

Consequently, the trajectories or goals of paganism and New Age are different. In New Age, the purpose of existence is to reunite with the primordial source—often represented metaphorically as reclimbing the ladder of being. The physical represents the furthermost emanation from the One or Good. The human body is a tomb (*soma sema*) from which the gnostic wishes to escape. There is a quest to return to the beginning.

Paganism, by contrast, celebrates the body and the physical. Evolution is not devolution, a furthering from the divine, but its perpetual and open-ended expansion. Consequently, there is no permanent return to the source, but a constant development from it. While the chief Pagan metaphor is that of the circle, the cyclic becomes an understanding of renewal: birth, growth, culmination, decline, death, rebirth. There is no ladder of unidirectional ascent but, instead, and at best, a spiraling evolution—as suggested, for instance, in the title of ecoactivist Starhawk's best-seller, *The Spiral Dance* (1979). With gnostic-centered New Age, by contrast, the cycle is not continuous but a one-time turning—completing when the divine spark that is the heart and soul of the individual remerges with that from which it came. New Age ultimately seeks a cessation of individuality rather than the endless exploration that is countenanced by the Pagan.

In this light, while both spiritualities generally entertain the notion of reincarnation, the cycle of birth-death-rebirth is radically different for each. Following in the understanding of Pythagoras and Plotinus as well as the Dharmic traditions of Hinduism and Buddhism, rebirth in New Age presents the opportunity to obtain gnosis or to clear one's register of karmic debt. Life is, in a sense, a punishment—a separation. Its final purpose is to merge with the One, the Good, Brahman and obtain *samadhi, moksha,* liberation, and release. Inasmuch as New Age primarily follows in the footsteps of these traditions, the New Ager's implicit goal is ultimately the transcendence of life. For the pagan, on the other hand, rebirth, or reincarnation, provides the opportunity for a return to life, its pleasures, and the occasion for further acquisition of understanding. While it is true that not all New Age is wedded to the idea of obtaining either a final state of Ascended Masterhood or extinction—such as James Jacob Hurtak considers in his *Keys of Enoch* (1987:909; see also York 1995a:80) where *samadhi* is presented as the false belief that no further evolution is required, New Age is almost invariably centered on a state or dimension that is "superior" or "beyond" the here-and-now of telluric human existence. The transcendence of earth, whether through cessation of repeated rebirths or absorption into "higher" realms of extraterrestrial beings (angels, space brethren, bodhisattvas, et cetera) is implicit in New Age theology. Nature is an illusory veil that the spiritual adept wishes to penetrate and pass beyond.

In its broadest sense, New Age is the present-day continuation of historic Western esotericism. Wouter Hanegraaff (1996) recognizes five elements as fundamental to the movement: (1) this-worldliness in a weak form, (2) holism, (3) evolutionism, (4) religion that is secularized while psychology itself is increasingly desecularized, and (5) the persistent expectation of the New Age as a return of emotionality, sensitivity, and spontaneity in Western society. In its own transcendental bias, New Age spirituality champions the divine individual's inalienable sovereignty—one that virtually pushes through the solipsistic threshold in the creation of the individual's own universe. Consequently, at the heart of New Age theology is its epistemological foundations. Unlike the prevailing Western empirical assumption that posits a "world-out-there" independent of our knowledge of it (epistemological realism), New Age tends to assume a metaphysical idealism that is less one that understands the world-out-there simply as independent but of the same nature of the mind and more one that holds that the only knowable world and range of reality are one's own ideas. This form of epistemological mentalism, or subjective idealism, when followed to its logical conclusion, holds that nothing exists other than "myself and my ideas." A classic statement of this position is made by Shirley MacLaine following a New Age New Year's Eve ceremony. She realized that "*I was the only person alive in my universe.* . . . [Human] beings feeling pain, terror, depression, panic, and so forth . . . were all characters in my reality, . . . only reflections of myself."[8] MacLaine is endeavoring to legitimize changing the world by changing herself, but she is articulating metaphysical and epistemological assumptions latent in the New Thought origins and core of the New Age movement.

## NEW AGE MAGIC

When it comes to magic, the New Age position is to be sharply contrasted from that of contemporary Western Paganism—in particular its ceremonial magician and Wiccan expressions—that tends to adopt Dion Fortune's understanding of magic as "the changing of consciousness at will." As Adler (1986:154) finds, "most Witches and Neo-Pagans do not link 'magic' with the 'supernatural.'" Crowley (1996:39) sees "magic as a system of spiritual development," and Starhawk (1979:142) recognizes it as a device for developing "power-from-within." Within modern-day Paganism, magic is essentially the practice of techniques that aim to alter consciousness.

For New Agers, on the other hand, magic as a concept or tool is not something that is emphasized. As Tanya Luhrmann (in York 1995b:136) explains, most New Agers "would not use the word 'magic' to describe their doings." Recognizing that "while much of Occult teaching has a direct bearing on New Age philosophy," Jane Alexander (1989:20) feels "it's fair to say that the overwhelming majority of New Agers would consider themselves neither magicians or witches." Nevertheless, hermetic affinities exist within both the New Age and Neopagan movements, and a New Age spokesperson such as Shirley MacLaine (1987:243) can affirm that the "loss of magic is the denial of unlimited possibility." In general, Wiccan magic may be understood as similar albeit not identical to New Age visualization (York 1995b:157).

But though magic may be nominally absent from most of New Age, it is nevertheless an operative notion throughout much of the movement. Magic itself, when recognized as a legitimate principle or force, represents a violation of the natural law of equal exchange.[9] What reputedly occurs in the magical act is the substitution of something for something else of greater worth or desirability. In this sense, it is akin to prayer as an attempted shortcut to the rewards sought. In traditional magic of the quid pro quo, an offering or act of limited, symbolic, or token value is presumably exchanged for an increased advantage or quality of greater worth—whether a magic word for a magical result or a tangible offering for health, wealth, success, or happiness. Much of the Human Potential Movement is constructed on this principle of violation, and the effort to exchange the lesser for the greater becomes the decisive factor in such techniques as homeopathy, aroma therapy, flower therapy, Qi gong, sweat lodge ceremony, crystal therapy, and acupuncture-acupressure. Magic as *techne* or the "art of craft" (Davis 1998:17) is the operative whether in mantra chanting or in the aim for health or pain relief through the acupressurist's stimulating a *chi,* or energy node, in the body.

In the more vernacular, traditionally religious and scientific understanding of magic, it is understood largely as a trick—an act of deception or beguiling. Believers in magic, of course, will usually deny its dissimulating nature and argue that magic is real although not subject to the usual observations of empirical demonstration. The paranormal aspects of New Age begin with Spiritualism and are elevated into a more intense transcendental mode with Theosophy and the resurgence of Gnosticism. From this direction, the "art" or "science" of channeling is to be seen as an extension of the animistic world of paganism to one of supersentient beings. In a sense, this is reenchantment with a message. The *devas,* bodhisattvas, and/or ascended masters are products of New Age's insistence on a cosmos of greater possibility than the limited opportunities understood as our more ordinary three-dimensional world of time and space. Whether the otherness of magical beings is translated into extraterrestrials and UFOs from outer space or into angels, fairies, elementals, and coincidental synchronicities inhabiting enchanted realms of inner space, it appears to spring from a New Age desire to extend the mundane world of commonplace reality. The paranormal and whatever actuality it may or may not represent become assisting means to expand the ordinary into a transcendental and preferred dimension. This expansion rests on the denial of an exclusively rationalistic world—the same denial that has allowed the persistence of astrological belief as well as the more esoteric arts or "sciences." While a confirmed empirical methodologist such as Carl Sagan would deplore and reject the human propensity for cognitive dissonance, anthropologist Pascal Boyer can at least recognize the natural tendency for people to consider what he terms "counter-intuitive" or "counter-ontological" information.[10] In that most religious concepts include counterintuitive perceptions, New Age ideas of magic are in this sense conforming to a universal faculty embedded within humanity's emotional consciousness.

But in addition to both the Human Potential violation of the law of equal exchange and the perception of a reality that supersedes the increasingly disenchanted mundane one, New Age magic finds its fullest expression through New Thought's doggedness on the denial of negativity. Once again we are in the realm of Human Potential (whether Neuro-Linguistic Programming, reiki, shiatsu, iridology, or creative visualization). Seeing the negative only as an opportunity and occasion to grow is not a magic of something for nothing but a magic of denial. In this respect, it comes closer to high magic and Pagan understandings of magic as the changing of consciousness at will. At the same time, it can be viewed as a magic of deception. The denial of illness, poverty, even the physical may perhaps be achieved as a "trick of the mind." But once again we are seeing New Age magic expressed by Fortune's changing consciousness through will. New Thought magic seeks to make the world conform to how it wills it to be. It constitutes an act or series of acts of volitional solipsism. If the world exists only within the mind, then it can be changed by changing the mind through determined belief—perhaps bolstered by training in various mental disciplines (yoga, Neuro-Linguistic Programming, reiki, self-help, eurthymy, and transformational techniques) used to develop concentration and perhaps bolstered further through physiotherapies and body enhancements (for example, rolfing, shiatsu, Feldenkrais method, massage, reflexology) to diminish physical distraction.

The major consequence of New Thought–New Age magic is that authenticity ceases to be the issue. This also allows the drive to appropriate and reproduce the exotic and esoteric. Even if the magical trick is one of fakery or deception, all that matters is the effect. New Age is, of course, often condemned for this inauthentication, even commodification, but this is a direct consequence of its New Thought heritage in which the seemingly real and authentic are devalued. If what the mind believes is real, then in New Age thought this is all that matters.

Coupled with this solipsistic insistence as a form of magic, at its most saccharine, New Age also espouses a form of love magic. This is, however, more usually a travesty in not being focused on a beloved but on either the self or an abstract reification of everyone. Perhaps the underlying impulse behind the declaration of love as a magical dogma derives from a Mahayana Buddhist understanding of compassion for all sentient beings, but in the prevailing superficiality that characterizes New Age in general there appears little of the substantiation—let alone altruistic demonstration—that the New Age declaration of universal love is little more than a ritual mantra in search of a real conviction to reinforce it with the power of effective magic.

In general, New Age oscillates between being a new religiosity looking for its own footing, understanding, and articulation, on the one hand, and a spirituality that is simply characteristic of the consumerism of its times, on the other. But like all religions, its essential effort is to provide a framework for approaching and evaluating the world and one's relation to it and within it. In a word, religions are attempts to superimpose a hermeneutical scheme from without. The astrological metaphor of the Aquarian Age provides New Age with its particular framework. The idea of the quantum leap may be understood as a successful act of magical structuring. Not only does it reenchant the world for its holders, but it also represents a violation-transformation of the law of equal exchange—namely, the belief and insistence that something become more than simply the sum of its parts.

CONCLUSION

As a sectarian response, the New Age movement, much like contemporary Western paganism, ranges between Wilson's understanding of the manipulationist and thaumaturgical sects. The latter differs little from the former but for a more personal and less universalistic response to the world. The primary characteristic for those of a thaumaturgical predisposition is to seek a personal experience of the supernatural. Rather than seeking gnosis in and of itself, one's interest is in communicating with spiritual powers and the dead for predictive and miraculous purposes (Wilson 1969:367; York 1995b:269). In its more gnostic or manipulationist tendencies, on the other hand, New Age is psychocosmologically or mystically oriented and centered on an essentially optimistic and esoteric eschatology. At the same time, and putting the New Age in many respects into a more dissonant footing vis-à-vis traditional Gnosticism, it conforms to Roy Wallis's understanding of the world-affirming movement and, as such, "is a modern version of the almost ubiquitous phenomenon of magic; the invocation, or manipulation, of occult forces or powers for personal ends" (Wallis 1984:122). As Wallis recognizes, the purposes of magic have changed from preoccupation with fertility and protection from witchcraft to "psychological well-being, enhanced self-confidence and freedom from socially ingrained inhibitions, but *the enterprise is essentially the same*" (Wallis 1984:122).[11] This personalization within the world-affirming context may suggest the ultimate transformation of New Age into the "Next Age" of Introvigne. Nevertheless, as a sectarian response, New Age is also similar to Wilson's adventist or revolutionist sect in its expectation of the world's (imminent) alteration.

New Age, like much of Neopaganism, is a development of the Western esoteric-occult tradition of theosophy, theurgy, astrology, and alchemy originating with the late Roman Empire's schools of Neo-Platonism, Neo-Pythagoreanism, Alexandrian Hermeticism, and Stoicism. In the Renaissance, the metaphysical current manifested in the kabbalah, alchemy and the works of Paracelsus. Subsequently, in the seventeenth century, Joannes Andreae fostered Rosicrucianism, which may be recognized as part of the broader tradition of Freemasonry. The eighteenth century saw the rise of Illuminism, which culminated in the visions and works of Swedenborg. Consequently, the thaumaturgical undercurrent has always been a part of Western culture since at least the days of the Hellenistic and Roman civilizations. The New Age movement is its continuation in today's late modern–postmodern world—now undergirded by a prevailing capitalist ethos that insists on the democratization and commercial availability of all esoterica and magic.

But in its concern with magic, New Age must share the contemporary

stage with Neopaganism and the schools of ritual magic. These movements
express interest, for instance, in the kabbalah, the esoteric tradition of He-
brew culture. For contemporary Western paganism, this pursuit occurs
mostly among ceremonial magicians. In New Age, cabalism is apt to appear
at any point within its consumer market. Overall, however, the present-
day occult tradition increasingly appears to polarize between not just New
Age and paganism but between New Age, Neopaganism, and high magical
expressions—with all three but especially the first two increasingly involved with psychological interpretations of magic. Paganism in general
in the West seeks its metaphors and understandings within indigenous
European and other traditions—whether Celtic, Greek, Roman, Norse,
Egyptian, and so forth—and questions whether the kabbalah is the true
root of the Western tradition. While Neopaganism—particularly Wicca
and Witchcraft—employs the ceremonial circle as a means to protect its
worshipers from external intrusion or disturbance—especially from the
mundane, the ritual circle is used by the magician as the means to confine
the demon or magical entity he or she invokes. As a protective device, the
magician and the pagan employ the magical circle differently. But in New
Age, the whole notion of the circle is absent for, as William Bloom explains, New Age denies the reality of the negative and, hence, has no need
for magical barriers (York 1995b:167). Consequently, in their respective
attitudes toward the supernatural, ceremonial magicians and pagans tend to
distinguish between either the good and the bad or the sacred and the
ordinary. New Age magic, on the other hand, denies evil or negativity and,
ultimately, the apparent world itself.

Judging from the 1991 census of Canada alone, and excluding the Aboriginal American indian and Inuit communities, the remaining paranor-
mal-religious groups may be seen roughly to divide between pagan and
broad New Age identities.[12] We can guess that approximately one-third of
either pagans or New Agers live in the province of British Columbia. Similar to what we know of the American West Coast, Bibby (1993:173) finds
there to be a "unique aversion to organized religion in British Columbia."
The greater success of new religious movements along the Pacific coasts
of both the United States and Canada has been attributed by Bainbridge
(1997:413) to the weakness of conventional denominations due to the generally high degree of geographic mobility throughout these regions. At the
same time, accordingly, this factor also prevents the new religions from
becoming substantial movements. Nevertheless, Bainbridge may in fact be
mis-seeing in the same way Western governmental leaders for many years
could not countenance the existence of the Palestine Liberation Organization. As Luther Gerlach and Virginia Hine (see York 1995b:324–27) indicate, an apparently leaderless segmented network is a long-standing means
for noninstitutional survival in a hostile environment. In other words, a

multicelled, grassroots nonconformist movement that avoids the higher profile of institutional bureaucracy and detectable leadership is an organizational means to avoid recognition and reduce vulnerability and possible elimination by the enforcement authorities of the state. With its incorporation of a magical theology and practices that are opposed by both traditional canonical religion and the scientific establishment of the mainstream, the loose confederation of spiritual innovation that characterizes the New Age movement throughout the United States and Canada may prove to be a spiritual innovation that will have a greater durability than its detractors contend.

# Witchcraft and Neopaganism

## Helen A. Berger

Contemporary Witchcraft, along with the larger Neopagan movement in which it is embedded, has grown and become better known since its arrival in North America from England in the 1960s. Contemporary Witches—or Wiccans, as many of its adherents prefer to call themselves—are not devil worshipers. Instead they are members of what they define as an earth-based religion, in which the goddess or goddesses and the god force or gods are venerated, nature's yearly cycle of seasons is celebrated, and magic is practiced. Wicca, which is the largest sect of Neopaganism, has provided the template for magical practices and yearly celebrations for many of the other forms of Neopaganism, or what are called by adherents traditions or spiritual paths (Berger 1999; Jorgensen and Russell 1999; Berger et al. 2003). Neopaganism has no set dogma or central leadership; this permits innovation and the possibility of each individual having her or his own form of the religion. Although there tends to be a great deal of similarity among groups and individuals, some forms of Neopaganism, such as Dianics (women-only groups) and those that worship the deities of a particular historic region (for example, Odinists or Druids) do distinguish themselves from other Neopagans. Some differences exist between the spiritual practices of Americans and Canadians and among regions in both nations; however, there is also a great deal of consistency, as Neopagans on both sides of the border read the same books, attend many of the same festivals, and interact on the Internet.

The religion is particularly appealing to white, middle-class, well-educated individuals. Approximately 65 percent to 66 percent of participants are female (Berger et al. 2003:27; Reid 2001:63–65). Women tend to be overrepresented in all religions, but this disparity is slightly higher within Neopaganism because of the appeal of a feminine divine for some women. Estimates range between 150,000 and 400,000 Neopagans in the United States (Berger 1999; Jorgensen and Russell 1999).[1] The category *Pagan* was offered as a possible religious affiliation in the1991 Canadian census, with the result that 5,530 people out of a population of 26,994,045 stated they were Pagans.[2] This would suggest a much lower proportion of Neopagans in Canada than in the United States. Canadian scholars of Neopaganism, however, contend that the proportion of Neopagans in both countries is approximately the same. Sian Reid (2001) explains the discrepancy between researchers' ethnographic sense of the number of Canadian Neopagans and the number reported in the census by arguing that many Neopagans avoided using the terms *Pagan, Witch,* or *Wiccan* when responding to the census, which were coded as *Pagan.* Twenty-five percent of respondents to her survey, all of whom are Canadian and consider themselves Neopagans, state that if they were filling out the census today, they would not choose the designation *Pagan.* It is possible that an even larger percentage may have chosen to not accurately complete the census form when it was administered.

Unlike religions with established churches that have membership lists, Neopaganism has no central bureaucracy to maintain records. Normally, individuals' self-definitions are accepted. The estimates put forth by scholars have been derived from registration numbers of participants at religious retreats, referred to as festivals; subscriptions to Neopagan journals; purchases of popular books on Witchcraft, such as Starhawk's *Spiral Dance* (1979); and survey results. In all instances these are only loose estimates. Some individuals subscribe to Neopagan journals or buy books about Neopagan or Wiccan spiritual practices who are not practitioners. In turn, friends and members of the same group, or coven, often share subscriptions or borrow each other's books. None of these methods accounts for those who chose to leave the religion but have at some point attended festivals, taken courses, or purchased books and journals. Counting the exact number of Neopagans is further frustrated by the fact that some individuals fearing that they or their families will be negatively impacted professionally, socially, or legally keep their religious affiliation secret. Reid (2001) argues that this may have been one of the reasons that Pagans were underrepresented in the Canadian census. The lack of clear boundaries of who is and who is not a Neopagan further confuses the issue of a reliable census. Because of the fluidity of practice and beliefs, individuals often speak of combining traditions or participating in more than one. Some individuals even consider themselves simultaneously Christians or Jews and Neopagans (Manning 1996).

*Neopagan* is an umbrella term for spiritual practices that share a view of the world as enchanted and the earth as sacred. Margot Adler (1979) credits Kerry Thornley with first using the term to refer to members of this amorphous religion and the early Neopagan journal *Green Egg* with popularizing it.[3] Most Neopagans venerate a female and male aspect of the divine, although some groups focus exclusively on the goddess or goddesses. Even in those groups in which the male deity is acknowledged, the goddess is usually viewed as more central. Most practitioners prefer the term *Pagan* to *Neopagan.* For some it is because they view their practices as a return to the old pagan religions. However, Macha NightMare, a well-known Witch and author, contends, "I say *Pagan* rather than *Neopagan* because the prefix *neo* implies that there was once a 'paleo' Paganism that had a group identity and some shared values, beliefs and practices. There was no such phenomenon" (2001:25). Throughout this chapter I will use the term *Neopagan* to differentiate this new religion from older pagan religions. Although all Witches consider themselves Neopagans or Pagans, not all Neopagan use the term *Witch*. Some, such as Druids, avoid the term because they define themselves as coming from an alternative spiritual path. Others feel the term is too loaded. Some Witches prefer to call themselves Wiccans, although in Europe and among some American Witches, most notably those from the Reclaiming tradition, the term *Wiccan* is reserved for those trained in traditional covens. Most Americans and Canadians have used the terms *Wiccan* and *Witch* interchangeably, but that is in the process of changing as more individuals reserve the label *Wiccan* for those who are initiated within the coven tradition. Many Witches say that they are practicing the Craft— viewing their religion as something that is learned and practiced and not as a devotion or set of beliefs.

Individuals' self-definitions as Witches, Wiccans, Pagans, or Neopagans are normally accepted. However, there are at times backbiting or sarcastic comments made about individuals' claims to some heritages and the quality of others' training. Arguments about who is and is not properly trained, or who is more magically adept than others, are referred to by members of the Neopagan community as "Witch wars." These sometimes result in personal rifts or bad feelings within the larger Neopagan community and may affect individuals' credibility but do not result in anyone being eliminated from the religion. Although individuals' status in the community may increase or decrease the number of individuals who want to be trained by them, it never precludes anyone from becoming a teacher. Some prominent Neopagans have raised concerns about the disparity of training that exists within the religion and the ability of some with little training or knowledge to train others (Berger 1999). In response to this, some groups offer courses of study to ensure the quality of training.

Like Eastern religions, Neopaganism puts a greater emphasis on spiritual experiences than on beliefs. Drumming, meditation, and ecstatic dancing are all used to reach an altered state of consciousness. Although there are beliefs and practices that are common among Neopagans, and interpretations of these are sometimes argued about, there is no required dogma or set of practices. Each individual is considered the ultimate authority of his or her own relationship with the divine. Because of the lack of dogma and the emphasis on having mystical experiences, it is possible to be a Neopagan and an atheist. Neopagans offer several interpretations of the meaning of the deities. For some, the goddess(es) and god(s) are divine beings, while for others they are representations of the divine, and for still others they are metaphors of natural processes. Individuals are not always consistent in their definition, and some suspend disbelief for rituals (Berger 1999).

Although individual inspiration is respected and it is possible for there to be as many forms of Neopaganism as there are participants, there are several important trends that have informed the Neopagan movement. The most important is Gardnerian Witchcraft that came first to the United States and subsequently to Canada from the United Kingdom. Gerald Gardner claimed to be initiated into a coven, which had secretly met and kept alive the teachings of a pan-European pagan religion that was practiced prior to the spread of Christianity, training only a handful of adepts each generation. In 1954, three years after the repeal of the 1736 Witchcraft act, Gardner published *Witchcraft Today* (1954) his first nonfiction book on the religion of Wicca. Gardner's claim that he was initiated into a coven that had passed on their rites and rituals in secret for centuries has been brought into question by scholars and some practitioners alike (Lurhmann 1989; Hutton 1999; Adler 1979; Bonewits 1989; Kelly 1991). Ronald Hutton (1999), who has presented the first comprehensive academic examination of the history of Wicca, concludes that although Gardner's sources of inspiration can be discerned in his writings, he nonetheless produced something original—a religion that was exported around the world.

Some practitioners continue to say that theirs is the old religion. Among these practitioners there are two schools of thought. One school of thought continues to argue that Gardner was initiated into a hidden coven. Some in this school ignore the evidence to the contrary, while others contend that Gardner was given incomplete rituals and filled in the gaps with existing materials. The other school of thought argues that even if Gardner created the religion in the early twentieth century, he was reestablishing an older spiritual tradition, and hence as practitioners, they are returning to older sensibilities, spirituality, and rituals.

Although the religion has changed since coming to North America, it retains the mark of its origins. Gardnerian Witchcraft continues to be practiced in North America as one form of contemporary Wicca, but more important, it has influenced other forms of Neopaganism (Jorgensen and Russell 1999). The religion as presented by Gardner is based on individuals' being initiated into covens which Gardner suggested were ideally composed of thirteen members, a high priestess, six men, and six women. The high priestess is the accepted leader of the coven but works with a high priest to ensure balancing of what are referred to as masculine and feminine energies. Although all people are believed to possess both male and female energies, the religion as Gardner presented it has incorporated a notion of innate differences between men and women. This reached its height when after the religion had gained popularity in England, he argued for the high priestess of a coven stepping down when she ceased to be young, as he stated that the young and beautiful would best represent the goddess. Doreen Valiente, who was a member of his original coven and wrote much of the poetry that is used in Wiccan rituals, broke with Gardner over this issue (Salomonsen 2002:92). Contemporary groups, particularly women only groups, have worked to eliminate what they view as lingering sexism within Wicca. For example, it is not a common practice in North America for there to be an emphasis on the high priestess being young or classically beautiful.

Those initiated into Gardnerian covens take an oath to maintain the teachings as secret. There have been so many books and journal articles written about Wiccan rituals and practices it is unclear how many, if any, secrets still exist. Gardnerians practice skyclad—that is, in the nude. They claim that nudity is used in rituals to ensure that all are equal and to put the participants in a more natural state. Other Wiccan and Neopagan groups differ in the degree to which they practice skyclad. Some groups prefer to use robes for rituals, others vary in whether they use ritual robes, street clothing, or practice skyclad, depending on the place the ritual is occurring, or the weather, and the participation of outsiders or children.

Among the techniques used in rituals by Gardner to help place people in an altered state of consciousness is the scourge. Although it has been suggested the inclusion of the scourge was an indication that Gardner had sadomasochistic tendencies, Hutton contends that it was just one among a number of techniques used to put participants into an altered state of consciousness. Hutton notes that Gardner's description of its use suggests that the scourging is slow and light, something that is employed to put someone into a trance, not as a beating. Nonetheless, most North American Witches have eliminated the scourge from their repertoire of techniques used to gain altered consciousness.

Gardner described the religion he was taught as a gentle earth religion in which the goddess of fertility and the god of the hunt were venerated. The goddess is eternal but changes from maid to mother to crone. The god is born of the goddess at Yule (December 21), grows to manhood and becomes the goddess's consort at Beltane (May 1), and dies to ensure the fertility of the crops at Samhain (October 31) to be reborn at the next Yule. The changing relationship of the goddess and god and the corresponding changes in nature are celebrated at the eight sabbats, which are evenly spaced at six-week intervals throughout the year at the solstices, the equinoxes, and in between these solar events at what are referred to as the cross points. Each sabbat celebrates either the beginning or the height of a season.

Esabats are traditionally held on the new and full moon. The phases of the moon correspond to the three aspects of the goddess: maid, mother, and crone. The moon is drawn down into the high priestess—that is, the power of the moon is viewed as entering into the priestess at the full moon, empowering the high priestess and through her those in the circle in their magical working. The new moon is associated with the crone, the element of death and destruction, which is viewed as an important part of the life cycle. For Gardner and for most contemporary Neopagans, life is viewed as a spiral in which death is an important element for the renewal of life and fostering of change. Reincarnation is a commonly held belief among Neopagans. In the United States, Berger et al. (2003) found that 75 percent of Neopagans believe in reincarnation as compared to 25 percent of the general American public. Even Neopagans who do not accept the concept of reincarnation may still use it as a metaphor for changes in nature and people's personal lives.

The basic ritual as presented by Gardner continues to be practiced by most Wiccan and Neopagan groups. Those leading the ritual create a sacred circle. For Gardnerians and most Witches, this is the high priestess and high priest. Typically, *athames*—ritual knives—are used to create the space. The cardinal points—east, south, west, and north, each of which is viewed as having specific colors and powers associated with it—are acknowledged. There is a ritual working that normally corresponds to the theme of the sabbat, esabat, or other ritual. For instance, at Beltane a celebration of fertility in nature and in the participants' lives occurs. As part of the ritual, participants are said to raise energy for doing magical workings; dance, mediation, and singing people direct their thoughts toward enacting change, such as healing the ill or helping the environment. After the magical working, the watch towers of the four directions are dismissed, the circle is ritually opened, and food is served to help the participants "ground"—that is, return to mundane world after participating in magic.

Almost as soon as Gardner made the religion public, sects began to form. Some individuals claimed to have been initiated into other covens that had survived in hiding since the witch trials. Some of these had marked differences from Gardnarian Witchcraft, offering, for instance, different correspondences between the cardinal points and the elements. Others who had been trained by Gardner or those knowledgeable of his system also created alternative sects. From almost the moment it became public, the boundaries of this religion were amorphous. Nonetheless, the basic elements of ritual presented by Gardner, his celebration of the cycle of the year, and his use of magical techniques are part of most forms of Neopaganism.

## MAGIC

As presented by Gardner and practiced today, magic is an important element of all branches of Neopaganism. As British psychologist Vivianne

Crowley (2000b:152) notes: "Wiccans believe in and practice magic: the science and art of causing change by non-physical means not as yet accepted by science. . . . The Wiccan word-view is that the material world is comprised of energy and that energy can be manipulated by mind and by the Witch's own *etheric energy*. Etheric energy exists on the border of matter and mind. Wicca accepts the idea, common to the Western magical tradition and similar to Hinduism, that there is an energy field around the body." Tanya Luhrmann, who as part of her ethnographic study of contemporary magical practitioners in England trained with Gardner's original coven, similarly notes that those practicing modern magic "learn to accept its core concept that mind affects matter, and that in special circumstances, like ritual, the trained imagination can alter the physical world" (Lurhmann 1989:7). Witches and most Neopagans participate in a series of exercises to train their minds. Through their training in covens, classes, or groups, and from books and Internet sites, Witches learn to meditate, to visualize, and to have out-of-body experiences. In rituals, all of these techniques are used to raise "energy" to do magical workings. The magical workings vary among individuals and groups, and from ritual to ritual. Magic can be used to heal the ill, protect the natural environment, bring participants jobs, housing, or lovers. As it is considered unethical to control another person through magic, most Witches adhere to the notion that it is acceptable to bring love to you but not a particular lover. Objects, such as a piece of jewelry, an amulet, or a stone, can be magically charged with energy at the rituals. These are then carried or worn by participants to help achieve some aim. Phyllis Curott, an American Witch, describes the instructions she was given by one of her spiritual teachers who helped her make a love potion. After handing her herbs enhanced with three drops of oil that had been magically charged at a ritual, Curott's teacher instructed: "You are to add all of these to three cups of pure spring water. Bring it to a boil, lower the heat, simmer for twenty minutes, stirring deosil, that's clockwise. As you stir, think about love. Strain the herbs from the liquid and pour the liquid into your bath water. Right before you get into the tub, add five drops of oil and the petals of three red roses to the bath water. Close your eyes, relax, and allow yourself to dream of love. But make sure you get out of the bath before the water gets cold" (Curott, 1998:78). Curott was instructed to be open to the different forms of love that could manifest. She describes the spell as working when she is able to regain her love for her work and is reunited with a former lover even though she had hoped to meet her "soul-mate."

Although trained minds and those knowledgeable about the magical associations between particular herbs and gems are believed to be most capable of performing magic, all individuals are viewed as doing magic. Thinking of someone who then calls you is one example of everyday magic. Among Neopagans, there is a belief in synchrony—that is, what might otherwise be interpreted as coincidence is viewed by members of this group as magic or as an element of the Web of Life. If, for example, one misses a train only to meet an old friend, a potential love interest, or someone who can help you find a better job while standing around the station, it would be a clear indication that one was meant to miss the train. Practitioners might suggest that the individual was guided by a higher force or that it was part of some other magical working that she or he had done.

Luhrmann suggests that as part of their training, magic practitioners learn to reinterpret data to conform to their belief in magic. Individuals use a wide definition of a spell working, just as Curott was instructed to do. Luhrmann views the magic practiced by these middle-class well-educated individuals as fitting the anthropological definition of the word, although how modern practitioners believe magic works differs on the whole from more traditional-interpretations. In explaining their belief in magic, Neopagans tend to rely on current social and scientific theories such as quantum mechanics or postmodern philosophy. It is common to hear Neopagans say that the magic of today will become the science of tomorrow. Still others claim they have no idea how magic works but know it does from their own experience (Berger 1994).

A growing number of contemporary Witches and Neopagans contend that magic works by changing the individual and not the natural world. In other words, magical practitioners, in doing a spell, focus on what they want to change in their own lives and are then better able to foster those changes. The ritual serves as a psychological tool to enable persons to recognize and focus on aspects of their lives they would like to change. For example, an individual might create an amulet to stop smoking, which she or he then carries with her or him at all times as a reminder and psychological aid to resist smoking. The charm works in part because the individual believes in it—a type of placebo effect.

The same individual may at different times offer different explanations for how magic works. Crowley (2000b) contends this is because there are different aspects of magic that are manifested in different types of acts. For example, in healing the ill, Witches may claim that it is the psychological effect of the individuals' belief in the healing ritual that helps them become well. At other times Witches may rely on other explanations for magic, such as that the world is a web of energy that can be influenced by the right rituals or that the effects are a manifestation of the gods or the goddess.

Healing, particularly healing the ill, is one of the most common forms of magic used by Witches (Crowley 2000b; Orion 1995). As Crowley notes, healing permits Witches, particularly those who are newly initiated, to both show their magical prowess and to be altruistic. Healing can take one of three forms: the sending of magical energy to help the person heal, the laying on of hands, or the use of herbs or other forms of alternative medicine. The last, although part of a more general occult underground, is not based on magic but on ancient folk wisdom that has been passed down through the generations. As many Witches note, some contemporary medicines such as aspirin are derived from folk remedies. Contemporary Neopagans often study herbal remedies, which they view as both an element of self-empowerment and a return to the old ways when folk healers guided people toward health. Margaret Murray (1971), one of the authors who influenced Gardner, presented an image of the pre-Christian European witch as an individual, most commonly a woman, who was beloved by her community and served it by using herbs and magic to effect healings and secure crops.[4] This image of the Witch continues to influence contemporary Neopaganism.

Although magic is viewed as having a practical end of transforming the world to the Witches' wills, it is also an element of their spiritual practice. For Witches and Neopagans, magic is a concrete example of the interconnectedness of the universe and their own spiritual empowerment. By performing magic, Witches believe they are influencing the core of existence. Raising and sending magical energy is, therefore, part of most, if not all, rituals. The techniques used to raise energy, furthermore, are the same as are used to place the individual in an altered state of consciousness in which they feel themselves in contact with the universe or the divine. As one Witch describes this: "Magic has always been an element of Witchcraft, but in the Craft its techniques were practiced within a context of community and connection. They were means of ecstatic union with the Goddess Self—not ends in themselves" (Starhawk 1979:192).

In doing magic, Witches and Neopagans adhere to the Wiccan Rede: "Do as thou will as long as thou harm none." Although Witches believe that magic can be used for positive and negative goals, they regularly argue that magic used negatively is a violation of another's will. Most Witches believe in the three-fold return: the energy one sends out will return to one with three times the force with which it was sent. Those that do harm, in other words, will ultimately be harmed.

NORTH AMERICAN INFLUENCE

Raymond and Rosemary Buckland are credited with bringing Wicca from the United Kingdom to the United States in the 1960s. Other immigrants to both the United States and Canada subsequently brought different versions of the religion (Marron 1989). Wicca spread quickly throughout North America, as it appealed to members of the counterculture, women looking for a female face to the divine, and environmentalists. These movements, as well as American individualism, helped to transform the religion by emphasizing, and therefore developing, its environmental aspects, feminist perspective (at least within part of the movement), and focus on individual innovation and experience. Although national differences exist, American cultural hegemony has resulted in American Neopaganism having an influence on the religion worldwide.

The religion was spread initially primarily through covens and face-to-face interactions. Although covens and classes at adult education centers and occult bookstores remain an important venue for individuals to learn about the religion, books, magazines, and the Internet have grown in importance. Hundreds of books on magic, Witchcraft, Paganism, the application of magical or medicinal herbs, the use of stones in healing and magic, how to run a coven or raise a Pagan child have been published. Llewellyn Press in St. Paul, Minnesota, one of the largest publishing houses for books on Pagan topics, has been instrumental in spreading information about the religion. In addition, newsletters, magazines, and online websites and forums are abundant. America Online's search engine offers over 40,000 sites and Google over 200,000 sites for those interested in Witchcraft and Neopaganism. As with all sites on the Internet, not all of these are active nor are they equally popular, but nonetheless the number of sites is increasing (Griffin 2002b).

The spread of the religion through printed matter and the Internet has helped to speed the process through which the religion has spread in North America. Although this is important, particularly in rural areas in both countries, it is even more important in Canada, which has a much lower population density than the U.S. The language barrier in French Canada has made the English-language writers somewhat less important, although most Neopagans in Canada, like those in the U.S., are well educated and hence are able to read English. Witchcraft, Wiccan, and Neopagan groups exist in Quebec and have some of their own literature that is published in French.

Several authors have made significant imprints on the religion through their writings, none more so than Miriam Simos, who writes under and is best known by her magical name, Starhawk. Her first book, *The Spiral Dance* (1979), sold over 300,000 copies (Salomonsen 2002). Although not all of these were bought by Neopagans, the book is widely read within the Witchcraft and Neopagan movement. In my fieldwork on the East Coast of the United States, it was common for Neopagans that I met to quote Starhawk. Some did so consciously citing her work, others took her words as their own—either because they had absorbed what they had read or because they had heard it from others and unconsciously made it part of their own thinking. Although many of these individuals do not see themselves as part of the Reclaiming Tradition that Starhawk helped to create, they have integrated aspects of her interpretation of Witchcraft and suggestions for organizing and maintaining a coven into their own spiritual practices. This is consistent with Starhawk's own aims. As she states: "The myths underlying philosophy and 'thealogy' (a word coined by religious scholar Naomi Goldenburg from 'thea,' the Greek word for Goddess) in this book are based on the Faery Tradition. Other Witches may disagree with details, but the overall values and attitudes expressed are common to all of the Craft" (11).

Starhawk, a feminist and political activist for liberal causes who is an initiated Witch in the Faery Tradition, created a bridge between feminist Witchcraft and more traditional Wicca. Feminist Witchcraft, which is discussed by Wendy Griffin in this volume, focuses on the goddess to the exclusion of the god force. Influenced by Wicca, feminist Witchcraft grew out of the women's movement and celebrates the goddess as an important element of women's liberation. Feminist Witchcraft, particularly as presented by Zsuzsanna Budapest, is separatist, involving only women. Although, recognizing its value for women, Starhawk argues that "in the long run, a female-only model of the universe will prove to be as constricting and oppressive, to women as well as men, as the patriarchal model has been" (1979:26–27). Nonetheless, Starhawk was influenced by feminist Witchcraft. The image of the god force presented by Starhawk is a nonpatriarchal view of manhood that is consistent with feminist values. Furthermore, Starhawk argues that it is the goddess that is central to Witchcraft. As she writes, "[T]he symbolism of the Goddess has taken on an electrifying power for modern women. The rediscovery of the ancient matrifocal civilizations has given us a deep sense of pride in woman's ability to create and sustain culture" (77).

In all of her writings, Starhawk's feminism is integrated into her spirituality. She presents Witchcraft as empowering women and helping to soften men. Her discussion of how to organize and run a coven is clearly influenced by feminist concerns about "power over" or domination. She suggests, for example, that there be a facilitator at each coven meeting to ensure that everyone's voice is heard (Starhawk 1982). Starhawk has been important in presenting one image of Witchcraft that is feminist, ecological, and politically active. Her writings have influenced the early movement, providing a bridge between feminism, environmentalism, and Witchcraft. Although not all Witches or Neopagans are feminists or environmentalists, many, particularly among the first wave of adherents, have incorporated elements of these movements into their beliefs and practices. Starhawk also provided individuals, particularly women with the tools for creating their own covens. Instead of being required to find a coven that would train them, individuals working with Starhawk's books could create their own group and form of practice.

There is a dispute among Neopagans about whether or not only those who have not been initiated in the coven tradition can truly be said to be Witches. A growing number of participants, however, are practicing alone and are self-initiated. Berger et al. (2003) found in a large-scale study that 51 percent of Neopagans in the U.S. are solitary practitioners and another 1 percent practice with only one other person. Because of the lower population density in Canada, it is estimated that a larger percentage of Canadian Neopagans are solitaries. Some of these people define themselves as Pagans, not Witches; others, however, take the label *Witch*. Authors such as Scott Cunningham (1988, 1994) have provided readers who want or have to practice alone with information on how to celebrate the sabbats and esabats, the ethic and techniques of magical practice and self-transformation, rituals for self-initiation, and the mythology of Witchcraft.

Many authors, including Starhawk and Cunningham, encourage their readers to be innovative. Some Witches and Neopagans are referred to as British Traditional Witches—that is, those that are initiated and practice Wicca as presented by Gardner or one of his disciples, or those trained by one of his disciples. Similarly, some Neopagans practice a very specific form of Paganism, such as Druidism. However, many Neopagans in North America are eclectic—blending several strands of Witchcraft, Neopaganism, Shamanism, and elements of spiritual practices from around world. Creativity is celebrated among North American Neopagans in the composition of arts, crafts, and in rituals (Orion 1995). Although there is a good deal of sharing and homogenization through individuals reading the same books and journals, and participating in the same websites, there is nonetheless a sense of religious creativity and freedom that is apparent among North American Neopagans. At times, rituals are taken as a whole from a book or from another person's Book of Shadows—that is, her or his personal journal of ritual and magical workings. At other times, people include their own poetry, artwork, and magical workings as part of the ritual. Rituals normally are playful. Adler (1979) and Luhrmann (1989), both relying on Huizungia (1950), refer to this lightheartedness that appears in rituals as deep play in which the rituals are simultaneously playful and serious. These primarily well-educated people dressed in robes or performing their rituals skyclad call on ancient gods and goddesses frequently taken from different pantheons. Most Neopagans are aware that they are involved in creating ritual and often are lighthearted or even joke about their endeavor. However, they are not just playacting but are involved in a serious spiritual endeavor.

A new generation of Neopagans is finding the religion. Some of these younger adults and adolescents are the second generation who are continuing in the family tradition, and others are a new generation of seekers. There is a general sense among Neopagans and scholars of Neopaganism that there is an increased interest in Witchcraft among teenagers. Although no statistics exist that codify the numbers of teenagers who are interested in Witchcraft, the growth in books, websites, and magazines devoted to young Witches indicates that there is a large contemporary interest. Silver RavenWolf is the best-known author writing for this young generation. She provides an overview of the religious beliefs, rituals, and magical practices geared to young people. Her books are widely read among teenage Witches, many of whom use her as a guide as they explore the religion (Berger and Ezzy 2003).

The interest among teenagers in part has been sparked by movies and television shows such *Charmed* and *Sabrina, the Teenage Witch*. Only a small percentage of those who explore Witchcraft or other forms of Neopaganism appear to decide to self-define as members of the religion. Some become disillusioned when they realize that they will not be able to perform magical acts like those performed by Sabrina or Harry Potter. However, some who are drawn in by the magical practices become more interested in the mythical and spiritual aspects of the religion (Ezzy and Berger 2004).

The teenagers who do more than dabble in Witchcraft but actually become initiated and seriously practice the religion appear to be drawn by a strong interest in self-development and transformation. This has always been an essential element of North American Witchcraft, but among the first generation of seekers this was integrated with concerns about gender equality and environmentalism. The greater emphasis among the young on self-development may change with age. As most people who join a new religion do not remain, it is probable that most of these young people will leave Neopaganism within a few years. Those that do remain may become influenced by some of the older Neopagans, although as most of the younger generation are solitary practitioners, they have little chance to directly interact with others except on the Internet.

The influx of a new generation of seekers, the aging of the original participants of the religion, and the growing number of individuals who practice alone are changing the face of this religion. The increased focus on self-development is one aspect of this. At the same time that there is a greater emphasis on the religion as an individual quest, there is also a growing number of organizations that have developed to provide services, to represent Neopagans and Witches, and to fight for greater legitimacy for the religion and its practitioners.

SPIRITUAL PATHS

Although some participants view their practice as a religion, it is more common for Neopagans to refer to their practice as a spiritual path. Some avoid the term *religion,* as they view it as referring only to institutionalized religions, such as Christianity and Judaism, that they have chosen to leave. For others, the notion of spiritual path is more open than that of religion, implying that each individual is responsible for his or her own relationship with the divine. Among Neopagans, the terms *spiritual path* and *tradition* can be used to describe either the practices of those trained in a particular form of Neopaganism, such as Druids, Reclaiming Witches, or Gardnerians, or to indicate an individual's unique version of the religion. Differences among spiritual paths may be very slight; for instance, the particular manner in which the circle is cast or the four quarter called, or more significant, as shown in the women-only groups that exclude men and the male divine. It is acceptable among Neopagans to combine elements of different spiritual paths or even elements of traditional religions. Crystal Manning (1996), for example, describes women who embrace both the goddess and Jesus—seeing no contradiction in worshiping both.

There are more spiritual paths than it is possible to discuss in this chapter. Graham Harvey (1997) in his work on Neopaganism primarily in England selects six groups, which he believes are particularly significant either because of their popularity among Neopagans or because they provide a clearly unique and different form of Paganism. The six he chose to analyze are Wicca, women-only Witchcraft groups, Shamans, Heathens (or, as they are also called, Odinists), and Druids. Shamans and women-only groups are both discussed separately in the volume. Because it is so central to the Neopagan movement, Wicca has previously been discussed in this chapter. Druids and Odinists are both important traditions in North America, as they are in England. The Reclaiming Tradition, which Starhawk helped to develop, is a North American creation that has influenced Witchcraft and the Neopaganism worldwide. Each of these traditions offers an important alternative form of Neopaganism and gives a sense of the variations that exist within the religion.

## Druids

Not all North American Druids are Neopagans. Some are Christians, and others view their practice as an ethical system consistent with any or no religion. Contemporary Druids all share a belief that their practices are in some way connected to those of the ancient Druids. Most contemporary North American Druids view their religion as a modern creation or a re-creation or new interpretation of the practices of ancient Druids. They openly acknowledge what archeologists have asserted—that there is no direct link between their religion and that of the ancient Druids. An earlier Christian revival in eighteenth and nineteenth centuries Europe and North America with links to Freemasonry made claims of antiquity, as do some contemporary groups. The Order of Bards, Ovates, and Druids—a British group with groves in North America—is one example of those that claim antiquity.

The best-known Druid organizations in North America are all offshoots of the Reformed Druids of North America (RDNA). This is in part because Isaac Bonewits, one of its members, is an outspoken Neopagan and prolific writer. The RDNA began in 1963 as a protest movement at Carleton College in Northfield, Minnesota, against the college's requirement that all students attend chapel on Sunday morning. The founders did not intend to create a religion but an ethical system in which the sky spirit, Ba'al, and Mother Earth were affirmed and in which students of any faith or no faith could comfortably join to avoid attending chapel. They had only two principles, both of which they summarize as "Earth is good." Initially the RDNA, while creating Druid-influenced rituals eschewed any magical practices (Adler 1986).

To the surprise of the group's founders, when Carlton revoked its chapel requirement, the RDNA continued, spread, and clearly became a religion. On its website the RDNA boasts 4,000 or more members but notes only 150 of those are in groups, which they call groves (www.geocities.com/mikerdna). They state that there are approximately 15 groves although they list more than 40 on the same website, two of which are in Canada—one in Ontario and the other in Alberta—while the rest are scattered throughout the United States. The group's statistics, particularly for members outside of groves, are not reliable. As their website indicates, they no longer have a national council, nor do they keep a record of all their groves, let alone those individuals who consider themselves part of the RDNA but are not in a grove. As they note on their website, each grove is a separate entity with no implied endorsement from the RDNA. Some of these groves are Neopagan, others are not. Adler (1979) notes that the RDNA, although serious about its religion, were always particularly playful and lighthearted. Their website continues to display a sense of humor about their organization, or lack of organization, and its membership.

The New Reformed Druids of North America (NRDNA), which is a splinter group of the RDNA, formed as a response to the RDNA's unwillingness to define Druidism as a Neopagan spiritual path. Isaac Bonewits, who had been ordained by RDNA in 1969, was an important voice for the creation of this new organization. Bonewits subsequently broke from the NRDNA to form ÀrnDraíocht Féin (ADF), which translates from the Gaelic as Our Own Druidism. ADF, unlike the NRDNA or the RDNA, defines itself as a national organization for the creation and dissemination of Druidism. In an open letter to the Neopagan community and all other interested individuals at the outset of the organization, Bonewits described his desire to create a form of Druidism that was at once appropriate to the space age and based on scholarship of what he described as pan-European Druidism. As he notes in this letter:

> I mean to include all the European Branches of the Indo-European culture and language tree—Celtic, Germanic, Slavic, Baltic, even the pre-Classical Greek and Roman. Paradoxically this would resemble the original Paleopagan Druidism far more than any efforts of the last thousand years. It would be based on the best scholarly research available, combined with what has been learned [about art, psychology, small-group politics and economics] through the theory and practice of modern Neopaganism, and my own knowledge of [the polytheological and practical details] magical and religious phenomena. (Bonewits 1983, 2001:2)

He subsequently states that technically Druids were Celtic but that other European pagan religions offer many complementary insights.

The ADF has been successful in creating a liturgy, a training program for clergy, and advocating for Druidism. It has also spawned its own splinter groups, including the Hendge of Keltria. The group, in part as a joke, pinned 13 theses, numbered 1 through 12 and 95 to the door of Bonwit's van at a Pagan gathering to indicate their desire to break from the larger group. Among their concerns was the formality of ADF and their own desire to have a Celtic form of Druidism (Taylor and Taylor 1996). All the Druid organizations and individuals whose practice is influenced by them that have grown out of the RDNA acknowledge that they are re-creating the religion and are influenced by what is known about ancient Druids but are not the direct descendents of the ancient Druids. As not all Druids are members of the RDNA or one of its daughter organizations, not all North American Druids may agree with this history. Nonetheless, it is less common in North America than in the United Kingdom for groups to claim antiquity.

Druids are polytheistic, celebrating several gods and goddesses. Mother Earth and the Sun are both revered. Contemporary Druids, like most other Neopagans, celebrate the eight sabbats that form the wheel of the year. Because of Druids' focus on the celebration of the Sun and its powers, they consider spring and fall equinoxes the most important sabbats. Unlike Wiccans who prefer to have their rituals at night, Druids are noted for having their rituals in daylight. Weather permitting, Druids typically hold their rituals in the woods, particularly in oak groves, as the oak is considered sacred to contemporary Druids just as it was to the ancient Druids.

Druids have been viewed by some in the Neopagan community as patriarchal. The older orders of the eighteenth and nineteenth century were composed completely of men. Contemporary groups are open to women and men on equal standing. In the United States, Druid groups have an equal number of male and female members, distinguishing this spiritual path from most other forms of Neopaganism in which there are usually more women than men (Berger et al. 2003). Shallcrass (1996), a practicing Druid, argues that the religion is not patriarchal but unlike Wiccan groups, is less concerned with feminist issues. He notes this does not mean that they are antiequality or necessarily sexist.

Within Druid groves there are three specialists: the Druid or priest; the Bard, who is the keeper of stories and poems; and the Ovate, who divines the future and uses herbs to heal. Druid rituals have a different feel than those of other Neopagan rites. Unlike Wiccan groups in which the high priestess or high priestess and high priest officiate, in Druid groups the three specialists perform the ritual. Stories and poems, divination, and the calling of the deities are all part of the ritual. Bonewits (1996:81–82) describes Neopagan Druid rituals:

> The primary deity worshipped by Neopagan Druids is the Earth Mother, also known as Mother Nature or Gaia. . . . She is mentioned prominently near the beginning and end of every Neopagan Druidic ceremony. ADF liturgy also focuses strongly on a Divine Gatekeeper, deities or other spirits of Bardic inspiration, the "Three Kindreds" of Deities, Ancestors and Nature Spirits, and even the forces of Chaos—very carefully. Every ADF liturgy has a specific Divine "guest of honor" or two, to whom the majority of our worship is dedicated. Our offerings consist of songs, chants, dances, ritual dramas, poems, and other works of art. These are "sacrificed" instead of the blood offerings of our Paleopagan predecessors.

Druid's cosmology speaks of three worlds, with humans inhabiting the middle one. There are variations about what these three worlds are composed of, whether divinity is above or below, and how they are connected. Nonetheless, there is believed to be an interaction among these three spheres (Bonewits 1996). Like other Neopagans, Druids participate in magic. In *Real Magic* (1989) Bonewits argues that magic is a form of science, which can be learned. Although Bonewits is an important voice for North American Druidism, not all Druids agree with his view of magic. Others see magic as a more spiritual activity and not solely a technique. Like other Neopagans, Druids use herbs for healing, viewing it as part of the knowledge that the "wise ones" held in traditional communities. Foretelling the future plays a more prominent part in many Druids' rituals than other groups, as Druids have the Ovate, who is considered an expert on these issues. However, this distinction is not strong, as several forms of divination, such as reading tarot cards, are common throughout the Neopagan community, and hence this is a matter of degree as well as form but not something that makes Druids unique.

## Odinists

Odinists are the most controversial Neopagan spiritual path because a subset of this group has revived Neo-Nazis' paganism and propaganda. Margot Adler, in her most recent edition of *Drawing Down the Moon* (1986), notes that she excluded any mention of Odinists in the first edition of her book (1978) because of her discomfort with the links between some Odinists and the Neo-Nazi movement. In their Megiddo Report, the FBI included Odinists as one of the millennial groups that they considered a potential threat as year 2000 approached. As an example of the threat posed by Odinists, the report cites William King, a self-described Odinist and one of the men who dragged James Byrd Jr., an African American, to his death. The Canadian Security Intelligence Service similarly, in anticipation of the new millenium, prepared a report on what it called "Doomsday Religious Movements." Unlike the FBI, the Canadian report did not specifically mention Odinists as a threat.

The year after the FBI report was published, the Southern Poverty Law Center (SPLC) included an article about racist Odinist groups in its newsletter. The article, an interview with Mattias Gardell (2001), professor of religion at the University of Stockholm's Center for Research in International Migration and Ethnic Relations, is a discussion of Professor Gardell's research on white supremacist groups in the United States. Gardell notes that older racists groups are Christian and patriotic. The newer groups are composed of young men who have rejected the Christianity and patriotism of their elders because they view both Christianity and the United States government as responsible for what they see as the evils of a liberal society. These young white supremacists are instead embracing Odinism. Jeffrey Kaplan (1997) similarly notes the growing interest in one form of Odinism among members of the radical racist right-wing movements.

The aggregation of both racist and nonracist groups under the heading of Odinist has confused the discussion about the threat of Neo-Nazi Pagans and has angered Odinists who are neither racist nor Neo-Nazi. Odinist groups responded to both the FBI and SPLC reports. Valgard Murray of the International Asatru/Odinic Alliance (IAOA) responding to the FBI report, asserts: "Our nation's founders felt so strongly about our inalienable right to religious freedom without fear of governmental harassment that they placed it first in the Bill of Rights at the top of the First Amendment. . . . Americans who support the Bill of Rights must question their government's efforts to vilify, demonize and even destroy a law aiding religious minority through what amount to a smear campaign based upon gross misrepresentation and outright lies. . . . What next, will we be fed to the lions" (Cesnur 1999). The SPLC report came under attack from Neopagan groups who were alarmed that the article treated all Odinists, and in fact all Neopagans, as though they were members of the radical right. The newsletter subsequently printed a correction noting that the groups mentioned in the article were not representative of all Odinists or Neopagans. The version of the article that appears on the SPLC web page includes this correction at the top of the page.

Contemporary Neo-Nazi Odinists base their spiritual and political practices on writings on Aryan Pagans in Nazi Germany (Kaplan 1996). Although these Odinists are a concern, particularly in the United States because of their links to other hate groups, they form a small percentage of all Odinists. Non–Neo-Nazi Odinists work to distinguish themselves from the Neo-Nazi variant. To help clarify the distinction, many Odinists prefer to use the term *Heathen* or *Ásatrú* instead of *Odinist* to describe their religion. Odin, as they note, is only one of the gods of the ancient Nordic religion. Ásatrú translates from the Norse as believer in the gods—and hence is more general designation. Unlike many other Neopagans who view each of the deities as an aspect of the one divine entity or of nature, Odinists are clearly polytheistic. They view the deities as having almost human foibles and attributes. Among Odinists, there are two categories of deities—the Aesir, who are the sky gods, and the Vanir, or earth deities. There is variation among Odinists, some focus their worship on the Aesir and others on the Vanir.

Odinists are not eclectic but focus exclusively on the Viking deities, which are noted for their emphasis on war and fertility, although each of the deities also has some aspects not associated with these attributes (Kaplan 1997). Like other Neopagans, most Ásatrú celebrate the eight seasonal holidays. In addition, they celebrate specifically Nordic holidays and personal days throughout the year. The Ásatrú, like the Druids, rely on scholarly research about the pagan practices in one specific historic area to help to re-create an older religious practice within a modern context. Central to the Odinists are Norse mythology and magical practices. The mythology postulates nine worlds connected by a tree. Some creatures, such as giants and the deities, can travel among the worlds and influence the lives of humans. All of these creatures are mortal, including the gods and goddesses. Jeffrey Kaplan (1997:72) describes the relationship between their gods and the Ásatrú: "[T]he relationship is less one of creator to creation or of distant, all-knowing, and all-powerful spirit to weak mortal flesh than it is one of father to child or of tribal elder to youthful warrior." The magical system of the Ásatrú is based on the use of the runes for divination and for transformation of events. Although aspects of Odinist magical practice, such as the use of runes for divination, have been absorbed into the general occult milieu and the Neopagan community, Odinists usually focus exclusively on Nordic magical practices.

Odinists draw more men than women to their ranks. In *Voices from the Pagan Census,* Berger et al. (2003) found that 65 percent of Odinists in the United States are men—the inverse of the proportion of men to women in the general Neopagan community. Most of those drawn to the religion are of German or Scandinavian heritage and view their religion as an aspect of their cultural heritage. Jeffrey Kaplan (1997) makes a distinction between racist Odinists and the racially aware but not racist Ásatrú. However, as Kaplan notes, this distinction is sometimes difficult to maintain. Margot Adler (1986) reports that in one interview a member of the Ásatrú Free Assembly told her "we are not racists, but we are racially aware." Another member said "she had never had a black person apply to be in her group, but she would wonder why they weren't interested in their own religious roots" (277). As Adler notes, the focus on one particular ethnic or geographically based form of Neopaganism does not necessitate this view. The Druids, for example, do not have a racially oriented perspective, although for many of the groups the focus is on Celtic mythology and magic. Not all Odinist groups are racially aware. In my own fieldwork in the Northeast United States, I attended the rituals and interviewed the members of one Odinist group whose members fit comfortably within the greater Neopagan community. They were not racists nor even particularly conservative. The group's leader was of Irish, not Norse, extraction. However, on the whole, Odinists, more than other forms of Neopaganism, see their spirituality tied to their ethnicity and directly or indirectly to their race.

Kaplan argues that the racial issue, which has plagued the Odinists since the AFA first formed, is in many ways minor for the religion. It has, he believes, been blown out of proportion. Among Odinists, like other Neopagan groups, emphasis is placed on reenchantment of the world and on the practice of magic. The issue of race and racism within this group is particularly thorny because of the fluid membership within Neopaganism. The religion has open boundaries that make it impossible to exclude anyone, including Neo-Nazi Neopagans whose values are so at odds with the norms of the larger Neopagan community.

*Reclaiming Tradition*
The Reclaiming Tradition bears the marks of Starhawk, who is one of its founders, but is more than merely an extension of Starhawk's writings. The tradition is maintained, modified, and taught by the Reclaiming Collective, which is also responsible for producing a glossy magazine four times a year and holding open rituals in their local area. Members of the collective describe themselves as "a community of San Francisco Bay Area women and

men working to unify spirit and politics" (Rabinovitch and Lewis, 2002:218).

Classes in the San Francisco Bay area and a set of intensive classes called Witch Camps, which have been held in California, Florida, Georgia, Michigan, Missouri, Pennsylvania, Texas, Vermont, and Virginia in the U.S. and in Vancouver, Canada, Germany, and England, have helped to spread the tradition throughout the United States, Canada, and parts of Europe. By encouraging those trained in the tradition to take what they have learned back to their home communities and teach others, the Reclaiming Tradition has been further disseminated. Starhawk's fame has brought attention to the Reclaiming Tradition.

The Reclaiming Collective grew out of classes taught by Starhawk and another member of her coven, Diane Baker, in the San Francisco Bay area around 1980.[5] Prior to this time, individuals had been trained within the coven system or through classes that Starhawk taught at a local occult bookstore and at the Open University. The initial set of classes taught by Starhawk and Baker was a six-week course called "The Elements of Magic," focusing on the four directions (east, south, west, and north) and the elements associated with each of them. Spirit, which is viewed as located in the center, was the last topic to be covered. The course emphasized the participants' learning to experience and to use the magical aspects of each of the directions to transform some aspect of their lives. Although the Reclaiming Tradition includes women and men, the initial set of classes were open only to women. Interest from the first group of participants resulted in a second and third set of classes being taught and more members of Starhawk and Baker's coven being drawn into teaching. Ultimately, members of the initial class formed their own coven and in turn began to teach the Reclaiming Tradition.

The Witch Camps, which were begun in 1985, were a response to requests by individuals who lived outside of and could not come for an extended period of time to the San Francisco Bay, but wanted to be trained in the tradition (Salomonsen 2002). At these camps, individuals live together for a week, during which time they participate in learning mythology, ritual creation, and magical practices as interpreted through the Reclaiming Tradition. Days are filled with classes, participating in and helping to create rituals, and socializing among the participants. These Witch Camps provide an immersion course in the Reclaiming Tradition as well as a place for individuals to meet others of similar interest. Some covens have sprouted from the friendships formed at the Witch Camps.

The Reclaiming Tradition has its immediate roots in the Faery Tradition, into which Starhawk was initiated, and the feminist Witchcraft teachings of Zsuzsanna Budapest, with whom Starhawk studied. Victor Anderson, Starhawk's teacher in Faery Witchcraft, claims that his tradition was in part bestowed on him by his grandmother and in part his own creation. He describes what he believes makes his tradition unique: "We worship 'God' as a feminine being. When we say 'Goddess' . . . we mean . . . the Ancient One, the Oldest of all Deities, the Mother of All the Gods, The Holy Ghost Herself. We speak of Her as the Holy Virgin. Not because She doesn't have sex, but because She is complete within Herself. She is both Male and Female" (Anderson 1996:78). Anderson claims that his tradition has its origins more than 20,000 years ago in Africa and was spread by magical creatures, "the little people," or faeries. Salomonsen (2002), contrary to Anderson, contends that the Faery Tradition's roots are firmly planted in British Wicca. The Faery and Reclaiming Traditions celebrate the same sabbats and esabats as Wicca and share similar magical practices and mythology.

The magical system taught within Reclaiming is influenced by the Faery Tradition, which uses a system of meditating on what are called the Iron and Pearl Pentacles. The second set of the initial classes taught by Starhawk and Baker were entitled the "Iron Pentagram" and focused on the use of meditation on sex, self, passion, and pride. This work is viewed as magical, as it is believed to help the individual, through the mind-body connection, to heal her- or himself and therefore to become more effective in the world. Like many forms of Neopaganism, the emphasis is not on dogma but on experiencing the magical through which the individual transforms the self and the world around her or him. Anna Korn (1996), a practitioner, claims the Faery Tradition, more than Wicca, focuses on the ecstatic union of the participants with the divine. This, as she notes, is a matter of degree more than kind.

Unlike Zsuzsanna Budapest, whose form of Dianic Witchcraft honors the goddess to the exclusion of the god, Reclaiming celebrations regularly honor both the goddess and the god. Although Anderson's teaching stresses a greater emphasis on the goddess than the god, Budapest's influence can be seen in the even stronger influence of the goddess in the Reclaiming Tradition than in the Faery Tradition. Furthermore, feminist concerns are reflected in Reclaiming's shunning of hierarchy, its lack of a required initiation, and the combining of the spiritual and the political. Salomonsen describes the Reclaiming collective as simultaneously embracing women's reproductive capacities as sacred and working to redefine women's roles inside and outside the family.

Although Salomonsen has documented instances of hierarchy within the collective, such as between those that are and are not initiated, the group has worked to address entrenched power differentials. In 1997, the same year that the group gained recognition as a tax-exempt religious association, it reorganized to give newer members more power. Both before and after the reorganization, the group was based on working cells. In the reorganization more cells were developed, permitting greater involvement of more people. Prior to reorganization those with the most experience in the collective had the most power in the group. The group has from its formation eschewed formal hierarchies. They do not, for instance, have high priestesses or high priests, or other leaders. The reorganization was an attempt to limit the power differentials that had developed based on longevity (NightMare with Willow 2002; Salomonsen 2002).

There is a strong commitment to liberal ideals and policies among the Reclaiming Witches. Starhawk and some of the other members of the group participate in demonstrations for social justice. However, others who are part of the Reclaiming Tradition are less politically active. It is, therefore, possible to be both a Reclaiming Witch and not politically active. Nonetheless, the Reclaiming tradition is an important voice of the blending of the political and the spiritual. The influence of this tradition is felt to varying degrees throughout the Neopagan community, even if only as something to respond to.

## NEOPAGAN ORGANIZATIONS

Each of the spiritual paths that were discussed in the last section have one or more organizations associated with it that provide services for members and other interested individuals, such as magazines and websites, and help seekers find groups or other individuals with similar interests. Not all spiritual paths have organizations associated with them, but the larger and more established ones have at least nascent organizations and websites. Although, as noted before, there is no single central Neopagan organization, there are numerous Neopagan umbrella groups throughout North America. These organizations provide services to the larger Neopagan community, including ordination, training, newsletters, festivals, and open rituals, and serve as representatives on interfaith councils and in public venues such as the Parliament of World Religions. Some of these groups have incorporated into churches, others have not. Through their newsletters, open rituals, gatherings, websites, and well-known spokespeople for the movement, each of these groups helps to shape the religion. Some groups and individuals involved with them have more influence than others, usually based on how large a network of Neopagans they have established, how well known their leaders or some of their most outspoken members are, and the types and usefulness of the services they provide.

The Church of All Worlds (CAW), which took its name from the Robert A. Heinlein's science fiction classic *Stranger in a Strange Land,* was one of the earliest Neopagan organizations in North America. The organization is best known for publishing *Green Egg,* one of the earliest Neopagan journals in North America. The journal helped to define the nascent movement by providing a forum for the sharing of ideas and disputes. The magazine, as noted earlier, popularized the term *Pagan*. Its greatest contribution, however, was its willingness to publish unedited articles and letters, providing an arena for Pagans throughout North America to communicate with one another. CAW also serves as an organization for its group's own form of Neopaganism, which combines elements of libertarianism, science fiction, and environmentalism.

The Covenant of the Goddess (CoG) offers an example of another type of Neopagan organization that neither advocates for a particular spiritual path nor has the majority of its leadership from one spiritual path or group. Although both Canadians and Americans can join CoG, Canada also has a similar but much smaller group, the Congregationalist Witchcraft Association (Reid 2001). CoG, which was established in 1975, states that its purpose is "to increase cooperation and to secure for Witches and covens the legal protection enjoyed by members of other religions" (www.cog.org). Both covens and individuals can join, if recommended by two members without reservation. The organization, among other things, provides Witches with clergy certification, which can be used by individuals to become legal clergy in some states. They also provide a network of covens and a newsletter and hold a yearly gathering called Merry Meet. In addition to the national organization, there are local CoG chapters that meet to provide local services to groups and individuals in their community. CoG often serves as a voice within the Neopagan community—speaking to issues and concerns of its members and for the larger Neopagan community. Most members of CoG belong to several other organizations. The first officer, who is sometimes jokingly referred to as the head Witch, rotates. Individuals from most of the major groups and forms of Witchcraft have at one time been first officer of CoG.

Many organizations have sprung up throughout North America. These differ in their influence and the number of people involved. However, the sheer number of groups stops anyone from becoming the only or even the main voice of Neopaganism. Some, like CoG, however, have gained centrality and recognition within the Neopagan community. Circle Sanctuary, which is run by Selena Fox and her romantic partner Dennis Carpenter, is one of the best known of these organizations. Amid controversy and legal battles with their neighbors, Circle Sanctuary bought 200 acres of land in Wisconsin, on which the group lives and maintains a nature sanctuary. The group has a website, runs festivals, and has a legal arm, Lady Liberty, that both collects information on law suits concerning the truncation of Neopagans' civil liberties and provides help to Neopagans who believe that they are being discriminated against because of their religious practice.

Circle Sanctuary, CoG, and several other organizations such as Earth-

Spirit Community and Elf Lore Family, have become well known for the festivals they run. These gatherings that draw together hundreds of Neopagans each year serve as an emblem of the community. However, each of these organizations do more than just run festivals or open circles. Earth-Spirit Community and Circle Sanctuary, for example, represented Earth Based Religions at the Parliament of World Religions. All the groups provide resources for individuals not only in their immediate area but also throughout North America. Although none of these churches or organizations can speak for all Neopagans, they are important structures in this polymorphous religion. They provide a forum through their newsletter, magazines, websites, and festivals for Neopagans to exchange ideas and to maintain their identities. They also contribute a public face for Neopaganism, as the leaders often are asked to speak for the community in the media. Furthermore, they furnish a series of services that more-traditional religions accomplish in their churches—that is, they help to create a community through which like-minded people can find one another and feel they belong. As well as being a source for information about the religion, these organizations normally provide either training for interested seekers or suggestions of where individuals might find an appropriate teacher.

FESTIVALS

Festivals are gatherings that occur yearly in the countryside and last over a weekend or a week. They provide a venue for Neopagans to come together, camp, participate in each other's rituals, and meet one another and some well-known Neopagans—often referred to as BNPs (Big Name Pagans). Because individuals usually camp or live in unheated cabins, most festivals occur in the spring and summer, although some for the hardy take place well into the fall. EarthSpirit Community, for example, has a large gathering for a week around Memorial Day weekend, which commonly attracts 500 to 800 participants and a much smaller one in the fall that may only have 200 attendees. Pike (2001) views festivals as combining elements of nineteenth-century religious retreats, revival meetings, spiritualist gatherings, and a tourist attraction (14). Neopagan festivals share with these earlier gatherings a separation of the participants from their daily life in the pursuit of the spiritual. Entering a festival, one has the sense of joining a summer camp for adults. Neopagans of all ages walk around in ritual robes, in clothing reminiscent of medieval nobility, in jeans or shorts, or skyclad or semidressed. There are often games played on grass, and sunbathing and swimming if a lake is nearby.

Festivals provide an image of what a Neopagan community might be like if one were to exist. There are normally several rituals a day that one can chose to attend, workshops on any number of topics of interest to Neopagans, such as astral projection, creation of rituals, and how to raise a Pagan child. Merchants' Row provides an area in which people can buy goods and services that have a Pagan flavor. Handmade ritual robes, paintings and small sculptures of gods and goddesses, magical or medical herbs, body painting, and jewelry are all for sale. Most of the merchants are themselves Neopagans and therefore sell goods as well as participate in rituals and other activities.

Individuals who attend often have a sense that they are part of a sporadic but ongoing community. Friendships are formed and maintained as the same people often attend the same festival each year. At many of the festivals, individuals are asked to contribute some of their time to the community, either working in the kitchen, helping with child care, participating in cleanups, or overseeing the parking. For most Neopagans there is a sense of excitement and magic in the air as they are surrounded by others who share many of the same religious beliefs and practices, and possibly more importantly, the same worldview. The intense interaction among people, the large number of rituals and magical workings, often result in people expressing a feeling of being "burned out" by the festivals.

A fire that is kept burning throughout the festival is often the spiritual center of the gathering. Throughout the day, but particularly at night, individuals come to the fire to talk, to meditate, and to participate in ecstatic dancing. The fire is also often the center of conflicts. Pike notes that festivals, while celebrating Neopagan creativity and sense of freedom, also provide a venue for the contradiction of the community to come to the fore. Individual freedom is something that most Neopagans see as central to their spiritual quest and worldview. Nonetheless, these freedoms often come in conflict with other's needs. There are complaints, for example, that sacrilege is committed by those who throw their cigarette butts in the sacred fire. Some women have reported having unwanted sexual overtures made to them as they dance ecstatically around the fire. Neopagans celebrate all forms of sexuality as part of the sacred. They also are supportive of women's rights and the right of both women and men to feel safe at festivals.

The sense of community that develops at Neopagan gatherings, although real, is limited. Festivals are temporary; food, clothing, and bedding are brought to them. Other than the merchants, those attending earn their living outside of the festival. There is, therefore, no sense of creating a real economically and socially sustainable community. What the festivals do provide is a sense of community and a place for Neopagans to connect with others. In any given year only a small percentage of Neopagans attend festivals (Berger et al. 2003). Nonetheless, festivals remain an important image of the Neopagan community, at least for those who attend or are integrated into groups in which some members attend. Like Neopagan churches and organizations, festivals provide a visible center for a polymorphous religion.

CONCLUSION

Magical practices, occult beliefs, and individualization of religious practice are all becoming more accepted and common within North America. It is within this context that North American Neopaganism and Witchcraft is growing and flourishing. The religion is international, having its roots in England, but has been altered in North America by the social movements of the 1960s and 1970s, by American individualism, and by the larger population and lower density than in Europe. The spread of the religion is being aided by books, journals, and the Internet. On the one hand, this permits the ultimate in self-expression, as individuals can pick and choose which websites and books or parts of books to use. There is no bureaucracy or immediate authority to determine practice or even who is and is not a Neopagan or Witch. On the other hand, the mass media has fostered a growth in homogeneity among individuals and groups as people read the same materials and interact on the Internet.

Although Witchcraft remains the most popular form of Neopaganism, there are numerous spiritual paths within the religion. Some of these offer minor variations from Witchcraft while others offer a more clearly differentiated practice. All of these, however, share a celebration of nature's yearly cycles, the veneration of goddesses and most commonly also gods, a belief that the divine is imminent in nature and in people's bodies and lives. The growth of a small number of Neo-Nazi Neopagans, the increased interest in the religion among teenagers, and its own growth are challenging the religion on many fronts. Although it is impossible to document the exact number of Neopagans in North America, both practitioners and ethnographers of the religion agree that there is an increase in the number of participants. The increased numbers of members, particularly the growth of solitary practitioners, is quietly changing the religion. The Internet and books are becoming increasingly important in the way in which the religion is practiced. The increased interest among teenagers, most of whom practice as solitaries, indicates another change in the religion. Witchcraft and magical practices are becoming more commonplace in North America. It is unclear if this religion, whose growth was in part a reflection of the social movements of the 1960s, will maintain its critical edge. In part that depends on how well the groups and organizations that exist are able to integrate the newer and younger members into their worldview as well as into their religious practice.

# Webs of Women: Feminist Spiritualities

## Wendy Griffin

When Hungarian immigrant Zsuzsanna Budapest first coined the term *feminist spirituality* in a 1972 issue of a monthly paper in Los Angeles called *Sister*, it was in the context of her argument regarding the interdependent dynamics of politics and religion. She posed the question that if patriarchal religion denigrated women and helped to perpetuate male domination, what would happen if women "rewrote the script" and created a religion based on feminist values, a feminist spirituality? In the succeeding thirty years, the phrase has been applied to groups as varied as Dianic Witches, generic goddess worshipers, Roman Catholic members of Woman-Church, and Protestant Christian Feminists (Caron 1992; Eller 1993; Stuckey 1998). In this time of increasing privatization of religion, the term more accurately describes several related worldviews instead of one. Rather than there being one feminist spirituality, as may have been true in the early 1970s, there exists today a family of feminist spiritualities. Like strands of color in a weaving, they are related yet not the same. They overlap and interact in many places. They all provide a feminist understanding of the divine, and each insists upon the importance of listening to women's voices and hearing their stories. In addition, they share women's empowerment as a major goal and the use of language, symbols, ritual, and what could be identified as ritual magic. Some threads reject traditional religions and function outside their immediate sphere; some work within them to transform them, to "call the patriarchal church to conversion" (Fiorenza as quoted in Caron 1992:161). While these spiritualities have some differences, together they form a tapestry. Members of groups within these diverse strands may even be part of intersecting webs, as it is not unusual to discover women in both the United States and Canada who comfortably participate in more than one spiritual group, weaving seemingly disparate elements into one syncretistic and idiosyncratic worldview. This includes those women who use both the goddess and Christianity or Judaism as the warp and woof of their spiritual lives (Winter, Lummis, and Stokes 1994; Manning 1996; Taylor 2001). Although the roots of this phenomenon cannot be traced back to a single source, multiple sources first become visible in the United States in the 1960s, with the second wave of feminist organizing.

## THE REEMERGENCE OF FEMINISM

In 1963, one year after Raymond and Rosemary Buckland brought Wicca to the United States, several things occurred that marked the reemergence of organized feminism. President John Kennedy, at the urging of Esther Peterson, director of the Women's Bureau, had previously established a Commission on the Status of Women and given it the charge to investigate women's status in the workplace. Shortly after the Equal Pay Act was signed in 1963, the commission published a report that demonstrated discrimination against women in almost every facet of American life and in particular in wage discrimination (Zelman 1982). In that same year, Betty Friedan published *The Feminine Mystique*. This book tapped into the discontent experienced primarily by white, middle-class, married women over the limitations imposed by their family-centered role. Thus, for the first time, women who worked only inside their homes as wives and mothers joined women who, in increasing numbers, worked outside the home as paid laborers, and together they began to give voice to their dissatisfaction and growing resentment.

In 1966, at the Third National Conference on the State Commissions on the Status of Women, delegates submitted a resolution calling on the Equal Employment Opportunity Commission to follow its legal mandate and enforce the sex provision of Title VII of the Civil Rights Act. The resolution was not allowed on the floor for discussion. Later that day, a small group of frustrated delegates met and formed the National Organization for Women (NOW). While NOW met the needs of many women who wanted social change, it could not be everything to everybody. Schisms formed within the organization, some claiming it was too radical, others that it was too conservative. Women who were unhappy with its goals or strategies broke away and started their own groups.

These women were joined by others who had dropped out of different social justice movements, women who had became discouraged when they realized these movements did not extend social justice to include gender issues. These smaller, splinter groups could focus on specific issues and strategies with which all members were comfortable. Here women acted from and drew on their own experiences. New York Radical Women, formed in 1967, was one of these splinter groups. It was the first feminist group to capture national media attention, doing so with a flamboyant protest at the 1968 Miss America pageant. However, not all members were happy with "guerilla theater," and the group split along political lines, with radical feminists founding Redstockings to write and do consciousness raising and "hip Left style politicos" founding WITCH to be a feminist action group (Morgan in Ryan 1992:198n7).

Calling itself the striking arm of the Women's Liberation Movement, WITCH took its name from I Samuel 15:23, which reads, "For rebellion is as the sin of witchcraft." WITCH made its first formal appearance on Halloween in 1968. A group of costumed "witches," cackling with glee in an action titled "Up against the Wall Street," theatrically disrupted and hexed a brokerage firm, the Chase Manhattan Bank, and the Morgan Guarantee Trust (Morgan 1970). Within weeks, small groups calling themselves covens had sprung up in Boston, Chicago, San Francisco, and Washington, D.C. In one town, WITCH hexed the transit authority for raising fares, in another the United Fruit Company for labor practices abroad and sex discrimination at home. Organized locally and completely autonomous, all the groups used the acronym WITCH, although in one place it meant Women's International Terrorist Conspiracy from Hell, in another Women Inspired to Commit Herstory, and in still another something entirely different.

The symbol of the witch was an inspired one for these feminists. This was neither Glenda the Good from Oz nor Samantha from *Bewitched*. This was the rebellious woman who had secret knowledge, the power to hex. As religious studies scholar Cynthia Eller (1993:55) points out, "By choosing this symbol, feminists were identifying themselves with everything that women were taught not to be: ugly, aggressive, independent and malicious." Members of WITCH frequently passed out cards to other women that read, in part, "You are a witch by saying aloud, 'I am a witch,' three times and thinking about that. You are a witch by being female, untamed, angry, joyous, and immortal" (in Morgan 1970:606).

Although unconnected to Wicca or any other system of shared spiritual beliefs, WITCH irrevocably linked second wave feminism with the symbol of the witch. Its manifesto accepted uncritically the work of first wave feminist Matilda Joselyn Gage, who in the previous century had written that nine million women were put to death for the crime of witchcraft (Gage [1893] 1980). In her writings, Gage drew on the sensationalistic *La Sorciére,* by French historian Jules Michelet, a book that portrayed witchcraft as a surviving pagan religion gone underground during Christian persecutions in the Middle Ages and passed on from mother to daughter (Hutton 1999). Gage linked these ideas to the then popular theory of universal matriarchy and concluded that witches were pagan priestesses of an ancient religion, skilled in the healing arts and persecuted by the Church in order to eliminate female power. WITCH brought Gage and her ideas into twentieth-century radical feminist consciousness.

This occurred in both the United States and Canada. Feminism had begun to make its appearance in Canada by the late 1960s, and WITCH manifestos and actions were thoroughly covered in Ottawa's *Free Press* and served as models for Quebec's "sorciéres," feminist activists in the arts, publishing, theo/alogy, and sociopolitical action (DuFresne 2002a). Later, when Witchcraft began to grow as a spiritual practice in British Victoria, WITCH stood for Wiccans Invoking Tolerance, Compassion, and Harmony and Witches Invoking Tolerance, Caring, and Healing (Marron 1989).

In 1970, more than 200 women from across Canada gathered in Saskatoon, Saskatchewan, for the first national conference on the women's movement. They heard sociologist Marlene Dixon announce in her keystone speech that race and class divided women too much to build an autonomous women's movement (PAR-L 2002). Nevertheless, a movement for women's rights did grow in Canada, consciousness raising (CR) groups began to spring up, and the first feminist courses were taught at York University in 1971. Major changes occurred in the law that affected issues such as divorce, contraception, abortion, and discrimination. For several years, government grants were available for community work and social services. Women took advantage of these to build support infrastructures, and a large number of them experienced the intense and empowering environment of small groups of women working together for social change, just as they did in the United States through the various state commissions on the status of women, NOW, and other women's groups. It was not long before Canadian women began looking for spiritual empowerment as well, and T-shirts that read "Womanspirit" could be seen by the mid-1970s (Slater 2002). Womanspirit was also the name of a women's art gallery and research and resource center in London, Ontario, which was in operation from 1975 to 1985, when the building was sold out from under them. Besides hosting exhibitions, cultural events, and rituals, Womanspirit was a member of the National Action Committee on the Status of Women, Canada's largest women's organization (Buyers 2002). As such, it deftly combined goddess spirituality, cultural feminism, and feminist activism for Canadian women.

Although it may have been an inspiration to early Canadian feminism, WITCH did not offer a spiritual belief system to replace what it critiqued with such flourish. However, it did link witchcraft and religion in a thoroughly feminist manner. In the winter of 1968–1969, a local coven turned out to hex Boston College because it denied tenure to a feminist theologian by the name of Mary Daly. Daly, a scholar with doctorates in religion, sacred theology, and philosophy, had been hired in 1966 as "token woman" in an all-male theology department in a Catholic university (Daly 1992:88). Her book *Church and the Second Sex*, a bold and critical examination of the Catholic Church and its relationship to women, had been written in Europe before she was hired. When it was published, the Jesuit college reacted by giving Daly a one-year terminal contract. The decision generated considerable controversy and protest, and was eventually reversed when Daly was awarded tenure. Daly initially believed that she could remain and find spiritual meaning within the Catholic Church as she called it to task for its historical exclusion and treatment of women. But she found that impossible, and by 1971, she was teaching her first feminist classes and challenging the entire symbol system of patriarchal religion.

That fall, Daly was invited to be the first woman in 336 years to preach at Harvard's Memorial Church. She met with a group of women to discuss the opportunity. Together they decided to turn the invitation into a "Call for an Exodus" from patriarchal religion altogether. On November 14, 1971, Daly announced from the pulpit that "We have to go out from the land of our fathers into an unknown place. We can this morning demonstrate our exodus from sexist religion—a break which for many of us has already taken place spiritually. . . . We cannot really belong to institutional religion as it exists. It isn't good enough to be token preachers. It isn't good enough to have our energies drained and co-opted. Singing sexist hymns, praying to a male god breaks our spirit, makes us less than human" (in King 1993:163). Although afraid she would lead only a handful of followers on the exodus, Daly reports that hundreds of women and some men marched out of the church, leaving her to rush along with them, "caught in the middle of the stampede" (Daly 1992:138). While some of these individuals returned the next Sunday, seeing the act as a symbolic rather than a definitive one, the impact of the exodus was significant, and Daly's reputation as a radical feminist theologian was established.

That same fall, she suggested the formation of a special section on women and religion at the annual meetings of the American Academy of Religion.[1] The women members enthusiastically accepted the proposal, and Daly was elected program chair for 1972. Not surprisingly, the conference in 1972 contained papers from various feminist scholars that explored the religious oppression and aspirations of women. By 1973, Daly's own personal exodus was reaffirmed in *Beyond God the Father: Toward a Philosophy of Women's Liberation*, and by the time *The Church and Second Sex* was rereleased in 1975, it carried a "Feminist Postchristian Introduction."

Although Daly typically prefers to refer to herself as a crone[2] or a spinster rather than a Witch, her work has had an enormous impact on the development of early Feminist Spirituality.[3] She points out that, "The word *craft* means, among other things, skill and cunning. Wild women sometimes refer to our strength, force, skills, and occupations as Witchcraft" (Daly 1992:109). Using ingenious wordplay that is designed to dis-cover patriarchal language and "be-spell" or awaken latent power in women, Daly defines the word *Witch* as, "an Elemental Soothsayer;[4] one who is in harmony with the rhythms of the universe; Wise Woman, Healer; one who exercises transformative powers: Shape-shifter; one who wields Labrys-like powers of aversion and attraction–averting disaster, warding off attacks of demons and Magnetizing Elemental Spiritual Forces" (Daly 1987:180).

The symbol of the witch as powerful rebel against male dominance was a popular one that caught on quickly and spread. In 1984, a large graffiti-covered billboard in Vancouver read, "April 30th. The Night of the Witches."[5] The graffiti was inspired by a German rape survivor who had sought refuge in the Vancouver Rape Relief House. She reported that German feminists celebrated April 30 by going into the streets to protest violence against women. Three-dimensional models of witches were fastened to the Canadian billboard. According to one woman involved in the project, "we are celebrating the witchiness in ourselves. Lots of women today feel an affinity to the witches. We are the carriers of culture and tradition. Midwives and herbalists today are the direct descendents of witches" (Kelly 1984). Her comments echo the analysis of both WITCH and Ehrenreich and English (1973), who argued that the European persecution of witches was a deliberate attack on women healers. Like these, the focus of the billboard was political, not spiritual. Its message was successful, as it quickly became an important feminist networking exchange, adorned with comments, notes, and posters from women's groups from all over the Lower Mainland.

Feminist scholar Johanna Stuckey argued that this kind of political work led naturally to Goddess Spirituality for some women. An early second wave radical feminist in Toronto from the late 1960s, Stuckey was one of the first academics to teach a course on goddesses. For her, discovering and being involved in feminism was a spiritual experience (Stuckey 1998). The consciousness-raising groups in which many feminists were involved provided an intensity, a ritualized sharing of experience, and community validation that were sorely missed when they disbanded. Stuckey believes that CR helped prepare women with spiritual needs to look elsewhere for nourishment. What some of them discovered was feminist Witchcraft.

## FEMINIST WITCHCRAFT

On the winter solstice in 1971, just over a month after Daly's Exodus on the East Coast, seven women on the West Coast created the first coven of feminist Witches. It was led by Zsuzsanna Budapest, who, as a teenager, had escaped the Soviet crackdown in Hungry and fled to Austria. By 1958, Budapest had immigrated to Chicago, where she married a childhood sweetheart, gave birth to two sons, and studied with Second City, an improvisational theater group. Inspired, she convinced her family to move to

New York where she studied at the American Academy of Dramatic Arts. But at the age of 30, Budapest found herself frustrated and depressed.

> Suddenly I had reviewed all of thirty years and I realized that nowhere near have I come to what I'm supposed to do, which I, of course, didn't know what it was. But I knew it was something much bigger than what I was involved in. And at that point, I talked about it with my husband, and I talked with my children for years about it. . . . So when I hit the Saturn Cycle, I was extremely unhappy. I was crying all the time. I acted out what somebody misplaced would do. You know, if you put a scientist into just digging holes, a scientist would want to be a scientist. Well, I was a High Priestess without me knowing it at that time, and I was intensely unhappy in every other role. (Budapest 1991)

Budapest left for a three-week vacation in Southern California and never went back. "I stayed in Venice, California and there I gave birth to myself. Other women gave birth to me by introducing me to the feminist movement" (Budapest 1991).

But although she became involved with feminist politics, the women's movement failed to meet her spiritual needs or address her growing belief that women needed to reclaim not only their bodies, but their "sweet womon souls"[6] from male-dominated religions (Budapest, Roslund, Hancken, Doczi, Nina, Kria, Braziel, Scmidtt, Jackson, and Joya 1979).[7] Budapest built on the feminist insight that the personal was political and went on to argue that the spiritual was political as well. It was the need for a feminist spiritual community that was behind her creation of the Susan B. Anthony Coven Number 1. Budapest agreed to be the high priestess and to create religious rituals for this women-only group. Members adopted the belief in ancient goddess-worshiping matriarchies and called their new religion Dianic Witchcraft, after the Goddess of the Witches in Charles Leland's *Aradia*. Budapest, who was familiar with WITCH's activities when she lived in New York, embraced the image of the witch as a symbol of women's empowerment and used it to create a feminist separatist version of Wicca.

Presented as a new religion with ancient roots, the Dianic Craft incorporated many elements of Gardnerian Wicca, although it delighted in creating new rituals and innovative practices. From Wicca it adopted the five-fold kiss used in blessing the set of ritual tools, including in particular the *athame*, or magical knife; the casting of the circle and the correlation of the four elements with the directions, the eight sabbats, and thirteen full, moon esabats; and the concept of the Triple Goddess originally promoted by English poet Robert Graves. However, unlike the British traditions of Wicca, the Dianic Triple Goddess was an autonomous deity who did not have a male consort. Nor did the high priestess, who was the sole leader of her coven. Men were not included in Dianic practice.[8] This reflected the separate space of women's consciousness-raising groups that had sprung up across the U.S. since the late 1960s, where women felt safe to experiment and discover who they were and wanted to be without the social constraints of mixed groups.

The Triple Goddess was mirrored in the changes of the waxing, full, and waning moon and was represented as the maiden, mother, and crone (see Griffin 1995). According to believers, this echoing of women's life stages allowed women to identify with deity in a way that had not been possible since the advent of patriarchal religions. Budapest talked about "Women's Mysteries," the celebration of the passages in a woman's life—menarche, pregnancy and birthing, menopause—things that most women were not discussing comfortably in the early 1970s, and certainly not celebrating and incorporating into their spiritual practice. Although seeing themselves as part of a revolution in consciousness, long "feared and prophesized by the patriarchs," the immediate goal for Dianics was, according to the coven's manifesto, "to congregate with each other according to our ancient womon-made laws and remember our past, renew our powers and affirm our Goddess of the Ten-thousand Names" (Budapest et al. 1979:1). The coven opened a small occult supply store in Los Angeles called Feminist Wicca, and it quickly became a gathering place for a growing spiritual community. Regular teaching and rituals were held there, and Budapest began giving lectures as well. Rituals were also conducted in the mountains outside Malibu. According to Budapest, as many as 700 women would gather to dance in ecstasy around the fire under the full moon. The rituals were broken up twice by the police, and in some cases participants were arrested.

In 1975, Budapest herself was arrested for reading tarot cards. Until that time, most feminists were unaware of the magical activities of feminist Witches in Southern California. But a small article in *Ms.* magazine covering Budapest's arrest made her a national figure and feminist hero to those who found her spiritual teachings empowering. Even feminists comfortable in their own religions and those who had rejected religion altogether took notice. Budapest points out, this "was very important because spiritual people were not enough seen as feminists in the movement, and by having a trial, they thought, well, Z. must have threatened patriarchy after all. And that was like a badge of honor, because every good feminist went to jail. We know that. So I did too" (Budapest 1991). As word spread, more women showed up for the rituals, and women whom Budapest initiated went on to form their own covens. With the publication of her books, women elsewhere in the country began to learn how and when to do their own rituals as well as to cast magical spells.

*The Feminist Book of Light and Shadows*[9] explained the origins of magic, drawing from Leland almost a century earlier to explain that Aradia, daughter of the Goddess Diana, was sent down to earth to teach the oppressed how to overthrow their masters. As the female avatar, Aradia taught magical spells, which were passed down from mother to daughter, surviving patriarchy in secret. The book went on to argue that the slaves today are predominately "wimmin," and so it is appropriate that women practice magic. "Anyone who tells wimmin not to practice magic because it is 'dangerous' and it comes back to them is propagating fear. Wimmin invented magic . . ." (Budapest et al. 1979:61). The general rules for spell casting were based on the belief that the power of the mind is behind magic. The ingredients used represent the four elements of air, fire, water, and earth, and the tools and objects used are tokens that relate to the "deep mind." The book explained the magical use of candles, oils, colors, and herbs, and provided spells for things such as health, love, money, and finding a job—all correlated with the phases of the moon. While emphasizing the power of one's will, the book cautioned that the woman casting the spell should remember that she may not always get what she wants; the Goddess has veto power. In her classes, Budapest taught that we live in a sea of energy so that "our brains are connected to each other. There is like one big brain and everything we think is a ritual, every thought we make is important. So if a lot of women get together and create one thought form, it ripples and touches other brains and may be stimulating the conclusion of it. . . . when you manipulate your own brain, you manipulate a large brain" (Budapest 1991). So although she provided specific spells in her books and teachings, Budapest also informed women it didn't matter if they followed these to the letter. There were things that were used traditionally, such as a particular herb or oil, but an aromatic herb could be replaced by an aromatic candle, and oil by saliva. The important thing was to trigger one's own deep mind and to work with the phases of the moon. Bringing something positive into one's life was to be done during the waxing moon, getting rid of something as it waned, and so on.

What was unique about Dianic magic was that it also dealt with the violence women experienced under patriarchy, against which they were beginning to organize. The Dianic Craft offered a spell for healing after a rape during a time when most women were still reluctant to admit that they had been raped because of the social repercussions. In addition, and even more radical, it provided a hex to cast on rapists. It is important to know that Dianics accepted the Wiccan Rede, the one rule for Witches that said, "Harm none and do as thou wilt" (Budapest et al. 1979:59). The corollary was that anything magical sent out returned to the sender threefold. That made negative spells downright unwise, as the energy sent out returned to those who cast the spell three times stronger than before. But violence against women was an exception for Dianics, who believed that "A witch who cannot hex cannot heal" (Budapest et al. 1979:81).[10] Rape was a weapon of patriarchy. Hexing a rapist was a righteous hex, not "black magic," because the rapist wasn't innocent. The only caution Budapest and friends offered was that the woman should *know* the rapist was guilty, not just think so.[11] This, of course, does not mean that all Dianics were or are comfortable with hexing.[12]

Dianic Witchcraft was a religion totally in tune with the new cultural feminism that grew as an offshoot from the original radical feminist impulse in the United States. Taking an essentialist stance, cultural feminists valued and celebrated "femaleness," saw patriarchy and masculine values as responsible for the world's ills, and called for a world separate and apart, a world based on celebrating feminine values, female imagery, and women's sexuality. For some women, feminist Witchcraft was a natural fit. Some feminists, however, saw Witchcraft in general as "flaky," and feminist Witchcraft in particular as an embarrassment. For over a decade, other Wiccans resisted the Dianic Craft as well, objecting to its highly improvisational nature, its lack of formal, structured training, and its female-only stance. Nevertheless, the ideas of the charismatic leader known as the Mother of Dianic Witchcraft continue to influence women in North America and elsewhere as Budapest's books circulate and the women she trained and calls her daughters train others in magic.

## THE RETURN OF THE MATRIARCHY

The concept of matriarchal prehistory that Dianics believe in was not new. British historian Ronald Hutton (1999) does an excellent summary of the development of this idea. It was first promoted by German classicist Eduard Gerhard in 1849, who proposed that behind all the Greek goddesses stood a single goddess, who represented Mother Earth. Other classicists adopted the idea to earlier, prehistoric cultures, such as Anatolia and Mesopotamia. In 1862, Swiss judge J. J. Bachofen argued that the earliest human societies had been women centered. It was only logical to believe that the same was true in their religion.[13] When Sir Arthur Evans excavated Knossos in Crete at the turn of the century, he believed that the female imagery he discovered represented a single, powerful goddess. He saw her as being both Virgin and Mother with a divine child. Within a few years, Evans associated her with the female figures from the Neolithic. Medical doctor and amateur historian Robert Briffault explained how she could be both virgin and mother by suggesting that the meaning of *virgin* was to be independent of men, a definition that would be widely embraced by feminist Witches fifty years later. About the same time as the early excavations, respected medieval scholar Sir Edmund Chambers announced that prehistoric Europe had worshiped a Great Mother Goddess. This goddess had two aspects as well, but these were Creatrix and Destroyer. As the idea gained in adherents, other scholars announced similar findings, and the idea of a Great Mother who had been universally worshiped took hold. Sir James Frazer, author of *The Golden Bough*, saw the same pattern in western Asia, adding the element of a son-consort who died and returned like the grain. These images inspired poet Robert Graves to write *The White Goddess* in 1948, and the belief in the Great Goddess was popularized even further. Hutton stresses that by the time Graves wrote, "The image of his goddess had been developing for about a hundred and fifty years. No temple had been built to her, and no public worship accorded; yet she had become one of the principal cultural images of the nineteen and twentieth centuries. She and the modern age had taken shape together, in polar opposition to each other, and truly she needed no tangible monuments as she existed so firmly in the hearts and minds of poets, novelists, polemics, and scholars alike; the natural world itself had become her shrine" (Hutton 1999:42).

Works on history began to accept the premise of the worship of a great Neolithic Goddess as proven fact and incorporate it into new analyses. Scholarship thus became circular. Three extremely prominent British archeologists, including oft-quoted author Gordon Childe, declared their belief that the Goddess had been venerated from the Atlantic to the Near East (Hutton 1997). Scholars of religion, history, art history, archeology, and psychology accepted the belief that the European Neolithic had been a peaceful culture that valued women, worshiped a single female deity, and was matricentric. This concept was not seriously challenged until 1962 when professional prehistorians rejected some of the findings that had been based upon the assumption of a Great Mother Goddess. Most other scholars quickly lost whatever enthusiasm they had originally had as closer examination showed more flaws in the circular reasoning. According to Hutton (1997), they didn't reject the concept outright but became carefully neutral about it. This, of course, was not true of everyone.

In 1971, Elizabeth Gold Davis published *The First Sex*, which gave new life to what is often referred to as "matriarchal theory." The book purported to "document" the rule of women in prehistory, the rise of male domination, and the "dethroning" of the Goddess. While primarily political and not spiritual, its creative vision of prehistory laid the foundation for the sacred history of what was to become Goddess Spirituality.[14] And in 1974, Marija Gimbutas published *Gods and Goddesses of Old Europe*. Eight years later, reflecting growing feminist interest, the book was republished as *The Goddesses and Gods of Old Europe*. Gimbutas was a respected archeologist, known for her work on the prehistory of the Slavs, the Balts, and eastern European Bronze Age cultures. In *Gods and Goddesses*, she argues for the existence of a prehistoric, peaceful, matrifocal, agrarian culture that worshiped "a Goddess incarnating the creative principle as Source and Giver of all" (Gimbutas 1974:9).[15] This Goddess civilization, which she called Old Europe, had been invaded over a period of two thousand years in a series of waves by horseback riding, patriarchal warriors from a proto-Indo-European culture who replaced worship of the Goddess with their own male-dominated pantheon. Her next book, full of stunning full-color photography, was an attempt to explain the symbol system in the art of Old Europe. In the introduction, she wrote that "The purpose of this book is to present the pictorial 'script' for the religion of the Old European Great Goddess, consisting of signs, symbols, and images of divinities . . . to identify the Old European patterns that cross the boundaries of time and space. These systematic associations in the Near East, southeastern Europe, the Mediterranean area, and in central, western, and northern Europe indicate the extension of the same Goddess religion to all these regions as a cohesive and persistent ideological system" (Gimbutas 1989:xv). Although this work has been seriously criticized by many scholars,[16] it was embraced by many women who were searching for spiritual inspiration and meaning in a time when feminists in the United States were rejecting male authority in general. At the very least, Gimbutas's vision of the past offered hope that a peaceful, egalitarian society that valued women and women's values was possible in the future.

As women became more outspoken in their feminism, their critique of male domination extended into other areas. The European persecution of witches, which came to be called the Burning Times by Pagans, was seen as a deliberate attack on women by patriarchal Christianity (Ehrenreich and English 1973). This idea rapidly gained supporters among feminist spiritual seekers. These critiques were further spread as *WomanSpirit* magazine began to publish. Put out four times a year from Oregon, the writing staff consisted of changing collectives of women in different states and so reflected the ferment that women were experiencing across the country. It provided a forum for women to explore their spirituality through poetry, art, prose, discussions, and descriptions of women's rituals that were growing in popularity. Further support for the growing movement was found in Merlin Stone's 1976 book *When God Was a Woman*, which attempted to explain the suppression of women's rites in the ancient Near and Middle East.[17] Stone argued that political attitudes had recast certain historical events to create religious rationale for devaluing women.

The 1970s also saw the first conferences on women's spirituality. In 1976 in Boston, approximately eighteen hundred women came together for three days to attend "Through the Looking Glass: A Gynergenetic Experience." The conference began with a ritual in an old church where Morgan

McFarland and a group of McFarland Dianic Witches cast a circle and invoked the Goddess who "arose from Chaos and gave birth to Herself" (Adler 1986:223). In 1978, the University of California in Santa Cruz hosted the "Great Goddess Reemerging Conference." The five hundred attendees heard religious scholar Carol Christ explain that religious symbols that are primarily male keep women subservient to and dependent on men. Women *need* the Goddess, she exclaimed; female iconography would liberate, celebrate, and spiritually strengthen women (Christ 1982).

Books appeared during the latter part of the decade that retold ancient myths with a feminist twist and urged women to find the "Goddess Within" (Spretnak 1978; Stone 1979; Goldenberg 1979). Canadian psychologist of religion and feminist theologian Naomi Goldenberg coined the word "*thealogy*" to mean the logic of Goddess religion. The first anthology that appeared brought together scholars, thealogians, poets, artists, feminist activists, and feminist Witches, and explored the diversity of women's spirituality (Christ and Plaskow 1979). They were devoured by women who were beginning to form their own small spiritual circles across the United States. Some of these women called themselves Witches, borrowing from the WITCH manifesto which said they were Witches simply because they were women and in rebellion. Training and apprenticeship were unnecessary. Others didn't take a particular label for themselves; they just met and did innovative rituals around a divorce, a birth, an illness.

At the end of the decade, a book was to appear that would become a classic internationally. Unlike the many women who came to Goddess Spirituality through feminism, Starhawk discovered women's spirituality and feminism at about the same time. Trained in Faery Witchcraft, an American tradition begun by Victor and Cora Anderson, and familiar with the teachings of Budapest, Starhawk was a member of two covens and also interacted with the women's spiritual community in California. Her book, *The Spiral Dance*, was both a how-to book with instructions for casting a circle, how to do magic, specific rituals and meditation exercises, and a "why" book with a lyrical interweaving of feminism, theology, and Witchcraft philosophy for both men and women. Subtitled *A Rebirth of the Ancient Religion of the Great Goddess*, it invoked the image of the great Neolithic Goddess rejected by most scholars, and at the same time, it built upon the contemporary scholarship and philosophy promoted by women like Carol Christ. Starhawk was clear that what Pagans called the Old Religion could "just as accurately be called the New Religion. The Craft, today, is undergoing more than a revival, it is experiencing a renaissance, a re-creation. Women are spurring this renewal, and actively reawakening the Goddess, the image of 'the legitimacy and beneficence of female power'" (Starhawk 1979:8).

THE 1980S

In 1980, Starhawk teamed up with her coven members in San Francisco and began to give classes based on the material in *The Spiral Dance*. The class was extremely popular, and soon graduates began forming their own covens based on the teachings they had received. A group of students and teachers began to publish a newsletter and do rituals to which the public was invited. By 1982, the group had become the Reclaiming Collective. While open to both women and men, the Reclaiming Tradition was to have a tremendous impact on women's groups. To begin with, it was profoundly feminist and, unlike almost all other groups at the time, it was nonhierarchical; the group made decisions by consensus and functioned without either a high priestess or high priest. Like Dianic Witchcraft, Reclaiming linked the personal and the political but did it in a way that involved very public displays of magical protest and activism. Its major focus was not on women's mysteries but on the health of the planet and peace. This was because Starhawk's thealogy was focused on the immanence of the divine. That made the planet and all life upon it sacred. While Reclaiming Witches might show up to escort women entering a family planning clinic and protect them against antichoice demonstrators, they were even more likely to be arrested for civil disobedience at sites where nuclear bombs were tested or nuclear plants were to be opened. Another thing that was unique about Reclaiming was that although it was open to both women and men as were traditional Wiccan groups, it taught that sexual polarity was not necessary for magic. In addition to Reclaiming groups that welcomed both men and women, there were single-sex groups.

By 1985, the classes had become so popular that the Reclaiming Collective began offering week-long summer "intensives." These grew in attendance to the point where the collective began to rent space in rural areas in order to house all the students, some of whom came from outside California to attend. These intensives became known as Witch Camps and, over time, spread to seven other states, and Canada, Germany, Norway, and England as well, as feminist Witchcraft went international.

These Witch Camps were especially important in Canada, where the national population is a little less than the population of California but spread out over an area that is slightly larger than the entire United States. Traditional, British Wicca had already made its appearance but never caught on to the extent that it did in the United States. Where Witchcraft spread, it was typically learned through limited circle experience with women who had limited circle experience in other cities. Urban groups thus became fairly eclectic. Some women commuted to major cities in the United States for more structured coven training, and others traveled to women's and Pagan festivals in Washington, Oregon, California, and Wisconsin seeking experience. The distribution of the population across the northern part of the continent meant that, outside of a few urban areas, Canadian Witches were largely solitary practitioners, used to practicing on their own and resistant to being organized (Slater 2002). Although the gatherings, when they occurred, were not necessarily secret, the secluded nature of people's homesteads almost made them seem so (Marron 1989).

These feelings of isolation were alleviated somewhat with the advent of the Reclaiming Witch Camps. These began in 1987 in Canada when Pat Hogan, who had organized workshops for Starhawk in Vancouver, convinced her and other Reclaiming members to come from San Francisco to British Columbia and teach a week-long intensive in magic and ritual. This was the beginning of an annual event that hosts approximately one hundred people, mostly women. The camp is regularly sold out and has probably provided experiential training in Goddess Spirituality and Witchcraft to over a thousand women (Slater 2002). When they leave, people are told to go right out and find new people to work with, thus facilitating the spread of Reclaiming's unique nonhierarchical and highly activist perspective. Soon after the first Canadian camp began, there was an annual Sappho Witch Camp, a Dianic-identified camp for lesbians and lesbian-positive women. Over the past years since 1992, women have come to Sappho each year from Canada, the U.S., Australia, and Europe. In addition to the camps in British Columbia, there is a camp in southern Ontario called Wild Ginger that hosts about sixty every Spring, an offshoot of the Reclaiming-style Witch Camp in Vermont.

Additional ways that Goddess communities were linked and teaching spread in Canada were though various Pagan groups that sprang up on almost every college campus and through Goddess magazines and newspapers. It is helpful to think of Canada almost as one would of the European Union, as a land mass made up of different "countries" or provinces with distinct rules and cultures. In addition, the north-south connections are stronger in some areas than the east-west so that Ontario and Quebec are influenced by ideas coming from New York City, Buffalo, and Boston, and British Columbia is influenced by those coming from Washington State, Oregon, and California. Of particular importance are the two languages spoken in Canada and their impact on Goddess Spirituality there.

It is undeniable that the spread of Witchcraft was facilitated through the Canadian publishing industry and women's bookstores, and Budapest's *Holy Book of Women's Mysteries*, volumes 1 and 2, and Starhawk's *Spiral Dance* profoundly affected the development of early feminist spirituality in Canada. However, this was true in English-speaking Canada, not French. Wiccan priestess and doctoral student Lucie DuFresne (2002a) points out that the Francophone market is generally considered too small to be profitable, and most English language books are not translated and distrib-

uted in Quebec. Eclecta Thunderstorm, a Canadian Witch and high priestess with years in both the Anglophone and Francophone communities,
reports that no writings on feminist or Dianic Witchcraft were available in
French. The movement was well underway before anything was even
known about it in French Canada, except by those women who read both
French and English. Thunderstorm (2002) also suggests that these beliefs
took a longer time coming to the Francophone community because so
many women there felt close to the Goddess through the cult of the Virgin
Mary. Nevertheless, by 1983, Goddess Spirituality was the focus of the
entire issue of *Canadian Women's Studies/les cahiers de la femme*.[18] By the
mid-1980s at York University in neighboring Ontario, college students
were enrolling in popular "Goddess courses" in increasing numbers, and
talks by Starhawk and Merlin Stone drew huge crowds.

Dianic Witchcraft had continued to grow as well. In the United States,
the Covenant of the Goddess (CoG) had been formed in 1975 to create an
umbrella organization for Witches from a variety of traditions and to seek
legal recognition for Witchcraft as a religion. Although originally hostile to
separatist groups, CoG began to admit Dianic covens in the early 1980s. It
may have been influenced in this decision by Starhawk who, as first officer,
had presided over the organization. Budapest herself had moved to Northern California, leaving the group in Los Angeles to her high priestess, Ruth
Rhiannon Barrett. Under Barrett, the group developed a new structure and
became a large religious congregational community known as the Circle of
Aradia. As a registered nonprofit religious organization, it has trained literally thousands of women in the art of magic and ritual.

Another center for the Dianic Craft was founded in 1984 in Madison,
Wisconsin. The Re-formed Congregation of the Goddess (RCG) began
to publish a quarterly newspaper, sponsor two conferences and national
gatherings a year, and specialize in training Dianic priestesses. Its classes
developed into a six-year program of self-directed spiritual-development
activities, with specific paths or specializations. Women did not have to be
Dianics to take the courses, though only Dianics could be ordained and
given legal ministerial credentials.

Feminist Witchcraft and Goddess Spirituality were given another outlet
and legitimization when the Unitarian Universalist Church developed a
course of study called *Cakes for the Queen of Heaven: A Seminar in Feminist
Thealogy* (Ranck 1986). A response to the general assembly of the church,
"Resolution on Women and Religion," *Cakes for the Queen of Heaven* was
a package of ten courses intended to help women explore religion from a
female perspective. The package included slides, lectures, exercises, and
workshop suggestions; it borrowed heavily from Graves, Davis, Budapest,
Daly, Gimbutas, Christ, Goldenberg, and Starhawk and also from feminist
psychologists and theologian within mainstream religions. It was divided

into three sections: why women need the Goddess, seeking the female presence in Judaism and Christianity, and contemporary feminist spirituality, which included both feminist Witchcraft and possibilities for a feminist and spiritual future. *Cakes for the Queen of Heaven* was sold as a kit and marketed nationally, both inside and outside of the Unitarian/Universalist Church.

This was also a time when the glossy Goddess magazines began to appear. *Women and Power* took over in 1984 when *WomanSpirit* magazine folded. The first objective listed in *Women and Power* was to nurture the development of women's spirituality as a worldview and political movement. Its large advisory council was multiracial and multicultural, including feminist Witches; Christian, Jewish, and Buddhist feminists; Native American feminists revisioning American Indian spirituality; and practitioners of the more generic form of Goddess Spirituality. Published out of Cambridge, it offered women profiles of other women, poetry, art, photography, and articles on anything the editors considered spiritually empowering to women. It made a point of including the work and lives of women of color.[19] The *Beltane Papers: A Journal of Women's Mysteries* began publishing in 1984 as well. It began as a collection of papers and expanded to a regular, nationally distributed magazine. Its publication was interrupted twice; nevertheless, it is the longest surviving journal devoted to women who celebrate the Goddess. *SageWoman* has been published regularly since 1986 and, with its print run of 21,000 copies quarterly (Niven 2002), it is the most popular Goddess magazine for women today. *Hecate's Loom: A Journal of Magical Arts* was published in Victoria and served the women's community in Canada until fairly recently, along with Goddess magazines from the United States.

The women's spirituality movement was developing in a variety of directions. Charlene Spretnak (1982) continued the tradition of bringing together insights of women from a variety of spiritual practices in her large anthology *The Politics of Women's Spirituality*. Although the practices were different, the contributors were similar in visioning the divine with a female face and form. In the same year, Marion Zimmer Bradley published *The Mists of Avalon,* a feminist novel that saw the tales of King Arthur and his knights as a clash between Christianity and the old Goddess religion of Britain. The book quickly became a staple in the growing Goddess communities. The therapeutic approach begun in popular Goddess books in the late 1970s continued with Jean Shinoda Bolen (1985) helping women to discover archetypes with which to empower themselves in *Goddesses in Every Woman.* Barbara Walker (1983) produced *The Women's Encyclopedia of Myths and Secrets.* A large volume that purported to uncover ancient, prepatriarchal meanings of sacred symbols, *The Women's Encyclopedia* became the major reference book for many spiritual feminists. Vicki Nobel

and Karen Vogel created a round tarot deck full of female imagery that
caught on quickly. They opened a Mother House in northern California
where women could study the feminist Tarot and Goddess Spirituality. The
innovative deck was followed quickly by feminist versions of astrology,
Qabala and the I Ching. Social scientist Riane Eisler (1988) came out with
the enormously popular *The Chalice and the Blade*. Eisler attempted to explore human culture from its inception into the future. Taking a cue from
Gimbutas, she proposed there were two kinds of cultures: the dominator
and the partnership. Patriarchy was clearly a dominator model, and, she
argued, the problems the world encounters today are in large part the logical consequences of that model and so cannot be solved within it. Eisler
wove together ideas from many academic disciplines, including history,
psychology, economics, sociology, and physics, to propose a way to move
into a partnership future. It was received as a Goddess-send by many
women and feminist men who were searching for a nonhierarchical vision
of ways to live together, and small "partnership" study groups formed.

The National Film Board of Canada produced three widely distributed
and visually stunning documentaries that have helped to shape and spread
beliefs in Goddess Spirituality and its sacred history. *The Goddess Remembered* (1989) looks at ancient myths and folk beliefs and uses conversation
among women leaders in the movement to show how and why it has
grown. *The Burning Times* (1990) revisits the witchcraft persecutions in
Europe and New England and relates them to the figure of the Witch as a
healer, both ancient and contemporary. The last film, *Full Circle* (1993),
shows how women are "coming back" to the practice of Goddess Spirituality and what it means for women today. These films make regular appearances on public television and in college classrooms. The fact that all the
women who are interviewed in them are American indicates the extent of
the influence on the movement from the United States. The only Canadian
voices are those of the narrator, Martha Henry, and the lovely vocals of
Loreena McKennitt. Naomi Goldenberg, a Canadian who was one of the
very first scholars to do serious work and publish in the field of Goddess
studies, is not in the series.[20] Yet practitioners insist that Canadian Witchcraft is also uniquely Canadian, in its fluid and eclectic nature, its use of
indigenous symbols, myths, and rituals, its connection with African goddesses through the Caribbean, and the tremendous influence of the Reclaiming Witch Camps and traditions (Klassen 2002; Slater 2002; Stuckey
2002).[21]

The 1980s also saw dramatic changes in how some Jewish and Christian
feminists spoke about the divine. In small groups of women they experi-
mented with innovative rituals, symbols, and language. A few Jewish
groups on both the East and West Coasts in the United States changed the
language in books of prayers. Instead of adopting exclusively female images,

they tended to describe the divine with alternating pronouns or as Adonai and Shechina.

> Adonai and Shechina, Lord and Presence
> Are separate names for an indivisible God
> In the One God sometimes we encounter Him
> In the One God sometimes we are addressed by Her (Dart 1985:17)

Christian theologian Rosemary Radford Ruether critiqued the metaphors used for God that were grounded in authority and hierarchy, such as *Lord* and *King*. She argued for language that would foster egalitarian relationships among people and suggested the unpronounceable word *God/ess*. ". . . we have no adequate name for the true God/ess, the 'I am who I shall become.' Intimations of Her/His name will appear as we emerge from false naming of God/ess modeled on patriarchal alienation" (Ruether 1983:71). Later, in the same work, Ruether went on to write, "The Shalom of the Holy; the disclosure of the gracious Shekinah; Divine Wisdom; the empowering Matrix; She, in whom we live and move and have our being—She comes; She is here" (266). Another important Christian theologian, Sallie McFague (1987), urged a multiplicity of God images, including mother, lover, friend, and healer. These metaphors from everyday life evoked nurture, erotic pleasure, and mutuality, and were warmly welcomed by some Christian feminists who felt these images better reflected their experience of the Divine.

The National Council of Churches changed the book of readings often used by Protestant churches. The word *God* became *Father and Mother*, but use of word *God/dess* was found unthinkable by the committee that deliberated on the changes. Nevertheless, some traditionalists still found the changes very disturbing, believing that even *Father and Mother* reflected pre–Judeo-Christian Paganism that worshiped goddesses (Ostling 1983).[22]

The power of naming is not just an exercise in creativity. It is the power to define, to delineate, to create reality. Feminists argue that this is a power that patriarchy has guarded jealously. According to theologian Melissa Raphael, when feminists name the divine, they change reality and make power provisional, something patriarchy cannot tolerate. She points out that Christian feminists are not saying that the divine is literally female but that they are borrowing spiritually nourishing images and transforming "their meaning and intention by setting them in a Christian context. In fact, feminist God-talk can represent heresy at its best: that is, as the challenge of the new that rouses the church and mainstream theology from its dogmatic slumber" (Raphael 1996:148).

These changes in language and image should not be confused with what was happening in groups of women outside the churches and synagogues,

especially not with the Witches. However, it would be naive to think these
expressions of the divine did reflect some of the same ferment, or that
feminist women in mainstream religious were not aware what was happening elsewhere. This can clearly be seen in the many books and articles
published during this decade.[23]

Goddess Spirituality became one of the original paths that lead to ecofeminism, the belief that the devaluation of women, nature, and natural
processes were linked products of masculinist consciousness. Thealogian
and ecofeminist Charlene Spretnak recalls,

> What was cosmologically wholesome and healing was the discovery of
> the Divine as immanent in and around us. What was intriguing was the
> sacred link between the Goddess in her many guises and totemic animals
> and plants, sacred groves, and womblike caves, in the moon-rhythm
> blood of menses, the ecstatic dance-the experience of knowing Gaia,
> her voluptuous contours and fertile plains, her flowing waters that give
> life, her animal teachers. For who among us would ever again see a snake
> coiled around the arm of an ancient Goddess statue, teaching lesions of
> cyclic renewal and regeneration with its shedding of skins, as merely a
> member of the ophidian order in the reptilian class of the vertebrate
> phylum? That period of discovery . . . inspired art, music, poetry, and
> the resurrection of long-forgotten sacred myth and ritual, usually held
> out of doors, often on the Earth's holy days of cosmic alignment, the
> solstices and equinoxes. They are rituals of our own creation that express
> our deepest feelings of a spirituality infused with ecological wisdom and
> wholeness. At the beginning of that period, ecology was not on our
> minds; since moving out of that period into activism, ecology has never
> left our minds. (Spretnak 1990:5–6)

THE 1990S

Until 1990 there was very little research done on what women's groups
were actually doing in their spiritual explorations. One exception was Margot Adler who had incorporated a chapter on women, feminism, and
Witchcraft in *Drawing Down the Moon* in 1979. Adler, a reporter for National Public Radio and a Witch herself, had done early and excellent
overview of Pagans in the United States. Based on participant observation,
survey and interviews, Adler concluded that

> . . . contrary to many assumptions, feminists are viewing the idea of
> matriarchy as a complex one, and that their creative use of the idea of
> matriarchy as *vision* and *ideal* would in no way be compromised if sud-

denly there were "definite proof" that few matriarchies every existed. In the same way, Amazons may prove to be fictions or creations of the deep mind, or, like Troy, they may suddenly be brought to the surface as 'reality' one day. In either case, the feminist movement is giving birth to *new* Amazons, a process that is bound to continue no matter what we unearth from the past." (Adler 1986:191)

One concern that Adler voiced was that focus on a single Great Goddess, even one with many manifestations, was not that far removed from focus on a single, transcendent god. Nevertheless, she concluded that "The women's spirituality movement is now so large and indefinable that it is like an ocean whose waves push against all shores" (Adler 1986:227).

Yet with all the questioning that was taking place, scholarly writing on what was happening in the women's spirituality movement was largely limited to thea/ology and psychology. There were the rare graduate theses and dissertations that focused on research (see, for example, Eller 1984; Liston 1985; Ludeke 1989; and Galdman 1988), but, by and large, if academic scholars were out in the field doing feminist spirituality, they were not writing about it. This changed in 1990 when several articles appeared almost simultaneously.

Sociologist Mary Jo Neitz (1990) compared some of the differences between covens that included both men and women and those that were feminist, women-only groups and argued that feminist spirituality was a cultural movement. Janet Jacobs (1990) described a ritual where female rape survivors dealt with their experience in an attempt at healing. She concluded that the symbol of the Goddess as Mother Protector against the violence and alienation of patriarchal culture inspired participants to bond, move toward healing, and engage in political action. Tanice Foltz and I published an article based on ethnographic research in which we explored the meaning of death for Dianic Witches. Although originally skeptical, we discovered that Dianic Witchcraft unites people into a moral community and meets the sociological definitions of a religion (Lozano and Foltz 1990). Nancy Finley (1991) used surveys she conducted at a Dianic conference to refute the common accusation by mainstream feminists that feminist spirituality was apolitical. Mary Farrell Bednarowski (1992) compared themes to be found in various forms of feminist spirituality to the New Age movement. The former, she argued, was engaged in sacralizing the cosmos and changing human consciousness. This involved belief that both the Earth and the body were sacred, and that focusing on changing consciousness alone was a privilege of class.

But the first book-length examination of the Feminist Spirituality movement was written by Cynthia Eller in a revised version of her doctoral dissertation in religious studies. She found that the women's rituals could

be very beautiful and their religious practices and magic were a "manifestation of the therapeutic ethos" (Eller 1993:92). Although rich in ethnographic detail, the book was not received with overwhelming appreciation
by practitioners. Eller's major arguments were that women were drawn to
this spirituality because of relative deprivation, to feel good about themselves, and to reconcile themselves to being female. Nevertheless, the book
was widely read by practitioners and scholars in the field alike.

Eller's focus is on feminist Witches and those in the loosely structured
Goddess Movement. But the "female face of the Divine" and women's
spiritual rituals that addressed feminist concerns were being felt within
mainstream religions as well. Charlotte Caron (1992) compares a Goddess
group in Oregon to a feminist Christian group in Saskatchuan and finds
the rituals are not all that different. She lists four major streams within
feminist spirituality: Christian feminism, Woman-Church, Goddess Spirituality, and a fourth that may or may not focus on the divine but does focus
on women's rituals. She posits that the divine, which she refers to as "God/
dess," is concrete for women in feminist spiritualities, not an abstract ideal
separate from their daily material existence.

> The earth, air, water, and fire are it. The holy is the natural cycle of
> birth-to-death-to-birth in human life and natural worlds. God/dess is
> sunsets, being in touch with the ground, bread for common meal, brid-
> ges across diversity. . . . God/dess is concrete and earthy. . . .
>     The holy grows, changes, is organic, and is manifest in many
> ways. . . . What if we were to know God in the care we give to the
> environment, the earth, and each other? At this point in history, it would
> mean that we have to be the healers of the holy. Distorted and damaged
> by patriarchy, the holy needs support and healing to be whole. (Caron
> 1992: 213–14, 217)

Such radically new understandings of the divine were bound to inspire
strong reactions, and certainly many of them were negative. Perhaps the
strongest criticism came of the Re-Imagining Conference held in Minneapolis in 1993. Conceived as part of the World Council of Churches's
"Ecumenical Decade of Churches in Solidarity with Women," it was attended by some two thousand members of thirty-two Christian denominations from forty-nine states and twenty-seven countries. One of the
conference's goals was to liberate Christianity from patriarchy's hold on
symbols and language (Smith 1998). In this context, a prayer was offered
to Sophia, presented as Scripture's personification of wisdom.

> Our maker Sophia, we are women in your image; With the hot blood
> of our wombs we give form to new life. With the courage of our con-

victions we pour out lifeblood for justice. Sophia, creator God, let your milk and honey flow . . . shower us with your love. Our sweet Sophia, we are women in your image. With the nectar between our thighs we invite a lover, we birth a child; with our warm body fluids new remind the world of its pleasures and sensations . . . Our guide, Sophia, we are women in your image: With our moist mouths we kiss away a tear, we smile encouragement. With the honey of wisdom in our mouths, we prophesy a full humanity to all the peoples. (*Minneapolis Star Tribune* 1993)[24]

It was not just the revisioning of the divine as female, although conservatives found that shocking. Even more, it was the focus on the divine through the earthiness of the female body that was upsetting. An additional cause of conflict was the open acknowledgement of homosexuality (see Cloud 2001). Part of the uproar was also that money from several denominations was used to sponsor scholarships to the conference. According to one attendee, "For participants it was a stunning experience. The backlash by the conservative U.S. church was just as stunning—and some good women lost their jobs in the church" (Benjamin 1998). Nevertheless, Re-Imagining conferences continue every year, although scaled down and participants usually have to pay their own way. Sophia is now being studied by groups of Presbyterians and some of the feminist theologians from the first conference are highly respected and published, their books being used on college campuses.

In the same year as the first Re-Imagining Conference, Pope John Paul urged American bishops to combat a "bitter, ideological" feminism among some American Catholics that had led them to replace traditional Christianity with worship of an earth goddess and "forms of nature worship and the celebration of myths and symbols."[25] He was particularly critical of Catholic nuns who performed rituals outside of traditional worship approved by the Vatican, saying that such practices were un-Christian (Cowell 1993).

HEALING THE HOLY

Mary Farrell Bednarowski (1999) examined what is happening today in women's religious thought across spiritual traditions and found tremendous similarities. She grouped these into five areas. The first was the ambivalence that women experience toward their own religions. The second involved the understanding of the divine as immanent, of matter infused with spirit. Bednarowski points out that this immanence and immediacy tend to make the divine accessible without the need of religious specialists. The third she calls the revelatory power of the ordinary. Women's rituals use the stuff of ordinary life, women's lived experience, to make the sacraments meaningful. This also means that knowledge can take many forms, including that understood by the body and never articulated verbally. The fourth has to do with themes of relationship, of interconnectedness. The fifth is that of healing, of restoring to wholeness. Here, the concept of healing has moved beyond the idea of simply healing from the wounds of patriarchy to include working to heal the religious traditions that have wounded women.

For many women, this requires the incorporation of female representations of the divine. Winter, Lummis, and Stokes (1994) surveyed some four thousand Protestant and Catholic women and found that they are participating in their faith traditions on their own terms. The authors define this as "defecting in place." They found that, for many of these women, the Goddess and Jesus are compatible god images. Christian women who participate in Goddess circles do not necessarily leave Christianity. The authors decided that women's spirituality groups meet some unmet needs for these women and appear to help many feminist women remain in the church. Uniterian/Universalist minister Shernie Schafer, for example, reports being approached by pastors from other Christian denominations to design religious rituals that deal with issues such as healing from incest (Schafer 1993).

Some Jewish feminists have also challenged the use of any male-centered language and imagery. Religious studies scholar Rita Gross has stressed the importance of "re-uniting" the male and female sides of the divine and more recently argued for the use of and need for "Goddess" because "She 'completes' and makes whole the image of God" (in Stuckey 1998:48).[26] Jewish theologian Judith Plaskow has presented a similar argument ([1983] 1995). Plaskow also points out that the simple alternating of pronouns or the use of gender neutral ones does not itself guarantee that images of dominance have been addressed (Plaskow 1991). This points to the importance of the religious rituals that Jewish women have created and, in some cases, fought to have integrated into temple practice: birth ceremonies for daughters, bat mitzvahs, and women's seders where the traditional tools of Passover are used to express women's suffering and liberation (for example, see Broner 1993).

Women's spiritual rituals, whether Witchcraft, Goddess, Christian, or Jewish, create a shared framework of meaning and so construct community. Sandy Sasso (1993) argues that ritual may precede belief and faith. In Goddess Spirituality, it is often said that one need not believe in the Goddess in order to experience her. Although the experience of the divine may occur when one is alone, it happens more frequently in those ritual moments when the focus is on the immanence and interconnectivity that change the consciousness of the celebrant. The emphasis is on *doing* ritual, participating in the mystery, not reading about it (see Griffin 2000). Theologian Rita Gross argues that in spiritual feminism, ritual development seems to lead to theological development. "More than mainstream religions, feminist spirituality understands both *that* ritual works and *how* it works . . . by changing the consciousness of the performer . . ." (Gross 1996:211). Scholar of religion and culture Leslie Northup (1993) says women's rituals focus along a horizontal plane, not on transcendence but on community. They reach across time and space, not beyond them, celebrating the human experience, not the divine. Religion and culture are experienced as part of an integrated whole. This shapes a social ethos that leads to demands for environmental protection, social justice, and nonhierarchical relations.

What then differentiates among these feminist spiritualities? Some women participate comfortably in two traditions or circles within and without mainstream religions simultaneously. Others practice exclusively in monotheistic Goddess circles and pray to "her" in very conventional ways. Many spiritual feminists take part in ritual magic; most of them reject the separation of the secular from the sacred. Witches circle with nuns and call the Virgin Mary the Queen of Heaven. "Green nuns" pray at the stations of the Earth (Taylor 2001). In truth, the divisions are not clearly defined, and the highly personalized nature of the spiritual practices adds new shades, new patterns in the weave. Christian feminists have begun to focus more on the life of Jesus than on the central mystery of Christ's death and resurrection, and Womanist theologians redefine sin as the defilement of the Creation, and use slavery, the abuse of women, and environmental devastation as examples (Williams 1993). Even the oft-quoted "All acts of love and pleasure are my ritual" of the Witches' Goddess finds its counterpart in the writings of feminist Christian theologian Carter Heyward: "The erotic is our most fully embodied experience of the love of God" (Heyward 1989:99).

As feminist spiritualities are living practices without fixed script, there is a fluidity about them. They shift, change, borrow from each other, and evolve. Theology comes from praxis, and shapes praxis in return. The differences among these spiritualities are more of texture than of substance. Dianic Witchcraft, once heavily weighted toward lesbian separatists, is no longer so. Its focus is still on empowerment and women's blood mysteries; the interconnectedness of immanent divinity and the links to the environment still receive less emphasis than in the Reclaiming Tradition. While Dianic organizations still train women to "priestess," the political nature of its spiritual feminism may not be as appealing as in the past, and much of the focus is on the self rather than on society (Griffin 2002a). The Reclaiming Tradition now links social justice issues and the environment in a way that moves beyond the nuclear threat to inspire social activism around the stranglehold of globalization. Chains of Witches become living rivers at protests in Seattle, Quebec, and Genoa. Nuns in northern Oregon sell small reproductions of Neolithic goddesses, and Christian feminists in ritual weave a Goddess web. The weaving is more than sympathetic magic; it is an affirmation of the biosphere and a commitment to community.

Mainstream scholarship, much of it by women, disputes the sacred history of the Great Goddess, and Pagan scholars have demonstrated that the number of Witches put to death during the Burning Times has been grossly exaggerated (for example, see Gibbons 1998). Nevertheless, as Adler points out, there is no denying the power and strength of ancient "goddesses from a thousand cultures where women wielded power. There is also no denying that the world will change as women take up their roles as priestesses once again" (Adler 1986:229).

And the world is changing. On June 17, 2002, a funeral was held for the Reverend Sue Hiatt, one of the eleven women ordained illegally in the Episcopal Church in 1974. The procession of ninety priests and bishops was composed mainly of women and the chapel of the Episcopal Divinity School was filled with many more women priests than those in the procession. The ceremony began with women drummers and the president of the school and former bishop of Alaska blessing the four directions. One of the prayers reciteds as:

> Hear us, O Brother Jesus,
> Hear us, O Sister Sophia,
> Hear us, O Spirit of Life,
> Hear us , O Christ our Mother,
> Hear us, our Friend and our Lover,
> Hear us, O Father in Heaven. (Roihl 2002)

As in early Christianity, Feminist Spirituality groups, whether in mainstream religions, covens, or Goddess circles, tend to be small and decentralized, and as they grow in numbers, they grow in influence. Today they provide safe places where women's voices are heard, their ideas explored, their *experiences* of spirituality affirmed. Women in these groups reject male interpreters for their spiritual lives; they are their own priestesses, their own mediators of the divine. They may not agree on exactly what she is or how best to incorporate her into their lives, but these women *know* the Goddess. They celebrate her in their rituals and use their magic to strengthen and align themselves with her and the interconnected Web of Life. Whether or not this will create a lasting change in religion as we know it today, clearly women are weaving new patterns into the mix. When new colors subtly blend with old, both can be transformed. Fresh textures may soften worn threads; shadings may create a slight shift in emphasis that makes the tapestry anew. Women across religions are joined in this new weaving, and, for now at any rate, the web resonates to their touch.

4

# Shamanism and Magic

## Michael York

From the 1980s if not earlier, the term *shamanism* has become the catchword for many of the most innovative efforts within contemporary spirituality. As any concept borrowed from an alien culture, it is one not without its controversial issues—ones which here raise questions of legitimacy, authenticity, and validation. The historic trajectory of the word alone encompasses many if not most of the contentions and raging debates concerning spirituality, its place in society, and its very raison d'être: What makes spirituality spiritual? Is there such a thing as "spiritual ownership"? What are the ethical issues raised by cultural appropriation? Can religiocultural institutions be transferred between contrasting societies? What is the relationship between religion and magic? What are the purposes of shamanism and magic?

To understand shamanism in its fullest implications, it is necessary to differentiate within a range of specific applications. In its primary sense, *shamanism* refers to indigenous practices to be found among tribal peoples of Siberia, particularly within the Tungus or Evenki communities. Consequently, in its most narrow usage, *shamanism* refers to the techniques of healing and trance of the Asian Altaic peoples and the religion associated with these. The irony is that the Yokut term appears itself to be a cultural import. Calvert Watkins (1969:1190) traces the Siberian *saman* to the *şamân* of the Tocharian peoples who migrated into West Central Asia around the beginning of the first millennium B.C.E.—an Indo-European tribal confederacy who apparently adopted from their southeast the Sanskrit designation for ascetic—namely, *śramaṇás*.[1] Throughout the Asian Northeast, the shaman refers to the office of the ecstatic priest-magician whose principle concern would appear to be that of healing. While the term *shamanism* is a Western construct, in its original context, a *shamanist* designates a Siberian follower of a (usually animistic) religion in which the shaman plays the pivotal part.

However, as the designation has come to be extended—initially through anthropological recognition, it is now more widely employed to refer to related ethnic practices found worldwide—for example, among North and South American Indians, African tribalists, Australian Aborigines, or such

Polynesian peoples in the domain of kahuna magic. As such, the term *shamanism* has provided religious studies scholars a convenient generic designation for an animistic worldview in which special medium technicians link the visible world with the otherworld of gods and spirits for the benefit of the local community. While much of this further application of the term may be traced to the work of Sergei Shirokogoroff, in the West we owe this development largely to the contribution of the Romanian scholar Mircea Eliade. Consequently, as Ninian Smart (1989:38) explains, the term *shamanism* is now used to designate any religious system that is centered on "a religious specialist who has great powers derived from ecstatic experiences in which he or she has contact with sacred forces." From this perspective, *shamanism* applies not only to the shaman of the Tungusic-speaking peoples but additionally to the *angalkut* of the Artic Inuit, the *noiaidit* of the Lapps, the Yoruban *elegun* and the equivalent medicine person, or "witch doctor," of other preliterate, oral traditional ethnicities. Beyond these, the term is nowadays also used for the office of similar practices in more-advanced civilizations—namely, the *chilan*, the *wu*, the *miko*, and the *mudang* of the respective Mayan, Chinese, Japanese, and Korean cultures.

However, there is a third or even fourth development within the arena of new religious formation that has emerged in the spiritual ferment of a North America and beyond that has questioned the prevailing rational utilitarianism of Western culture. These further developments occur within and against the backdrop of New Age and Neopagan spiritualities that are steadily gaining recognition in both the United States and Canada. In fact, shamanism—along with earth religions and Native American practices—provides the strongest link between these divergent spiritualities. But at the same time, both New Age and contemporary Western Paganism are developing radically different understandings and applications of shamanism in the modern Western context. In this light, shamanism has become one more spiritual commodity available in the religious consumer market that has emerged as an integral part of the quest for meaning and significance within North America. Among the paradigms of new shamanisms, we now have differentiations that, at least incipiently, can be labeled as New Age or neo-, urban, and psychonautic.[2] The baseline of all these is the Siberian shamanism studied by Shirokogoroff and Eliade and, more recently, by Piers Vitebsky, Vilmos Diószegi, Mihály Hoppál and Juha Pentikäinen. But beyond the indigenous launching point, contemporary Western shamanisms constitute a new breed of extensions, applications, and transformations and have perhaps as much to tell us about ourselves at our own crossroads between the social and the cosmic as they do about understandings or possible realities of the supernatural otherworld. In the new anthropology of nonreductionistic comprehension, as seen for instance in the work of Greenwood (2000), magic is not simply dismissed as primitive science or elementary religion but is accepted as veridical legitimacy in and of itself.

## TRADITIONAL INDIGENOUS SHAMANISM

But in order to understand the newer developments, it is first necessary to delineate original shamanic expression in situ. We are then afforded the possibility of recognizing continuities and innovations alike. As a spiritual technique and accompanying religious orientation, *Shamanism* has now permanently entered the lingua franca of the magical register. Along with the mystical and contemplative, it expresses a fundamental religious approach. Smart (1996) sees it as the likely origin of all further religious coalescing whether bhakti or *dhyâna*.

In its Siberian and affinitive indigenous manifestation the basic shamanic trajectory begins with a call, crisis, or initial illness and is followed by the training that culminates with initiation and transformation.[3] A common feature is the shaman's acquisition of a familiar or "spirit-animal," but invariable is the shamanic performance and experience of trance. Death symbolism appears frequently if not universally, and, with the return and/or reincorporation of the mediating figure of the shaman himself or herself, knowledge is dispensed on behalf of the community or concerned individuals. These last will often include that shaman's own apprentices to whom magical implements (feathers, ceremonial pipes, special drums, ritual rattles, and so forth) may be bequeathed. In its indigenous forms, shamanism is always transmitted through lineage and carefully prescribed lines of succession. In some cases, it is hereditary.

One of the main contrasts between contemporary Western Shamanism and traditional tribal forms is the general reluctance of the would-be indigenous shaman to assume the shamanic mantle. Despite the reverence and respect shamans receive, there is also traditional fear of them by their communities at large. Typically, the shaman is quasi-solitary—living separately and differently from those who constitute the mainstream of society. Consequently, the shaman's life may be a lonely one.

Often coinciding with sexual maturity, the candidate experiences a powerful crisis in the form of a physical or mental illness (Siikala 1978; Noll 1983). Among the Yokuts and similar tribal peoples it is not all that unusual for people to endure a six- to nine-month period of temporary schizophrenia. Without the sequestering and hospitalization that would be the Western norm, suffering people are integrated into the social fabric as much as possible and through which they are comforted. Most eventually recover and proceed to live normal lives henceforth. If, however, they have demonstrated during their illness an above-average capacity for dreaming or extraordinary perception, such people may be selected as potential shamans and given special ascetic, hermetic, and/or necromanic training.

The severe Artic environment may induce nervous disorders or forms of hysteria. The pre-shamanic condition might in some cases even be epilepsy. While the training may be a series of prolonged and repeated ordeals and hardship, it nevertheless constitutes a cure. The epileptic learns to develop the skill of control. Ecstasy is managed, and the shaman is the person who chooses when to enter trance. This mastery of the physical and psychological is honored by the community. Among the more typical demonstration of superhuman powers is the ability to walk barefooted across red-hot coals, even to swallow them, to remain unharmed by scalding water, to endure physical mutilation, to extricate oneself from bonds, and to exercise kinesis.

Among the Manchu-Tungusic, the Nivkh, and other peoples of Siberia, a well-nigh universal feature of traditional training involved visionary dismemberment followed by eventual reintegration (Eliade 1964:36 passim). The candidate may undergo skeletal reduction, cooking of the body's pieces, and subsequent reconstitution—only now with reputedly more powerfully and magically enhanced organs and body parts. This initiation involves journeying to the sky world or underworld or both to learn esoteric language skills by which to communicate with gods and spirits. There is also the acquisition of special or tutelary spirits who henceforth become the shaman's personal assistants. Subsequent Shamanic performance is, in effect, a reenactment of the initiatory experience. Using the acquired powers of divination and clairvoyance, the shaman seeks to heal, recover lost objects or persons, predict or even control the weather, harm those he or she wishes and, in general, augment the communal welfare.

In its original Northeast Asian forms, the quasi-religious underpinning of shamanism is both animistic and a belief in the duality of spiritual self (cf. Hultkrantz 1953). An individual is understood as ill if and when the absenting dream-soul cannot return to the body—usually perceived as a theft by some malevolent spirit or an imprisonment by a sorcerer. The shaman's task is to retrieve the soul of the patient and, if necessary, do battle with the offending demon or negative entity. This involves the vision quest to discover and transform the cause of illness through soul-loss. In some cases, illness is seen instead as having been projected into the sufferer's body by otherworldly spirits. The shaman's endeavor here is to remove the malevolent projectile—usually by sucking out the harmful object. In either case, the shaman's function is the communication with particular gods or spirits for the purpose of magical healing.

Among the various roles of the shaman in traditional Yokut and Evenki society, there are those of healer-physician, psychopomp, animal-charmer, prophet, sacrificial priest, lawyer, mythologue, epic singer, and keeper of the tribal calendar.[4] In Siberia, the classic cosmology behind shamanism is the three-storied view of the universe, whether the vertical arrangement of the heavens, the earth, and the underworld or their concentric enfoldment with the nether regions at the center and the celestial forming the outermost spheres. The three realms are linked together through the *axis mundi*—a world tree, pillar, or mountain—and it is this that provides the route by which the shaman's soul travels to the upper and lower or inner and outer regions (see Eliade in Nicholson 1987).

The world-supporting axis is often symbolically represented in shamanic rites. It is this cosmic link that allows the alleged communication between the three levels. The basic belief is that spirits, deities, sorcerers, demons, and ghosts of the invisible worlds are capable of influencing human life. But conversely, this view also suggests that terrestrial life can influence that of spirit. In the religiosities of the indigenous Siberian peoples, information from the otherworld and the exertion of influence on it are centered on the person of the shaman, the specifically empowered people who are believed able to enter the spirit worlds to interact directly. These are those who possess exceptional talent for recurring altered states of consciousness.

Much of the shaman's abilities are akin to those of the medium, who also communicates with the spirits of the otherworld. However, there are some fundamental differences. The medium is a person who, while in a trance, is *occupied* by the extrasensory entity. The medium functions as a channel for the words of a bystanding spirit or the ghost of a deceased person. In essence, he or she acts as an oracle. Consequently, the Yoruban *elegun* and Japanese *miko* are more like mediums in that they undergo spirit possession. The Yokut shaman, on the other hand, and unlike the more passive medium, actively travels to the afterlife—whether in the nether or celestial worlds. And it is this capacity for soul-travel that distinguishes the shaman and provides the initial understanding of the term in contrast to that of the medium.

The Asian heartland of shamanism, including the Mansi, Khanty, Ket, Dolgan, Evenk, Even, Yukaghir, Koryak, Chukchee, and even Inuit peoples, has extended its influence into Mongolia, Tibet, and Nepal, and perhaps into the Caucasus mountain regions as well. Typical features of the traditional paraphernalia include the shaman's robe, or caftan; headgear; mask; footwear; the pectoral that forms the shaman's mirror; a hazel or willow wood staff or wand; and drum (Rutherford 1986:44–53). As a microcosmic structure relating to the *axis mundi*, the drum is virtually indispensable for traditional shamanic vision quest (Eliade 1964:168–76; Pentikäinen 1998:26–48). Masks are used to incarnate a mythical personage, and during the shamanic performance, rather than mediumistic possession, the shaman is frequently believed to transform into the particular animal spirit or god represented by the mask.

The Siberian shamanic rite centers on divesting the outer layers of the self and reducing to a skeletal state as symbolic of the inner essential self. Vision quest is often undertaken through solitude and physical suffering in such sacred places as mountains or sweat lodges. Physical austerities such as sleep deprivation, fasting, and body pain may be accompanied with the ingestion of entheogenic substances. For Shirokogoroff, the key purpose of these undertakings is to heal through communication with spirits, but Eliade identifies the propensity for entering trance through "techniques of ecstasy" as the defining feature of shamanism.

What is clear, however, is that, thanks to Soviet persecution, shamans in Siberia have been virtually eliminated. Shamans were taunted to prove their flying capacities and pushed out of helicopters. This liquidation culminated centuries of persecution that was earlier begun by Christian and Buddhist missionaries. The result is that today in an area roughly the size of India containing about one million inhabitants there may be less than a handful of surviving shamans.[5] As a lineage system of succession, indigenous Siberian forms of shamanism that traditionally negotiated the animistic contours of the regions' numerous micro-variations and micro-climates have been lost, and the ability to reconnect with the "shamanic impulse" is dependent on the formation of links with other indigenous peoples such as the Tamang in Nepal—ones that are often mediated through the scholarly work and contacts of anthropologists and the like.

## TRADITIONAL NORTH AMERICAN SHAMANISMS

Until recently, anthropologists have tended to reject the notion of a unitary shamanism as a romantic view developed by Eliade. Invariably, shamanic spirituality is a local expression of local peoples, but increasingly the Western concept of shaman*ism* is being recognized as an acknowledgment of the similarities that do exist between the variations. At the University of Newcastle conference on shamanism in June of 1988, Piers Vitebsky argued that the first region of shamanism may actually be engendering a world religion. Though this may comprise an artificial development akin to the British colonial labeling of the diverse dharmic practices of India under the single rubric of *Hinduism* and the use of the term *shamanism* to describe the medicine people and witch doctors of ethnic peoples beyond the Tungusic, Samoyedic, Paleosiberian, and Mongolian Buryat tribes, a Eurocentric misnomer, it nevertheless provides religious studies scholars a convenient generic designation for an animistic worldview in which specialist medium technicians connect the visible world with the otherworld of gods and spirits for the benefit of the local community.

One of the major extensions or reapplications of the Siberian-inspired term *shamanism* has been to similar practices of the native peoples of the Americas. While the South American *curañdero* has come into vogue throughout much of the more-exploratory forms of Neo-Shamanism, the America Indian of North America has furnished the chief link between the practices of Northeast Asia and the Euro-American adaptations. But once again, even here we must remain mindful not only of local variations but also of differences from the Siberian standards that bespeak contrasting spiritual nuance. For instance, the Algonquin shamanic practice of the Eastern United States and Canada is closer to that of the Japanese *miko* and Yoruban *elegun* in that instead of soul travel per se, medicine people are mediums who undergo spirit possession. On the other hand, the North American Plains people practice what could be considered a democratized form of shamanism in that, in place of the emphasis on the religious specialist, everyone is encouraged to participate in vision quest.[6]

The Plains Cree spanning both sides of the U.S.-Canadian border are an interesting ethnological phenomenon in themselves in that they represent relatively recent arrivals in the prairie country at the beginning of the nineteenth century—departing from their parent stock, the Eastern Cree, entering as invaders but quickly assimilating to a full-fledged Plains way of life that was centered on buffalo hunting until the last of the herds were killed off around 1880. Comprising a congeries of different bands (the River People, Calling River People, Rabbit Skin People, House People, Cree-Assiniboin, Touchwood Hills People, and Parklands People), even today on such reserves as the File Hills, Touchwood Hills, Qu'Appelle, Duck Lake, and Carlton Agencies, shamanic ceremonialism is continued— particularly the Sun Dance, and shamans are feared and respected. Here we find such typical features as flight to the otherworlds to achieve soul retrieval, cure of illness, securing important information (future weather conditions, hunting predictions, recovery of lost objects), or some other (usually communal) benefit. The shaman also conveys gifts or sacrifices to the gods or spirits or, in the role of psychopomp, may escort the souls of the dead to the afterlife. (See Mandelbaum 1979.)

Shamanism in general is not associated with millenarianism. However, in the United States, the early nineteenth-century Handsome Lake revival and the Ghost Dance movements of the 1870s and 1890s became religious celebrations of the imminent disappearance of the European descendents, the restoration of traditional lands and ways of life, and the return of revivified ancestors that were predicted and launched by mediumistic shamans.[7] Consequently, while indigenous shamanism is concerned primarily with maintenance of the social status quo, we can observe that in times of colonial oppression and extreme stress, the shaman's function may extend to inspiration of a millenarian movement that provokes fear and the necessity to follow codes of strictly observed conduct as the means to prepare for— and remain safe in—the anticipated changes. All these movements, of course, following a millennialist trajectory that predicts imminent change, ended in failure; but the net effect was the eventual Evangelical Christianization of the American Indian communities in both the United States and Canada.

Typical of this transformation are the Tsimshian and other Athapaskan peoples of the North Pacific Coast whose territory stretched along the Pacific Ocean coast from southern Alaska to Washington state. Among the Carrier Athapaskans, their original religion polarized the supernatural between the continuous, legitimate *haleyut* and the unwieldy, antisocial *naxnox*. The former represents the supernatural, as it may be controlled and used though simulative ritual that could occur at any time of the year. The *naxnox*, on the other hand, is depicted only during the dramatic masked performances conducted during the winter season. In both types, the shaman (*swansk*) plays the central role. However, with the influence of Christian missionary work and the Evangelical conversions that swept the American Indian communities, such peoples as the Tsimshian came to repudiate their previous beliefs as pagan and "low class." The *swansk* has become understood as a "witch doctor" or "devil worker" considered to be in league with Satan. They have become largely replaced by a line of *bini*, or prophets (for example, of the Beaver Phratry or exogamous social clan that employs the beaver as totem), who still undergo successive visits to the sky and who have mediated Aboriginal concepts and healing practices with quasi-canonical Christian understandings. While most people of the Tsimshianic language group are now devout Christians, the Gitksan tribe alone among them, relatively isolated by their interior homeland, retain recognition and patronage of the *swansk* who now derives power from the Christian God. Although a Christianized version, the Gitksan continue a practice of shamanism (Miller and Eastman 1984:137f).

Among the reawakened awareness by the American Indians of North America of their past traditions and appreciation of their organic vitality, the Lakota-Sioux peoples have formed much of the vanguard. Foremost has been the rediscovery and spread of the Sun Dance ceremony as a Shamanic initiatory experience available to all tribal individuals. Few Native Americans would consider themselves pagan; Christianity has become the norm and accepted religious framework. Nevertheless, lineages of ceremonial pipe holders have been revived, and there is a growing effort to retrace and discover lost practices. Much of this endeavor represents a desperate attempt to ensure ethnic identity, and, during the 1993 Parliament of World Religions in Chicago, a Lakota-sponsored initiative attempted to launch a "Declaration of War" against the appropriators of American Indian institutions such as use of native sweat lodges by Euro-Americans, display of traditional medicine bags in museums, and sale and commercialization of American Indian cultural artifacts. This issue divided the Native American community and was only privately endorsed a year later by the Lakota peoples themselves. The consensus of tribal elders at the Chicago venue was against ratification, but the issue remains highly contentious and retains unsettled ramifications for Euro-American shamanic practice (York 1994).

Another vexing issue is that of ethnology and the rights and wishes of the people being studied. As John Bauman disclosed on the Nature Religion list (natrel@uscolo.edu), Barre Toelken, director of the folklore program at Utah State University, chose to return his tapes of Navajo stories to his informant's family for destruction rather than risk that they could be employed in ways which were unacceptable to the tribe. But as Lucie DuFresne (November 11, 2001) in response pointed out, Alaskan and Yukon women elders at the Circumpolar Woman's Conference in Whitehorse, Yukon, in November of 1999 emphasized to the younger women that "it was 'white' curiosity that had 'saved' their cultures from total obliteration." Publication of the older genealogies, songs, stories, myths, and legends have in many cases allowed cultural memory to become reestablished. In following the ethnographic legacy of Frederica de Laguna, DuFresne allows that de Laguna was respecting the wishes of her informants to "[get] an ethnographer to write down as completely and accurately as possible, get the information published and disseminated as widely as possible, get the information stored in as 'permanent' and public a manner as possible and hope that it is still there for future generations to find and use." But as DuFresne also makes clear, many people as a form of cultural-political resistance invented myths, ownership claims and false legacies as "good jokes." These have now often become, to the detriment of the native communities themselves, subsequently enshrined in law and statute. And as Vitebsky warned at Newcastle, without the continuity of direct lineage, the "shamanic impulse" of local customs and institutions does not always work out correctly.

NEW AGE SHAMANISM

At the same Newcastle conference, Hoppál classified between continuous, recontinuous, and noncontinuous shamanic traditions. He also distinguished between urban and rural forms. Some classic continuous shamanisms would be those of Nepal and Siberia, and even, as with the latter, shamanism may appear to have died out, because locality is more significant than globality, an apparent discontinuous tradition can, according to Hoppál, sometimes demonstrate an ability to redevelop and become recontinuous. Hoppál is, of course, referring to indigenous Shamanisms, but his distinction may also be applicable to the North American Pagan resurgence. In this light, we can differentiate between native traditions that are being appropriated, eclecticized, and invented on the one hand and those that are being rediscovered and resurrected from the European cultural legacy on the other. The first of these is what we may essentially understand as New Age Shamanism, and its seminally informing appropriation is taken from the American Indian.

New Age Shamanism, in the sense I am employing it here, is an ideal type. In practice, Neo-Shamanisms range between New Age and contemporary Western identities, between invention and resurrection, and between different degrees of conformity with indigenous understandings. Both the new Shamanisms and Native American spirituality are, broadly speaking, part of North American alternative or countercultural spirituality that increasingly affirms the self as authority and self-autonomy as spiritual ideology. Jon Block (1998:21) recognizes the constituent features of alternative spirituality to include belief in Shamanistic or kabbalistic magic, the earth as spiritual, a willingness to participate in other kinds of spirituality and a disenchantment with organized religions. People who orient toward New Age Shamanism are found in both urban and rural regions of North America as well as Western Europe, Australia, and New Zealand. While much of the development has occurred in the metropolitan areas of Canada and the United States, inasmuch as there is a back-to-the-earth affinity with this orientation, there is a constant movement between city and country. In general, those involved could be described as mainstream, middle class in origin and economic and social lifestyle.

While Shamanism provides one of the strongest links between the contrasting poles of contemporary spiritual practices, its New Age variety represents a new breed of Shamanism with new goals and means. Though all contemporary forms of Western Shamanism are innovative, the New Age variety is less a re-creation as it is a creation. In short, it is a new religious movement.

The "legitimacy" question raises various possible assessments of contemporary Western Shamanism as a new religion. If the construct of "shamanism" is itself largely a Western academic fiction, the influence initially of Carlos Castaneda is that to which the popularity of this "fiction" is to be traced. Daniel Noel (Vermont College of Norwich University) considers Castaneda the inspiration behind what he calls the West's "shabby imitation" of indigenous shamanism (expressed during the Newcastle conference). But in the wake of Castaneda and the series of books he launched starting with *The Teachings of Don Juan* (1968), Mircea Eliade has become retroactively significant in the subsequent development of neo-shamanism as a polyglot, pluralistic movement that parallels the eclectic and multicultural-mulitperspectival proliferation of contemporary North American spirituality. A third major influence comes through the work of Michael Harner.

Originally, as an anthropologist, Harner conducted some substantial ethnographic work in South America (Harner 1973). In time, however, he developed the concept of what he terms "core shamanism" to describe what is reputedly the essential features of shamanism. His seminal work is his 1980–1982 *The Way of the Shaman: A Guide to Power and Healing* in which he presents his version of shamanic transformation and the experience of ecstasy. But he has also engineered a shift in emphasis and focus and does not seek to master the spirits as is found among both the Siberian shaman and the Latin American *curandero*. In fact, Harner has replaced shamanic journeying itself with the exercise of guided imagery, and what occurs in a Harner workshop or under the auspices of his Foundation for Shamanic Studies will not be found among any extant tribal peoples. Knowledge is now understood exoterically rather than esoterically. Perhaps here influenced more by American Indians, the aim in Harner's "core shamanism" is to eliminate the specialist altogether and foster power directly within the common person himself or herself. Eschewing both the imaginary and the archetypal of Jung, this New Age Shamanism places emphasis upon what is increasingly termed the *imaginal*—the imagination made powerful and constituting in some sense a reality of its own. And at least as Noel sees it, this particular process of imagining becomes a pragmatic way *not* to appropriate from other cultures.

Core Shamanism defines itself as "the universal and near universal basic methods of the shaman to enter nonordinary reality for problem solving, well-being, and healing" (*Common Ground* 1999:108). Harner's workshops, weekend intensives, and experimental courses in shamanic training have spawned numerous centers throughout North America and especially on the North American West Coast: for example, the Foundation for Shamanic Studies (Mill Valley, California),[8] Friends Landing International Centers for Conscious Living (http://www.friendshipslanding.net), Sacred Circles Institute (Mukilteo, Washington), Inward Journeys—Leah Maggie Garfield and Edwin Knight (British Columbia and Eugene, Oregon), and Dance of the Deer Foundation Center for Shamanic Studies (Soquel, California).

The Foundation for Shamanic Studies places particular emphasis on the "classic shamanic journey" as an awe-inspiring visionary method for exploring "the hidden universe" of myth and dream. Friends Landing combines Shamanic orientation with hypnotherapy and the ideokinetic study of how imagery affects movement. Sacred Circles Institute, Inward Journeys, and Dance of the Deer Foundation hold camping retreats, Mount Shasta pilgrimages, wilderness treks, and/or similar experiential encounters with nature in order to attain personal and spiritual transformation. According to Garfield and Knight (*Common Ground* 1999:47), "Shamanic development is a pathway that brings understanding and meaning to your life through mastery and cooperation with the natural world." It includes stargazing; interconnection of the soul's different parts; mastery of elements; use of yoga, herbs, and power sites; and "Vision Quests." One is encouraged to become the person one always knew he or she was born to be. The candidate is reputedly "provided with methods for journeying to discover and study [his or her] own individual spiritual teachers in nonordinary reality" (*Common Ground* 1999:108). The purpose of "core" shamanism, therefore, is to restore spiritual power and health into contemporary daily life for the healing of oneself, others, and the planet.

Using the "magic of focused attention," Neo-Shamanism endeavors to help its practitioners secure habit and lifestyle changes for both oneself and one's clients in order to transmute suffering, relieve stress, gain personal understanding, and locate a core of wellness that can implement one's life dream. While part of its effort is to train the would-be aspirant to supply fee-based healing and training services to others, the main concentration of Neo-Shamanic activity is directed toward the self. In this sense, it is in full accord with the essential thrust of New Age concerns with personal transformation.

In comparing core shamanism with traditional shamanisms, there is still the fundamental understanding that the physical world is infused with spirit power. The new Shamanism shares the animistic perception that under girds the rationale of various indigenous frameworks. But in the new, neo-, or New Age forms of contemporary Western shamanism, there is also a tendency to confuse the peak experience as the goal rather than the means—even when the overall emphasis is on self-development. Rather than seeking to make the individual more powerful, as in the sorcery of original shamanisms, Harner-based shamanism attempts to develop the individual's ability of spiritual surrender in order to discover his or her true humanity.

While Harner's "core shamanism" may be recognized among the leading motifs informing North American New Age Shamanism, it is not the only source of the matrix that can be so identified. Inasmuch as Neo-Shamanism shares in the New Age spiritual consumer market, there is a range of other influences and even formulations. Along with North American Indian legacies, New Age Shamanism is just as apt to borrow from the Australian Aborigine or the Hawaiian kahuna. The key concept behind all these derivative forms in the New Age context, however, is that of "spiritual evolution."

Typical, in this sense, would be the collection of ideas expressed by the rock group Enigma 2 in its 1993 album titled *The Cross of Changes*. Here we find the notion of evolutionary development, dolphin consciousness, spiritual purpose, reincarnation, and, employing ideas taken from the Sufi poet Mevlana Jalaluddin Rimi, inner truth. Enigma 2 traces humanity's origins in the deep "to help and understand but not to kill," to return to oneself, to innocence, but recognizes too the subsequent error of conquest, the liquidation of the American Indian and the need "to avoid the mistakes we made." As with most New Age spirituality, there is the picturing of the supernatural both beyond or external to the individual and internal as one's divine inner spark: "There's a universal justice and the eyes of truth are always watching you." This composite of New Age ideas is centered on the light at the center of every color and the crystal at the heart of every stone, and Enigma 2 advises to "Remember the shaman, when he used to say: 'Man is the dream of the dolphin.'"

Consequently, New Age Shamanism in North America is to be seen as an innovative if not also controversial development of the wider New Age complex. It differs from original shamanisms on two significant issues. The first of these concerns New Age Shamanism's adoption of New Age theodicy. Whereas, in their environments of origin, shamanic practices tend to approach a spirit of illness as a negativity, in Core and New Age perspectives there is no endeavor to destroy such spirits—either to kill them or boomerang them back for their sender's destruction—but instead to approach spirits of cancer, AIDS, and so forth not as evil but as respectable. The intent is here to appeal to them in a process of extrication. Following a New Thought–New Age ontology, the negative does not exist. It is instead a figment of one's own imagination. The shaman ceases to be the warrior he or she is in the Aboriginal community and instead concentrates on a power of the mind's concentration if not a New Age expression of universal love for all beings.

But the key "weakness" of Neo-Shamanism in its New Age variety is not its holistic as opposed to dualistic understanding of good and evil but its overemphasis on the self without a community framework. In traditional shamanisms, the shaman's entire endeavor is shaped by his or her role vis-à-vis the community. In a Western cultural context, sending forth one's (free-) soul to explore and encounter the spiritual realms of the otherworld would be an enterprise beyond the bounds of normal behavior. But the Westerner who transgresses standard limits courts with the dangers of insanity. In indigenous animistic societies, there is an inevitable understanding of soul-duality. There is both the life-soul that animates the body and the dream-soul that absents the corporeal self during dreams, in trance, and at the time of death.[9] The mentally ill is considered to be a person whose departed soul does not return to the waking body. This constitutes the general understanding of madness or schizophrenia in tribal ethnic society, which, in addition, becomes a prelude to physical illness and eventual death as well. For the ordinary person, such soul-loss is an accident or misfortune, but for the shaman, on the other hand, this very propensity for entering an altered state of consciousness is his or her trade. But the trance state is still not the goal, as it has often become in the contemporary West of North America, Europe, and Anglo-Oceania. The raison d'être for the shaman's shift in consciousness is always ultimately the community welfare.

Even for the experienced shaman in the traditional, indigenous setting, to navigate the dangers of the spirit world within an altered state of consciousness, there is the inevitable risk of soul-loss. Consequently, it is the vitally important social functions of the shaman that provide the means by which to return to this world. Without the community orientation, the shaman could become permanently lost in the otherworld. The function is of course a twofold one in its original milieu: it is through the shaman's mediumship capabilities that the traditional community is provided an access to the spiritual. Without this, the community itself risks the possibility of collective madness. But at the same time, it is the community and the shaman's duty to serve it that provides the shamanic safeguard against the specialist becoming perpetually imprisoned in a world of purely analogical and magical effervescence. To date, in core shamanism and the related forms of shamanic activity that follow a New Age agenda concentrating on self-development and self-empowerment alone, this key dynamic that is essential in all indigenous shamanisms is only incipient at best. There is a pursuit of altered states of consciousness without a concomitant sense of social responsibility.

## PAGAN SHAMANISM

In contrast to the New Age varieties of contemporary Western Shamanism in North America and beyond, there are also those practices that conform more to a Pagan spirituality, sometimes supernaturally oriented, sometimes more clinically fixated, that places the locus of value *primus inter pares* in the natural if not more broadly the tangible world. Again in contrast to New Age Shamans, Pagan Shamans comprise a greater number of people who tend to feel marginalized through such variables as gender politics, sexual orientation, and/or countercultural spirituality. A particular type of contemporary Shamanism is that which is increasingly designated as the psychonautic. Once again, with all these constructs—whether New Age, psychonautic, or pagan, we are speaking here in terms of ideal-types, but more like the New Age, the experimenter with power plants and consciousness transformers engages in soul-flight often without the context of a supporting and grounding community. Indeed, this lack of social responsibility may be considered a current characteristic of contemporary North American Shamanism in general. Nevertheless, this pursuit of urban Shamanism in today's world is increasingly occurring within a broader understanding of, if not the human community per se, the ecological environment and an increasing awareness of the fragility of the natural equilibrium.

Pagan expressions of contemporary Western Shamanism tend either to attempt revivals of lost European traditions (Druidism, Heathen *seidr,* some forms of Wodenism/Odinism, elements within the classical Greco-Roman religiosity of pre-Christianity, Baltic, and Finno-Ugrian legacies, even the *kemetic* heritage of ancient Egypt) or to institute techno-shamanic innovations. Those attempts that look into the cultural origins of the West itself, in other words, are endeavors to resurrect a spiritual essence of nonextant traditions. They tend not to appropriate from living practices. While they may borrow inspiration from Native American, Aboriginal, and Polynesian peoples, the tendency is to use this inspiration to find similarities and parallel institutions within their own legacies rather than to reproduce paraphernalia that may already belong to or be claimed by others.

Certainly here is residual influence from Harner's Foundation for Shamanic Studies, but there is perhaps less of the eclectic combination of shamanic journeying with Human Potential techniques such as hypnotherapy, ideokinesis, yoga, and lifestyle change. But more important, pagan shamanism refuses to follow the New Age route that cannot countenance the *ira deorum*—namely, the fear or wrath of the gods. In both its spiritually pagan and scholarly psychonautic expressions, in non-New Age contemporary Western Shamanism there is recognition of fear itself as a profound reality. In this encounter with the emotion of terror, there is an attempt to work through the kind of fright that Otto (1928:19) recognized "must be gravely disturbing to those persons who will recognize nothing in the divine nature but goodness, gentleness, love, and a sort of confidential intimacy." From the pagan shamanic perspective, evil is extrinsic rather than intrinsic and is understood as disease. It is to be cured rather than by-passed as an illusion through enlightenment. The pagan shaman is seeking to regain a natural balance that includes "disinfection" and disruption-removal and not simply a mental denying of its ontological reality. In a word, in the New Age variety of Shamanism, there is the effort to move beyond fear toward a state of complete spiritual and emotional freedom. With the Pagan variety, by contrast, there is more the endeavor to manage or outwit fear in the process of bringing benefit to the individual and community.

But while earth-centered forms of contemporary Shamanism in North America concentrate largely on gleaning and recovering metaphors, conceptual frameworks, institutions, and practices from their own Euro-American heritage and related traditions, surviving as an additional countercultural legacy from the 1960s, shamanic psychonautica has perhaps a more direct affinity with traditional shamanisms that employ drug-induced trance states as a major recourse for achieving soul-flight. Modern Western psychonauts comprise a quasi-scholarly and quasi-experimental alliance of explorers in entheogenic experience. Their point of departure is undoubtedly Eliade's identifying shamanism as techniques of ecstasy.

Not all of this contemporary Western pursuit is conducted within a religious or spiritual framework, but much of it is—and most of that is pagan. The seriousness of this kind of undertaking is to be seen in the prevailing refusal of present-day psychonauts to employ hallucinogens as a form of recreational tourism. Instead, use of shamanic techniques is directed toward self-discovery and imaginal exploration. If the more traditional understanding of community to be served is now absent in these North American endeavors, the present-day community for American and Canadian psychonauts is generally the psychonautic community itself.

In some senses, North American psychonautica brings the New Age and Neopagan branches of contemporary Western Shamanism together. The key feature is of course the use of different hallucinogenic substances to induce psychomimesis, *entheoi*, or catalepsis.[10] Harner's initial studies involve Latin American *ayahuasca* consumption as the medium by which to experience a world of spirit and vision. Castaneda launched his shamanic career through jimson weed, peyote and *Datura stramonium*. In the world-wide and traditional employment of "power plants," first century Thracian shamans resorted to hashish. Pythagoras consumed a plant known as *kykeon*, which is translated as "disorder." The Vedic peoples of the Indian subcontinent ingested *soma*—identified currently as possibly the Eastern Mediterranean pine *Ephedra fragile* or the fly agaric mushroom (*Amanita muscaria*). The Jivaro Indians of Ecuador use tobacco; the people of Surinam, the takini plant. Such "teacher plants" or "power plants" are usually those with psychotropic properties capable of producing a trance state, which can then be directed toward healing and divining purposes. From a traditional shamanic perspective, modern synthetic drugs such as LSD are considered to have no tutelary spirit. Consequently, there is an incipient division within the North American psychonautic community between those who resort to artificially produced hallucinogens and those who consider these to be dangerous.

Techno-shamanic practice is itself a wider orientation within which psychonautic shamanism is only one component. More broadly, it includes technological experimentation and inducement of trance state that began perhaps with the 1960s use of strobe light and laser beam and have progressed through the rave and trance dance phenomena of the 1990s youth culture. Further techno-extensions involve exploration of possibilities offered in cyberspace and through online network communities. Baudrillard's acknowledgment of hyper-reality alongside the more traditional realms of the real, the symbolic and the imaginary suggests a technological medium that offers nonimaginal ontologies. All of these dimensions become avenues of techno-shamanic exploration and its desire to shift and/ or expand consciousness (Davis 1998).

The wider context of all these emerging North American innovations, from psychonautic, techno, and even in some cases New Age Shamanisms, falls within the rubric increasingly known as urban Shamanism. Here the traditional community of indigenous shamanism has been replaced by the cosmopolitan worlds of the United States, Canada, and the West in general. An emerging recognition of the needs of a modern society that has become depersonalized and mechanized through a Weberian understanding of disenchantment is probably the single most motivating factor behind the various developments of contemporary urban Shamanism. In general, this disenchantment and search for a reenchanted world have turned to a quasi-romantic and ecologically activist understanding of nature. But in all forms of urban Shamanism there is an underlying yearning for organic, holistic, and natural balance, and even the largely high tech rave culminates with its participants greeting the rising sun. Behind most if not all forms of emerging contemporary Western Pagan Shamanism, there is an ultimate grounding in natural metaphor and natural reality.[11]

MAGIC IN THE SHAMANIC CONTEXT

Shamanism is invariably contextualized in some kind of an animistic world. Unlike the world of New Age, however, in which the animistic becomes one dimension or more of supersentience, in Pagan and traditional shamanisms, the animistic conforms more to an idea subsumed by the terminology of *other sentience*. In other words, there is an avoidance of such directional assessments of 'higher' and 'lower' in terms of *better-superior* and *worse-inferior*. Shamanism, in a word, attempts to engage fully with otherness per se, and in this light could be considered postmodern in a Derridan sense (Martin 1992).[12]

The other in a shamanic animist context becomes intimately related to the observer himself or herself and what becomes the heart of shamanistic technique—namely, shifting perspective. This is akin to Dion Fortune's understanding of magic as the changing of consciousness at will. Unless one is willing to accept that the ontological reality behind the shamanic otherworlds and the beings or spirits encountered within them are pure delusional fictions, the phenomenon of magic as it appears through the technology of trance has less to do with unequal return, the substitution of something of lesser value for a reward of greater value, but more as a mental operative. However the shaman constructs his or her world, whether through cultural conditioning or the deliberate adoption of a particular ideological framework within which to work, his or her magic is that which intimately relates to mind rather than the necessarily *creatio ex nihilo* of apport. It is not trance or ecstasy that is the shaman's purpose but a kaleidoscopic shifting of perspective in order to see things in new and different manners. In this development of the multiperspective, pagan, and traditional shamanic magic retains an affinity with the conjurative propensities of high ceremonial magic on the one hand and with the health affirmations and prosperity consciousness of New Thought on the other. In all these, magic may be interpreted as an attempt to trick the imagination.

Nevertheless, the enterprise of "tricking" or changing fundamentally a current state of imaginative perception—whether to encounter spirits, gods, ghosts, or demons, or to "see through" illness and poverty—when undertaken within an understanding of a world animistically alive, participates in league with magic not just as the art of deception but as a real force in and of itself. In traditional and pagan forms of shamanism, the magic resides, like the animistic forces themselves, within certain objects or entities. In native traditions, one resorts to "power plants" above all else. With the psychonautic extension from the integrity of a plant with a magical soul into a purely mechanical world of chemicals (lysergic acid, MDA, ketamine, etc.), there is still the technical similarity, though here one that employs a nonanimistic *techne* to trick or change the imagination—now usually termed *expanding consciousness*.

What remains the same for traditional and psychonautic Shamans alike is the engineering of consciousness by an entheogenic principle: namely, by adding a god-substance or god-provoking substance to one's already psychosomatic mix and getting something greater than the constituent parts. In this way, we can discern that the evolving complexity theory that is concerned with the nonlinear aspects of the universe and how something becomes more than merely the sum of its components (explored by the Santa Fe Institute and other "think tanks") is modern, scientific terminology for age-old magical "dis-equality."[13]

CONCLUSION

In recapitulation, the shaman's range of activities, his or her stock in trade so to speak, includes the development of vigilance, the mastery of both invisibility and flight or kinesis, and cultivation of multiple perspective, ritual knowledge, and spirit contact. Depending on locality and cultural context, these pursuits are interpreted differently. In indigenous Siberian and related Asian shamanisms as well as among native peoples with similar traditions elsewhere, flight and invisibility for instance might be literal expectations. Informants in Rajasthan, for example, have told me that they have seen magician sadhus levitate demonstrably. And while the same achievements might be sought in modern North America, more often than not, invisibility and flight are here understood as metaphors. The contemporary Shaman is one who can move about anonymously. He or she remains undetected by the world at large in the general pursuit of the shaman's trade. And the ability to fly occurs rather as the experience of trance—whether induced through ingestion or through some kind of austerity and/or mental concentration.

In all cases, however, the shaman's task is one of vigilance—the cultivation of awareness of the conditions and contours of his or her surroundings, the environment, the community, and the forces that exert influence and change upon them. The Shaman knows the local holy places, the power centers of old, the sites of major or significant events. He or she also knows the seasons, the cycles of sun and moon, the sacred days on which access to the otherworld of magical effervescence is the greatest. The shaman is the keeper of the sacred calendar. In the American and Canadian context of the new Shamanisms, these same pursuits are continued in countless variations and local interpretations. But the shamanic impulse that mirrors the more original function of the intermediary specialist who operates between the worlds springs from a perceived deficit within North American society and its need for renewal through the perception and experience of enchantment.

It is important, however, to keep in mind the different understandings of shamanism by Shirokogoroff and Eliade. While the latter considered shamanism to be a development of techniques of ecstasy, Shirokogoroff argued that the purpose of this profession is spiritual healing—a curing that ultimately occurs within and for the community. New Age Shamanism may stress this healing aspect but more often than not focuses it on the individual alone. Eliade may have, through Castaneda and, to a lesser extent, Harner, set the framework for most contemporary Shamanic pursuit within North America. But it ought nonetheless be kept in mind that it is not ecstasy or trance that is the goal of shamanism. What is desired is the development of mindfulness and multiple perspective—ultimately to attain as rounded and complete an understanding as possible of the world in which we live. Ecstatic experience is a means toward augmenting the ordinary viewing of things in the process of developing the multiple perspective.

Within North America, shamanistic practice occurs among two diverging communities: the Native American and the largely Euro-American Neo-Shamanic. This last has more often than not developed in urban and/or suburban regions of the continent—in and around such places like New

York, Chicago, Los Angeles, Vancouver, and Toronto. Rarely for Neo-Shamanists is there a definitive illness or crisis that leads to the initiation of the shaman as occurs among American Indians. It remains unlike traditional shamanism where those selected for training usually display an initial reluctance to become shamans. Among indigenous North American ethnic communities the trade of shamanism is not something one usually chooses. In fact, from the Native American perspective, this neocolonial intrusion is seen as a fake practice.

Moreover, in its original formulations, shamanic apprenticeship is arduous and prolonged. Knowledge of medicinal herbs and power plants is required along with an intimate familiarity of the local terrain and its geography of the sacred. Much of the training occurs in seclusion or isolated conditions. As Rutherford (1986:38) explains, "Beatings, burning with fire, slashing with knives, suspension often upside down from a tree for hours or even days, ascending a ladder of upturned sword blades are all to be found." By contrast, the Neo-Shamanic tyro more often than not comes out of New Age's concern with anxiety and phobia treatment. The primary focus becomes personal anxiety disorder that the contemporary North American tends to perceive as functionally impairing. Shortness of breath, dizziness, racing heart, trembling, depersonalization, paralyzing terrors, panic attacks, and fear of dying are the kinds of anxiety symptoms that Human Potential, New Age techniques, and Neo-Shamanism claim to eradicate.

The basic idea of shamanism as the institutionalization of a socially recognized intermediary who liaisons between the world of pragmatic realities and the more subtle realm of spirit is more clearly witnessed among the American Indian than among the Euro-American new variations. The new Shamanism, by contrast, exists more as an attempt to bypass the specialist and give power directly back to the people. But for both communities, there is an attempt to fill a lacuna that is perceived when communication between this world and the spirit world is not deemed possible on the part of ordinary persons or at least people in an ordinary state of consciousness. For the Native American, there is general conformity with the theological notion that, at the close of the primal era, the high god receded and became inactive in the affairs of this world (for example, Eliade 1964:105n140, 505). In this void that ensued, numerous ancestor spirits or spirits of nature come into prominence as interveners, and it is these beings with whom the shaman becomes an adept in communicating with and controlling.

In the historical progression of shamanism from its origins among hunter-gatherer societies, as a spiritual orientation it has given birth to a number of offshoots: the practice of magic, the development of healing techniques, and, in some cases, the creation of epic and lyric poetry. In fact, Richard Noll (Nicholson 1987:56) likens shamanism to the Western occult traditions of alchemy and ceremonial magic "in that they, too, cultivate mental imagery in order to contact imaginal beings." Nevertheless, there is frequently an element of the "sham" in shamanistic artistry. Although the words are presumably not etymologically related, there is undoubtedly a degree of fakery in the shaman's perceived ability to fly, to become invisible, to walk on red-hot coals, or to pierce stakes through vulnerable parts of the body's midriff or elsewhere. This does not mean that all supernormal shamanic feats are necessarily shams, but the shaman is a magician in both senses of the term: someone who performs tricks through sleight-of-hand techniques *and* someone who manipulates through magical power and/or is capable of changing consciousness at will. To these ends, typical shamanic devices include hypnotism, ventriloquism, legerdemain, and, above all, trance-like states. These last are achieved through dance, music, fasting, meditation, drug taking, and/or self-hypnosis.

Indigenous shamanisms are primarily concerned with maintaining the status quo of society, but as already mentioned, in times of colonial oppression or extreme stress, the shaman may inspire a millenarian movement as seen in the early nineteenth-century Handsome Lake revival or the Ghost Dances of the 1870s and 1890s. Nevertheless, Robert Pirsig (1991) compares the social roles of the priest vis-à-vis the shaman in that the ecclesiastic former is the conservative functionary preoccupied with social order while the shaman is the innovator, the iconoclast, the disrupter, and the source of new ideas. In that the shaman's very raison d'être is his or her expertise in crossing from this world to the next—and back—the shaman's movement occurs in the liminal zone that bridges both this world and the other, the inner and outer, the literal and the symbolic. The shaman's propensity to reach the other depends on his or her skill in traversing the liminal. And it is this realm between the worlds, this edge between chaos and order, in which the kind of spiritual innovations central to a creative, dynamic society are most likely to emerge.[14] The development of contemporary North American Shamanisms may constitute a response to perceptions of social and cultural rigidification. Like shamanisms more generally, Pagan Shamanisms explicitly and New Age Shamanisms at least implicitly rely on a worldview that understands tangible reality as animate and the divine as immanent within it. Both traditional American Indian and contemporary Western Shamanisms adopt a basically magical stance vis-à-vis the world, humanity, and the supernatural.

# Lucumí: The Second Diaspora

## Ysamur M. Flores-Peña

This chapter is concerned with Afro-Caribbean religion as it has taken form in North America. Caribbean Spiritualism, Palo, Curanderismo, and Voodoo have all been brought to North America with Caribbean immigrants. However, the most popular and most important of these religions is Santería, the religion of the Yoruba people as it developed in Cuba during and after the slave trade. As the use of the term *Santería* has racist connotations, I will use the emic designation *Lucumí* when speaking about this religion and its culture.[1] Largely misunderstood, Lucumí has produced a brilliant and vibrant diasporean culture, which has appealed to Latinas/Latinos, African Americans, Asians, and West Indians. Part of Lucumí's ability to draw a wide mix of ethnic groups in both North America and the Caribbean is due to its flexibility. The religion, while maintaining a core set of beliefs and practices, has appropriated elements of other cultures with which it has come into contact. In North America a new mixing and blending of traditions, some of which had previous contact in the Caribbean, is occurring. Cross-fertilization is particularly pronounced between Lucumí and other Afro-Caribbean traditions. The ability of the Lucumí culture to absorb other traditions and to change in new social contexts has helped to make the religion potent and appealing to both those in the African Diaspora who are seeking an African-based religion and members of other ethnic groups who have made Lucumí their religion.

Since its inception Lucumí culture has been an urban phenomenon. After the Cuban Revolution, the religion was transported with immigrants to North America, where it again flourished in an urban environment. Immigrants established temple houses (*ilés*) primarily in the cities of the U.S. and Canada. The religion has been particularly appealing to individuals in North America of African descent who are attempting to reclaim their ancestral history and spirituality. It has also, however, gained adherents among Latinas/Latinos, Asians, and West Indians. The appeal of Lucumí to urban ethnic minorities in North American cities is, at least in part, because, like in its country of origin, Lucumí provides immigrant groups with medical and psychological services as well as religious practices. These nonreligious services are particularly important for these groups due to the gap in access to social services that immigrants often experience. All of the ethnic groups that have joined the religion bring with them their own cultural and spiritual heritage, which has contributed to the religion's renewal, growth, and change in North America. Even New Age philosophy has had some influence on the Lucumí culture in North America. Although Lucumí culture has brought together people of different ethnic groups, division has also developed. This conflict can most clearly be seen in the interpretation offered respectively by African Americans and Latina/Latinos of the roles of Africa, Spain, and the Catholic Church in the religion's heritage.

LUCUMÍ RELIGIOUS CULTURE

The Lucumí religion has its origins in Cuba during the period of the slave trade. The religion combines the beliefs of the Yoruba people with elements of Bantu and Catholic cultures. Contrary to scholarly reports (see for example, Murphy 1983; Brandon 1993; and Matibag 1996) Lucumí culture did not begin with the religious associations or *cabildos*.[2] According to Rodríguez Reyes, the emergence of the religious culture began with a much humbler melange of cults and cultures in the slave barracks: "In the aforementioned communities [Calimete, Manguito, and Amarillas] the Yoruba cult of the *orichas* had as a result a cultural variant called santo parado or santo de manigua. One of the most striking characteristics of this religious variant is that it emerged in the slave quarters in close contact with Bantu traditions. Santo Parado amalgamates both practices, the cult of the orichas and the Npungus"[3] (Rodríguez Reyes 1993). The practice of *Santo Parado* can be identified as a proto-Lucumí practice. Due to its syncretic nature and its cross-cultural philosophy, many scholars have ignored its existence. Both cultural elements, Bantu and Yoruba, coexisted until a formal religious practice emerged in the *cabildos*. Although Lucumí culture is in its majority Yoruba centered, elements of Bantu culture are also present. The existence of dual priesthoods where individuals are initiated in both Lucumí and Bantu traditions is a lasting practice within the religion.[4]

Two institutions—the Catholic Church and slavery—shaped Lucumí culture in Cuba. The public practice of the religion from its inception in Cuba has included the use of Catholic rituals and sacramentals as well as the use of churches as extensions of sacred space. Furthermore, some Lucumí practitioners have adopted Catholic aesthetics and ritual performance into their ritual language. The use of the monstrance to represent *Obatala* and the tabernacle-like altars to present the *santos*, among others, gives a glimpse of the close ties between the two practices. It was the conditions of slavery that forced the Yoruba to interact on a daily basis with European culture and religion and other African groups, such as the Bantu. According to Rodríguez Reyes, the Yoruba were among the last African groups to be brought to Cuba as slaves: "By the Nineteenth Century the majority of African slaves introduced in Cuba belonged to the Yoruba ethnic group" (Rodríguez Reyes 1993).

The Yoruba arrived in a society in which intercultural relations between the dominant Spanish Catholic culture and other African cultures were firmly established. The Yoruba, although accommodating those established relationships, also challenged them with their own worldview. The result was something new. The Yoruba combined the Catholic saints and the use of written language from the Europeans with African spirits. Although the culture remained mostly oral in its transmission, clear attempts were made to make use of the written word. Beginning with the *libretas*, simple notebooks used to document ritual protocols and divination practices, the Lucumí culture attempted to create a written record for those in training as priests and priestesses. The Yoruba's ability to adapt European traditions and customs and to fit into the urban environment provided Lucumí culture with a series of alternative ritual languages that last to this day.

The establishment of the *cabildos* in cities like Habana and Matanzas in the nineteenth century gave the Lucumí a canvas to create the character of the culture as we know it today. *Cabildos* were religious associations created by the Catholic Church to Christianize the slaves. Each association placed under the patronage a saint, brought members of the same ethnic group together. This fertile environment not only promoted the transmission of Catholicism but also preserved the memories of the land of origin. *Cabildos* provided a safe heaven for the reconstruction of Yoruba society under the apparent guise of a Catholic religious association. In the *cabildos*, for example, the royal courts of the Yoruba and its etiquette were re-created. According to Ortiz: "Not much is known about the internal organization of the cabildos beyond the fact that membership was by election and that the cabildos each elected a person called *el rey* (the king) or *capataz* (boss or overseer) who mediated between the cabildos and both the church and the police"(Ortiz in Brandon 1997:71). Royalty is an important element of Lucumí ritual culture. Priests and priestesses in Lucumí culture are not consecrated but crowned. All Lucumí ritual language is expressed in the rhetoric of royalty. From the title of the individual in charge of the ceremonies Obá Oriaté (the king that enthrones) to the wearing of royal paraphernalia during the consecration ceremonies Lucumí culture views itself as regal and heirs of kings. To this day the expression used when referring to a person who became initiated is that he or she is "crowned Ocha." According to Castellanos and Castellanos (1992:19), "These Afro-Cuban rules [*reglas*][5] emerge as a result of a long process of acculturation between the religions brought to Cuba by the slaves and the Catholicism of their masters. They illustrate the cultural resistance of the newcomer to an over-whelming ethnocentric pressure and the attempt of cultural absorption." The enslaved African population in Cuba learned to "read" and interpret the complexity of a sign system that negotiated culturally specific practices and provided for a dialogue between the different culturally specific ideas of heaven and earth. This ability proved to be an efficient tool of cultural survival.

*Cabildos* evolved into ethnic-based associations that ultimately gave rise to the *ile*, which was a center for religious practice. The *calibildos* also became an avenue through which immigrants to Cuba and their spirituality could enter into Lucumí culture. In the nineteenth century the influx of indentured Chinese laborers came to Cuba to supply the absent slave labor. In 1853, according to Jiménez Pastrana, "more than 5,000 Chinese were imported. Almost a fifth died in transit. Between 1853 and 1873 it is estimated that 133,435 Chinese [entered Cuba] of which 13 percent died in transit or shortly after arrival" (1963:31). The newcomers found themselves in similar conditions to those of African descent who had arrived before them. Lucumí social structure provided a framework for these and other new immigrants to grasp the intricacies of Cuban culture. Some Chinese immigrants became initiated in the Lucumí religion and added another layer to the already complex culture, as is attested to by the pervasive use of Chinese art and aesthetic elements in Lucumí ritual. Similarly the Yucatecos, Jamaicans, and Haitians, who came to Cuba because of the sugar trade, joined Lucumí as a way of integrating into Cuban culture. This complex mélange of ethnic societies contributed their esoteric, pharmacological, and aesthetic experiences to the already rich heritage of the culture. Lucumí religious culture since its inception has been open to the "secrets" of others.

The Yoruba people in Cuba became polyglots of ritual language by virtue of their interaction with the beliefs, rites, and rituals of a multiplicity of pantheons that claimed the land. Every ethnic group that came to Cuba brought its gods and beliefs with them. The encounter of so many divinities was negotiated by devising a system of equivalence, placing together all *santos* who are deemed similar. For example, *Lucumí Ochún* is equated with the Congo *Mamá Chola*, the Haitian *Erzulí*, and the Catholic Our Lady of Charity. All of these are defined as river-dwelling or sweet-water–related deities.

BELIEFS

Yoruba-Lucumí religion postulates the existence of one God (Olofin, Olorun, Olodumare) who created the world and a series of divinities that take care of Creation in His name, permitting God to more or less retire from his Creation.[6] No specific cult, priesthood, and/or major offerings are directed to Him. This absent God, however, is the dispenser of life (*emí*), and many sacred stories or *Patakí*[7] explain His role as the owner of life.[8] Under the Supreme God, the divinities called *Santos*[9] and *Orichas*[10] populate Creation and take care of humanity. According to Lucumí beliefs, each human being is under the protection of one of these divinities. In Lucumí tradition the most popular are Echu (Echu Eleguá), Ogún, Ochosi, Obatalá, Oyá, Yemayá, Changó, Ochún, Babalú Ayé, Ibeyi, Oricha Oko, Agayú, Osaín, Obá, Naná Burukú, Ideú, Olokun, Olosá, and Inle. Each one of these *santos* possesses characteristics and domains that define their character, position in the hierarchy, natural abode, and particular colors and numbers associated with them. Cuban scholar Natalia Bolívar Aróstegui (1990:11) asserts: "The Orichas and their roads are described like personalities with human and divine characteristics, and some few peccadilloes and outrages that as gods they carry with them. These help to explain and give answers to existence and natural phenomena. We can see them with their garments and colors receiving offering from their acolytes, ruling the benefits of the herbs and 'palos'[11] they own; allowing us to peek inside their pots where their sacred stones are treasured and worshiped with drum music."

A brief discussion of the most important Orichas will give a better picture of the religion. These divinities have personalities with stated qualities, likes, and dislikes, which creates a complex ritual universe of reciprocal obligations between the devotee and the *santo*. Eleguá, or Echu Eleguá, is the trickster god. His abode, depending on the particular avatar, can be the crossroads, the prairie, a solitary place, or the trash dump. He is Olofin's (God's) messenger as well as that of the other *santos*. Spoiled and contentious, he is the absolute master of the oracular system. His colors are red and black and white and black. Ogún is the deity of war, iron, and life struggles. He is the blacksmith and the creator of industry. Violent and powerful, Ogún rules every weapon and violent act. His dominion extends from the sacrificial knife to the doctor's scalpel. Ochosi, the deity of the hunt and chase, is also the dispenser of justice. These three *santos* collectively constitute The Warriors. After initiation, every Lucumí worshiper receives them as the protectors of his or her person and possessions. Obatalá, the king of the white cloth, is Olodumare's deputy and hence the senior and wisest of all *santos*. He represents ritual purity and high moral character. Obatalá, depending on his avatars, can be male or female. He or she is responsible of carving the body of the newborn in the womb so Oloduamare can breathe life into the fetus. *Oyá*, the amazon of the pantheon, is the goddess of the winds and gatekeeper of the cemetery. She represents the transformative powers of life and death. Yemayá is the mother of humanity and the Orichas. She rules over the sea and maternity.

Dignified and commanding, she is the guarantor of the peace of the home. Like her element, the ocean, she is always in motion, working for the benefit of her children. Changó, one of the most popular santos, is the god of fire and lightning. His voice is the thunder. He is the incarnation of virility and the enjoyment of life. He rules over the sacred Batá drums and the mortar used for consecration. His colors are red and white.

Ochún, goddess of love and beauty, rules over the rivers, and the pregnant womb is her laboratory. Skilled in medicine and healing, Ochún is invoked by expectant mothers. She is considered the most beautiful of the female *santos* and is coquettish and vain. Babalú Ayé, dreaded god of infectious diseases and epidemics, has been transformed in Cuba and Brazil into a beloved *santo* known as "the doctor of the poor." Babalú Ayé is universally regarded simultaneously as a healer and the agent of death. His wrath is to be avoided at any cost. His colors are red, brown, and black, among others. Ibeyi, the twin gods, are the protectors of children, the sacred, and ritual space. In their manifestation as children these twin gods are propitiated to bring blessings to the home and to fight those who seek to disrupt ritual and life. *Oricha Oko*, the deity of farming and agriculture, is the male aspect of *Ilé*, the earth mother of all.[12] Oricha Oko is concerned with both the fertility of the land and protection against sorcery. In some Pataki, he and Yemayá are responsible for making the earth fertile. Agayú, the deity of the volcano and wastelands, whose domain extends over the internal fires of the earth and as such his name is Oroiña. Osaín, the deity of healing, magic, and the use of herbs, is a mystery, but as many elders of the religion say, "Without Osaín there is no medicine; there is no santo."[13] Oba, the deity closely associated with Changó and Ochún, is wise and stately and the perfect example of the devoted wife and administrator of family fortunes. Naná Burukú, a very ancient deity, is the mother of Babalú Ayé and in some instances the mother of the pantheon. Her domain extends from the moon to the quiet and secret inland lagoons. Ideú, one of the prodigious children of the religion along with the Ibeji, is known as Ochún's lost child. Custodian of Ochún's fortune, Ideú rules over the bestowing of blessings (usually in the form of money) from Ochún's hands. Olokun, ancient deity of the ocean, is mysterious and powerful. Olokun is the patron of merchants and creator of the market. Like the ocean, he is largely unknown, but his ceremonies allow for the prosperity of human society through commerce. Olosá is Olokún's wife and goddess of the lagoon. Inle is the divine doctor. If Osaín is the owner of the secret of leafs and healing, it is Inle who translates such knowledge and puts it to use in human society. Refined and mysterious, Inle's wisdom is sought when diseases of body and soul afflict humanity.[14]

All Lucumí *santos* can be approached through a series of offerings (*ebo*) and supplications. Once the devotee understands the source of his or her problems, be that through divination or by self-analysis, he or she must identify the particular *santo* to approach. Offerings can be taken to the natural abode of the spirit and deposited there after a series of prayers. These offerings may be fruits, cooked meals, and objects of ritual or symbolic significance. The offering can also be placed at the shrine or (*cuarto de santo*) were the sacred symbols are kept for a specific number of days, which is determined by the number sacred to the particular *santo*. After the prescribed days, the offering must be disposed of appropriately. Offerings to some *santos* have taboos or prohibitions associated with them—for example, whether or not there is an interdiction to prevent or allow the offering to spoil before they are disposed.

Lucumí religious culture is based on a strict hierarchy in which age is equated with knowledge, prestige, and power. Power rests in the hands of elders of both sexes, and it is shared through the institution of Olochas with the Obá Oriaté and that of the Babalaos. Both of these institutions (Babalawos and Oriates) are characterized by the instruments of divination: the *diliogún* (sixteen cowry shells) and *Ifá* (divining chain and *ikin*). Since its beginning, Lucumí priestly society, following the African model, has been open to both genders. The culture was (and still is) contained in the sacred stories memorized by the ritual specialists. The revelations contained in these stories are the main tool to negotiate all the affairs in the believers' everyday lives. No topic is too mundane and no question is too idle for these stories and their narrators. A veritable oral library, these stories provide a cognitive map to decipher the enigmas posed in everyday life.

The journey into Lucumí society begins with initiation. The path to the acquisition of knowledge depends on the authority one has to attend a specific rite or ceremony. At any given time a person can attend only those rites and ceremonies to which he or she has been initiated. Therefore, access to particular ritual knowledge depends on levels of initiation. The first ceremony is the imposition of the most tangible sign of the *santos*, the *collares*. These are coded necklaces that correspond with colored patterns and numbers of the deities of the pantheon. An initiate in the religion will receive those of Eleguá, Obatalá, Changó, Yemayá, and Ochún. With this ceremony the individual will begin a journey in which his or her existence will be permeated by the presence of nature made tangible in the multicolored strands of beads. As the initiate progresses in his or her levels of initiation, he or she will receive the icons of the Warriors, Eleguá, Ogún, and Ochosi. After a series of initiations, the individual may become a priest.

## LUCUMÍ DIASPORA

In 1959 the Cuban Revolution sent an exodus of Cubans to different parts of the world. These exiles brought the *santos* with them to the countries they entered. Initially the religious culture moved to Puerto Rico and New York City. Other countries also received an influx of Cuban refugees, but it was in North America where the religion would experience unprecedented growth. Historical events brought Lucumí culture face to face with the national dialogue of the Civil Rights movement in the United States. America was engaged in a period of self-examination that forced her to openly acknowledge the disparities created by segregation.[15]

*Lucumí* culture had developed in a climate of segregation and prejudice, but because of historical realities, the Spanish-speaking Caribbean faced different racial problems than those experienced in North America. These differences have their roots in the alternative visions of colonial power between the English and the Spanish, French, and Portuguese. Contrary to the English colonialists who came to the new lands to stay, and therefore moved with their families, the Spanish, French, and Portuguese for the most part never intended to remain in the Western Hemisphere. Many came with a "get rich quick and return to Europe" mentality. Historical documentation shows the political and social problems this attitude created. Population mobility prevented a firm settlement of Europeans in the New World. This promoted the mixing of populations with the resulting *mestizaje*, who became a sizable free population of color. As Jacques Lafaye notes apropos, the Mexican *mestizo,* which can be applied to the whole *mestizo* population in the Latina/Latino world: "Mestizos began life as children of the European rape of America, or *hijos de la chingada;*[16] but they rapidly acquired more complex traits primarily through the black importation of African slaves" (Lafaye 1998:81). Although racial mixing occurred in the English colonies in the Western Hemisphere the Afro-Latino experience was more complex. The presence of individuals of mixed race was much more visible in Spanish, French, and Portuguese colonial and postcolonial societies. Their presence can be felt in the arts and the emergence of nationalism in Latina/Latino society and in the very texture of Lucumí culture. Segregation of the type experienced in the United States never occurred in Latin America.

For many African Americans the encounter with Lucumí culture was an avenue to reclaim their history and to re-create their ancestral past. But many hurdles had to be conquered before a meaningful dialogue could exist between African American and Afro-Cuban cultures. Most central was the issue of the incorporation of Catholic iconography and aesthetics into the very fabric of Lucumí culture. Within Lucumí religion, participants can be said to pray and sing in an "African language" but to acknowledge the Catholic saints. Most African Americans, like most white Americans, were raised as Protestants and were not comfortable with the use of Catholic symbols and rituals. Furthermore, for many African Americans who were searching for a religion that spoke to their African heritage the marriage between African and Western aesthetics seemed odd at best. Nonetheless, for many African Americans initiation in the religion provided a venue to reclaim their connection to Africa. However, the issues of language and race brought both communities to a mutual impasse when many African Americans rejected the use of Catholic iconography and the allegiance to Spain expressed by the Latina/Latinos. In Latin America, Spain is the Mother Country, and regardless of ethnic origin, many feel part of the philosophical continuum of La Hispanidad. As a concept, La Hispanidad unifies all Latin Americans under the idea of a racial destiny defined not by the culture of Spain but by the language. Spanish has become an icon of racial and historical purpose. The Spanish language as a vehicle of culture is the lifeline that articulates the ideals and common purpose of those who speak it, regardless of their origin.

A tense discourse developed between Latina/Latino and African American members of Lucumí. The Spanish-speaking community asserted their claim to be part of the Spanish and African cultural continuum. The African Americans, to the contrary, affirmed their claim to an exclusive African cultural continuum. During the fifth World Congress of Orisa Tradition and Culture in San Francisco, August 3 through 10, 1997, the proceedings were marred by racial divisions between the African American constituents and the Latina/Latino, Anglo, and Asian constituents. The African American contingent wanted the religion to be exclusively for those of African heritage, which was unacceptable to the other contingent. Another disagreement grew out of the African Americans' desire to recognize the supremacy of the Oni of Ife as the religious head of the culture. This was viewed by many of the others as paramount to electing a pope. It was believed by some of the other members that the African American organizers had eliminated papers, which were not Afro centered. This resulted in many Latina/Latino Lucumí and Vodoo practitioners leaving the congress and destroyed hopes of unity.

Currently two factions exist: African American Lucumí practitioners who espouse the idea of Africa as the ultimate source of authority and the Caribbean faction who claim that the source of authority is in Cuba. For many members of this diasporean religious culture the language and cultural barrier highlights a profound divide in the history of the African Diaspora. This division, rooted in colonial experience, has resulted in each faction making one place, either Africa or Cuba, into a mythical paradise. This division between the two factions is epitomized by Oba Ofuntola Osejiman Adelabu Adefumi I, an African American initiated in Cuba who broke with Lucumí religious culture and established an African Village (Oyotunji) in South Carolina. Subsequently he was crowned *oba* (king) in Nigeria. He contends that the religion must be defined by the African American experience. Adefumi's first initiate into his form of Afro-

Caribbean religion, Orisha-Voodoo[17] asserted: "the Cubans had decided for themselves how they wanted to reorganize the religion and so, too had the Brazilians. Therefore it was time for Black Americans to decide what the religion and culture meant to them and how they were going to pre-serve it" (Hunt in Brandon 1997:119).

Issues of authority have deeply divided the community. Both groups claim final authority over the other. The Latina/Latino faction has created *cabildos*, (temples and churches),[18] while the African American contingent has created their own organizations. This division can also be seen on the Internet, where even the most rudimentary search reveals a plethora of sites and chat rooms devoted to the exchange of ideas about the Orichas from both sides of the aisle. The racial tensions that exist in the United States, which are alien to Lucumí in its country of origin, have become reflected in the religion in the United States.

## HEALING AND BOTÁNICA

Besides a well-organized body of beliefs, Lucumí religious culture rests on an extensive knowledge of herbal and natural remedies. The diviner, male or female, has at his or her disposal, aided by the oracle, the wisdom of a green pharmacy. This medical service is not ideally in lieu of Western medi-cine, but in addition. The interest in spiritual healing among the Lucumí is two-fold. First, good medical attention is often not available in the com-munities in which Lucumí is most popular. Second, the doctor cures the body, but, like Ana M. Peña, my late mother, also a Lucumí priestess and healer, used to say, "machines do not see spirits." Therefore, many people will seek the advice of their elders on which rituals to perform prior to seeing a doctor. For those who cannot afford medical care, the priest or priestess provides their only hope for a cure. Healer, psychologist, confi-dant, and priest or priestess, the Olocha is expected to assert the origin and solutions to ailments and to provide adequate counsel at all times.

The oracular system in Lucumí religious culture claims to have access to every spiritual language that exists. A diviner in Lucumí culture is said to be able to converse with spirits regardless of their origin and open channel of communication that can be of use for those seeking advice. America became a meeting place for the diverse cultures of the African Diaspora. The great migrations from the Caribbean prompted almost the same reali-ties as those of the colonial period. Traditional beliefs had to be disguised, and a new process of merging and representation had to be devised. Just as the prevalent belief in the supernatural and its constant influence in human affairs brought together all the diasporean beliefs during the slave trade, it is currently helping to unite other disparate spiritual forms. Central American and Mexican religions are carving a new facet in the spiritual practices of Lucumí culture, as to a lesser degree are New Age and Neopagan practices. As Lucumí culture has never been static, each wave of new practitioners leaves their mark and creates their own sense of community.

The normal port of entry for many into Lucumí culture is the *botánica*—a veritable market of the divine. In the Spanish-speaking Caribbean, *botánicas* provide services and paraphernalia for those who follow the traditional beliefs. These establishments, which are usually in humble locations, have migrated north with the religious practice, bringing with them the Caribbean pharmacology. The proliferation of *botánicas* in North American cities provides a glimpse into the beliefs of America's Caribbean immigrants. Murphy (1993:39) aptly characterizes these establishments: "If we would walk along the streets of any Hispanic neighborhood in New York, wedged between the busy groceries and newsstands we might see small retail stores called *Botánicas*. To the uninitiated, their merchandise must look mysterious indeed: candles and beads, herbs and oils, cauldrons and crockery, and plaster statues of Catholic saints. Yet for those who know their meaning, each of these items has a part to play in Santerìa, the religion of the *orishas* in New York." These establishments are usually the entry into the religious world of the immigrants from the Caribbean and their converts in America, and for many seeking an alternative spirituality. *Botánicas* are clearinghouses; they signal the existence of a religious community and also constitute a market of the divine. At present many groups use *botánicas* for their religious needs. These businesses can be aligned with diverse philosophies: Mexican *curanderismo*, Lucumí tradition, Palo, Espiritismo, and its newer cousin, the New Age. The array of services they provide goes beyond selling icons. It is at the *botánicas* that most individuals will encounter the gods and spirits of the diaspora for the first time. Spiritual consultations, spiritual cleanings, and advice in every aspect of life are some of the services provided. The owner of a *botánica* is often initiated in the Lucumí tradition, practices spiritism or *Curanderismo,* or, as is often the case, holds membership in more than one tradition.

It is not unusual for individuals to have multiple spiritual allegiances. Members of the African Diaspora have learned to accommodate other spiritualities in order to survive. Unlike Western religions, those of the Caribbean do not claim to possess the absolute truth. "La sabiduría está repartida." In other words wisdom has been distributed (to all), claims the old Lucumí proverb. Based on this approach, every spirit or supernatural force is believed to offer potential help. An examination of a typical diaspora altar is a lesson in history. Not only can one find the saints of the Church but the *santos* of all the theologies that have come in contact with the religion. That is the reason for the *botánica's* assemblage of diverse cultural and religious icons. This complexity must be negotiated in the altars.

As one practitioner offers: Santería has taught me that the spiritual world is complex, composed of guardian angels who see us in different ways, and of gods and goddesses. . . . Among my ancestral spirit angels are the Native Indians of the Caribbean, the Moors, the Congos, and Yorubas of Africa, Gypsies and Europeans from Spain and the Caribbean (Vega 2000,17). The idea that both the religious and the vernacular pantheons can be inclusive means that they are always in a state of flux—ready to be transformed in a new area or with another spiritual system.

## CANADA

Although practice in Canada shares many similarities to those in the United States, it has developed a particular style of African-based traditions and Lucumí culture. In Canada, West Indian immigrants brought the beliefs of Obeah, Shango, and Orisha Baptists. These practices found fertile soil in Canada; however, in the United States, where there are large numbers of West Indian immigrants, these beliefs are not prevalent. This one can speculate is due to the strength of Latina/Latino practices in the United States that have arrested the spread of such beliefs. In Canada the dominant immigrant culture of the Caribbean is West Indian, which has permitted this culture to better develop and thrive. Obeah, Shango, and Orisha Baptist beliefs—which became integrated with European cabalistic traditions as portrayed in the *Sixth and Seventh Books of Moses*, an esoteric manual, well known in the Caribbean and in the African American community—have resulted in the center of worship focusing on the use of Africanized seals and cryptic ciphers that express values of African and Creole hagiographies. Butler (2002:155) describes this combination of European and African elements in Canada: "Among the more interesting aspects of traditional immigrant culture is the manner in which supernatural and magico-religious beliefs have been transplanted and are maintained or transformed in the new cultural setting. One such tradition is that of *Obeah,* a magico-religious practice representing a synthesis of African spirit worship and European Christian principles. Obeah is widely known and, at last to some degree, continues to be believed and practiced by Canadians tracing their origins to Trinidad and Jamaica."

As in the United States, the Canadian Lucumí tradition has maintained its urban character. Lucumí temple houses, for example, are primarily located in Toronto. Practitioners maintain strong connections and communications across the border between the United States and Canada. However, Canadians maintain their own contacts with practitioners in Cuba. Currently the contact is particularly intense, with many Canadians traveling to Cuba to consult with Lucumí practitioners. There are many Canadian-based groups that sponsor cultural trips to Cuba and facilitate encounters with practitioners and interested North Americans.[19] Returning Canadians typically seek their counterparts in America, creating a dialogue that facilitates the exchange of ritual knowledge in North America. In other words, Canada has developed a distinct tradition based on an uninterrupted Caribbean connection while at the same time having access to and influencing those traditions in the United States. It is common for individuals to regularly travel between Canada and Cuba and New York City, providing cross-fertilization among practitioners in all three locations.

As Canada has attracted many immigrants from the English-speaking Caribbean, language has not served as a barrier for these immigrants as it has for their Spanish-speaking counterpart in the United States. Furthermore, the dynamics of politics in Canada facilitates the continuity and expansion of the Caribbean religious practices. As a rule I have experienced a more tolerant attitude toward these practices in Canada than in the United States. Speaking with practitioners, I have heard of fewer official prosecutions, and therefore, the community is less afraid of official intrusions. Based on my own ethnographic research, the American authorities appear to more often interfere with Caribbean religious practices than do the Canadian authorities. American practitioners appear to have a greater fear of the authorities than do the Canadians. Because their tradition is firmly established, Canadian practitioners have been well placed to make contacts with others in the Afro-Caribbean religious community whose native language is Spanish or Portuguese.

## ALTERNATIVE SPIRITUAL FORMS

Caribbean history has been marked by migration to the industrial centers of North America. An exploration of vernacular beliefs became part of the process of cultural survival and for many became a journey of self-discovery. People set out to find those individuals that provided services similar to those available in their countries of origin—for example, spiritual healing, ritual cleansings, and liberation from evil spirits. For nonnative English speakers, learning the language provided among other things access to other forms of spirituality. This cross-pollination has evolved in America to the point that vernacular ritual languages are no longer separated by their old boundaries of culture of origin. Within immigrant communities the services of spiritual specialists from many different Caribbean spiritual lexicons can be found within a few blocks of one another. The language barrier that kept these traditions separate in the Caribbean is fast fading in North America. Furthermore, the need for basic social services that each of these spiritual forms offers encourages people to interact and seek help from specialists and individuals from different cultural backgrounds. As Africa is a large and diverse continent, Afro-Caribbean religions from their beginnings have been influenced by a number of different spiritual systems. Robert Farris Thompson asserts apropos this state of affairs: "Also widespread across the black Atlantic are the signs and insights of the great Kongo people of Zaire, Angola, Cabinda, and Congo-Brazzaville. There is a clear connection between the cosmographic signs of spiritual renaissance in the classical religion of the Bakongo and similarly chalked signs of initiation among blacks of Cuba, Haiti, the island of St. Vincent, the United States, and Brazil where numerous Kongo slaves arrived" (Thompson 1984:xv–xvi).

This experience also holds true for the Yoruba in North America. Members of the current diaspora are bound by both by a shared past and the contemporary reality of economic migration. The bridge that connects the sacred ritual languages of Afro-Caribbean religions is *Espiritismo*. Spiritism, or Espiritismo could be designated the official folk religion of the West Indies. It is practiced widely by members of many different religions in the West Indies, and it also part of the Cuban spiritual heritage as well as that of other Afro-Caribbean religions. Holloway (1991:120–21) provides an excellent characterization of the role of Espiritismo within Caribbean religions: "When Espiritismo reached the lower classes and the rural areas it became mixed with the prevalent forms of folk Catholicism. Starting out as a non-Christian, European occult science, Espiritismo became much more Christianized in Cuba and assumed for many the role of noninstitutionalized form of Catholicism—including the cult of saints." Spiritism provided a metaphysical lingua franca that unified the area. Afro-Caribbean practitioners truly achieved the "gift of tongues."

Kardecian Spiritism that came to Cuba from France via Spain in the nineteenth century is based on the writings of Hippolyte Rivail (1804–69), better known as Allan Kardek to Spiritualists in the region. It was further developed in the writings of Amalia Soler. A parallel movement developed in North America. The Fox sisters in Hydesvillle, New York, are credited with creating America's Spiritualism movement (Wehmeyer 2000:6). American Spiritism found its way to Cuba where it was practiced primarily by the upper classes as "Espiritismo Científico." This form of Spiritualism was viewed by its adherents as the scientific study of the phenomenon. Vernacular Kardecian practice was believed by "Espiritismo Científico" to be mere superstition and a form of sorcery. The best-known form of Espiritismo Científico in Cuba is *Espiritismo de Cordón*. In this variant, individuals hold hands and form a circle while moving until possession occurs. Kardecian Spiritualism, however, is the best-known and most used form of Spiritualism throughout the Caribbean.[20]

Spiritualist practices were important in the success of Lucumí culture once it left Cuba. Trance possession is an integral part of Lucumí culture, but the inclusion of Spiritism gave voice to spirits not contemplated in the original pantheon. The ancestral spirits of the Indians (Arawak), African ethnic groups, Asians, Arabs, East Indians, among others, are given voice through Spiritualist practices, although they are not celebrated as deities. The use of Spiritualism to give voice to a wide range of ancestral spirits provided another tool for the Lucumí to negotiate cultural differences outside Lucumí sacred space. As a rule, Orichas and other spirits do not mix. They are considered parallel lines that should never cross. Because of the different ritual styles, each group of spirits must be propitiated and served according to strict etiquette. As practitioners say, "they are two different lands."

The *velada,* or séance, in the Spanish-speaking Caribbean has a very specific pattern. It begins with the recitation of prayers from Kardek's *Colección de Oraciones Escogidas* and also from the *Evangelio Según el Espiritismo* by the same author. Both books, along with the Bible, reside permanently on the altar. After the prayers, the religious spirits or "religious entities" will manifest to counsel and preach. These spirits represent God. After those spirits that represent God, the spirits of the Indians are the first to appear, since they are considered the true owners of the land. These spirits are wise and skilled in the art of herbal healing. Because of their stature in the eyes of practitioners, it is likely that almost every practitioner will count an Indian as a spiritual protector. After the Indians, the Africans arrive, generically identified as Congos. The African spirits are fierce and abhor sorcery, even though know it very well. Their warrior like nature justifies their choice of cutlasses, spears, and axes as part of their weaponry. Both Indians and African spirits speak in broken Spanish, or *bozal.* The rest of the séance is open to the spirits of other races.

The Spiritualist's altar and séance reflect in their composition the history of the region. The religious performances of the different spirits embody the migration patterns to the island. The spirits of different ethnic groups descend into the temple in the same order that migrants came to the Caribbean. Politics and faith have always been interwoven in the Caribbean. By ritually codifying history, the Spiritualist's séance gives presence to groups who did not have a voice in society. It is true that Indians also put appearances in the séances of high society, but in those they are envisioned as part of a concept of "the noble and wise savage." Because there are no unified doctrines or canons in Espiritismo, every medium is free to manipulate the doctrine to accommodate his or her views. This results in constant evolution of the spirits, although always within a Christian framework.

The massive Puerto Rican migration to New York brought the Madamas (female black spirits) to the United States. In New York the first recording of sacred Spiritualist music appeared in the late 1950s. Songs such as "Homenaje a la Madama" (Homage to the Madama) and singers such as

El Madamo Joe are familiar to many in the U.S. and the islands. Spiritualism gained a following of its own in the United States as well as serving as
a bridge between varying Afro-Caribbean religions.

The most pervasive of Spiritualist practices among Latina/Latino Americans is Espiritismo Cruzado. It amalgamates the doctrines of traditional
Spiritualist practices with those of Lucumí, Palo Mayombe, and Palo
Monte. Contrary to those practices that require extensive initiation rites
and long apprenticeships, Espiritismo Cruzado relies on the practitioner's
idiosyncratic interpretation and creativity, although practitioners do use the
symbols and rituals of other religious practices. Each medium is believed to
receive the call from the spirit world. True to the Caribbean religious spirit,
many individuals move from this practice to more formally participate in
any of the doctrines associated with it. *Espiritismo Cruzado*'s allure rests in
the liberty their practitioners have to develop their own theology and in
that way advance their views of the spirit world. Furthermore, there is no
hierarchy as in Lucumí or Palo traditions. Each individual is autonomous
and free to interpret their own experience and that of their followers.

PALO

Bantu practices in Cuba also migrated to America alongside Lucumí religious culture. In many instances both carried by the same individuals, who
(often) maintain membership in both traditions. Bantu religious practice,
which centers on the cult of the dead, for many years enjoyed an infamous
name in Cuba. Termed *sorcery* even by its practitioners, the mention of the
name *Palo* or any of its multiple variants was not an acceptable topic in
polite conversation. With its migration to North America, Palo came out
of the cultural shadows and has gained popularity among young people in
the urban areas of America. Many West Indians find its practices very similar to their own Obeah. More secretive than any other of the Cuban African-based religions, Palo resembles the characterization of Obeah. As
described in *Sacred Possessions* (Olmos 2000:6), "The practice of Obeah
involves the 'putting on' and taking off of 'duppies' or 'jumbees' (ghosts or
spirits of the dead) for either good or evil purposes." This can be compared
with Lydia Cabrera's (1983:118) characterization of a Nganga the magic
receptacle of *Palo* practices in Cuba: "[The] cemetery and the bush are
equivalent and complement each other in either one are the *fumbis* (ghosts,
spirits of the dead) and the and the forces that act as the invisible executors
of the sorcerer's good or bad deeds." Obeah and Palo share both an emphasis on secrecy and ritual practices in which the spirit of the dead play a
principal role. It is possible that both traditions cross-pollinated in Cuba
where there has been a Jamaican community since 1925. Further links

between the two religions have been strengthened in the U.S. and Canada by museum shows on the Palo tradition. The most recent by noted Cuban artist José Gabriel Malostikaas in 2002 at Maison de la Culture Plateau-Mont-Royal Québec, Canada. The fact that a mainstream institution such as the museum showcased this otherwise maligned practice helped to give legitimacy and popularize it. Practitioners felt their beliefs validated. Furthermore, the shows have helped to spread the religion's popularity among individuals of different social backgrounds. The fact that mainstream artists and institutions are paying attention to and finding inspiration from these practices inadvertently helped to raise the status of one religious practice over others. Official sanctioning is seen as offering legitimacy to the religion—something that all theses traditional practices have striven for since their inception.

## CURANDERISMO

Curanderismo, which originates in Mexico and Central America, is very popular in America's Southwest. With the migration of Mexicans and Central Americans to Chicago, New York, and Toronto, the religion has also made inroads in these cities where contact has been made between Curanderismo, American Indian beliefs, particularly as expressed in the New Age; and Lucumí. Many Curanderismo practitioners have adopted the Lucumí religious tradition while maintaining the core of their indigenous practices. *Curanderismo,* like Lucumí, is a mixture of vernacular beliefs and Catholic theologies. Herbal and spiritual healing practices are used to cure diseases believed to be caused by taboo violations or sorcery. The *curandero* or *curandera* possesses an extensive knowledge of herbs and their medicinal and ritual uses. Not constrained by ritual canonical rules of African-based religions, Curanderismo does not have elaborate rituals of consecration for individuals to become practitioners. Those who are believed to have the spiritual call by their community can become members. A successful *curandero* or *curandera*'s knowledge is validated by his or her community. Because of the close proximity of this practice to Lucumí ilés, many Curanderismo practitioners are integrating the hagiography of the Caribbean with their own. A sign of this integration can be seen in the change in name of stores that cater to the *curanderos*. Originally these were called *yerberías* signaling the preponderant role of herbs in their practice. With the increased contact with Caribbean practices, many are changing their names to *botánica* and integrating both belief systems.[21]

It is noteworthy that Curanderismo effectively named some psychosomatic conditions that are now part of the vernacular parlance among those of Caribbean descent. The most significant is *susto,* or fright. Immigrants, many of whom have become migrant workers, experience a condition that is believed to frighten the soul and renders the individual weak. Very frequently *susto* is the result of spiritual and cultural shock and the inability to negotiate effectively new and stressful realities. To help this condition, the Curanderismo use specific rituals and call on the intercession of saints, *santos*, and spirits to cure the affliction. The Curandero, like the priest and priestess of the Lucumí, work to help the immigrants to deal with *susto* and in turn become integrated into their new homelands and its demands.

CONCLUSION

The complex history of Lucumí religious practice provides a laboratory for the development of a unique culture that at once has been able to adopt to new circumstances while continuing to maintain its core. Lucumí is an oral tradition, with its roots in Africa, that developed during and after the slave trade in Cuba and now is finding a new home and new language in North America. Several developments are helping to change the religion. In the United States, the search among African Americans for an African religion has resulted in Lucumí, both growing and being challenged by new practitioners who do not feel comfortable with the Catholic symbolism that is part of its traditional practice. Canada has provided a different environment for Lucumí culture to develop. A large West Indian population in Canada has helped to foster bonds between West Indian, Cuban, and American practices. The West Indian spiritual practices share some basic elements with those of Lucumí, as both have their roots in Africa. Some assimilation of the two practices may have occurred earlier, as there has been a group of West Indians in Cuba since the first quarter of the twentieth century. But it is in Canada that this is coming to fruition today.

Lucumí culture, always inclusive, allows for diverse, culturally based spiritual expressions. However, language barriers between Spanish speakers and English speakers in the Caribbean have served as a break to interchanges between the groups. This is changing in North America as participants learn to speak English. Through the use of Spiritualism, which permits a mixing of different spiritual lexicons, there has been a further blending of Caribbean spiritual practices. Both Palo and Curanderismo, although remaining distinct practices, have also been integrating into Lucumí culture. Although divisions have developed between African American and Latina/Latino practitioners, the Lucumí culture serves both groups as a way of exploring their past and working toward negotiating a better future for themselves in North America.

# Satanic Cults, Ritual Abuse, and Moral Panic: Deconstructing a Modern Witch-Hunt

Stuart A. Wright

During the 1980s and early 1990s, reports of alleged satanic cults, child abductions, baby breeding, ritual torture, infanticide, and cannibalism became quite commonplace. This phenomenon has been described by a number of scholars in North America and Great Britain as forms of collective behavior leading to "rumor-panic" or "moral panic" (Cohen 1972; Goode and Ben-Yehuda 1994:57–65; Jenkins 1992; Richardson, Best, and Bromley 1991; Victor 1993). As the panic spread, the claims of interest groups grew more outlandish, bordering on mass hysteria. Parents feared that missing children were objects of diabolic efforts by devil-worshiping cults seeking to secure sacrificial victims or, in some cases, turn captive children into sex slaves for pedophiles in child pornography rings. National and regional conferences on occult crime, Satanism, and ritual abuse were held annually, training thousands of police officers, social workers, and mental health professionals to recognize mysterious signs of underground Satanist activities. Hospitals offered new treatment programs for "adolescent satanism," and psychologists, therapists, and family counselors carved out new specialities in treating satanic ritual abuse victims or "occult survivors." In the venues of popular talk shows and tabloid journalism, everything from heavy metal rock music to serial murders was linked to satanic cults. The traditional practice of Halloween trick-or-treating declined nationwide in North America as parents worried about children receiving candy tainted by poison, sewing needles, or razor blades. Proctor and Gamble was bombarded with thousands of letters and phone calls from angry consumers accusing the corporation of using a satanic symbol in their logo. In Newfoundland, Canada, graveyard vandalism sparked rumors of satanic cult activity when crosses on tombs were knocked off and set upside down. Reports of mysterious cattle mutilations surfaced in Texas believed to be the ritual work of Satanists. Taken together, these varied incidents had a measurable impact on public attitudes. By 1994, one survey reported that 70 percent of Americans believed in the existence of sexually abusive satanic cults and that nearly one-third thought these groups were being ignored by law enforcement (Ross 1994:88).

The allegations of threat dissipated, however, as the satanic cult scare received greater scrutiny by researchers, responsible investigative journalists, and law enforcement. A comprehensive, eight-year study by the FBI on occult crime was unable to find evidence of a single homicide attributed to organized satanic cults, despite popular beliefs to the contrary (Lanning 1989). A number of high-profile legal cases involving claims of satanic ritual abuse fell apart in the absence of material evidence and with the discovery of "witness contamination" by overzealous social workers who interviewed allegedly abused children (Nathan 1992; Nathan and Snedeker 1995; Wakefield and Underwager 1992). Many claims of ritual torture or abuse were later recanted by victims, and other claims were found to be contrived (Coleman 1989; Coleman and Clancy 1990). One occult survivor, Lauren Stratford, authored a detailed autobiographical account of her travails in a book titled *Satan's Underground* (1988), which was later determined to be groundless. When investigative reporters attempted to corroborate her stories, they found that friends, neighbors, and relatives could not confirm alleged pregnancies or claims of mutilation. For example, she claimed to have given birth to three children as a "breeder" for a satanic cult during her late teens and early twenties, but none of her family, friends, or teachers could substantiate any pregnancy. Some who knew Stratford said she was deeply disturbed and reportedly observed her engaging in self-mutilation, which she later attributed to Satanists. The publisher of her book, Harvest House, subsequently withdrew the book from the market (Victor 1993:100). In another case, Missouri law enforcement officials investigated two incidents of satanic sacrifices of fetuses reported by a woman in a highly publicized *Geraldo* television episode on Satanism, which first aired on Halloween night in 1987. But a police investigation later concluded that the incidents were fabricated. One woman who claimed to have seen Satanists "cut an infant's stomach, pour gasoline on the baby and set it on fire" later admitted to police that she made up the story (Religious Freedom Alert 1989:9).

Victor (1993) evaluated sixty-two cases of satanic cult incidents reported in the U.S. and Canada between 1983 and 1992. Conducting a content analysis of newspaper reports, he determined that the peak years of occurrence were between 1988 and 1989, catalyzed by two events given sensational media coverage, the *Geraldo* Satanism episode and the Matamoros cult murders in 1989. The Matamoros cult murders grabbed national news headlines when authorities discovered fifteen bodies in a shallow grave only weeks after the disappearance of twenty-one-year-old University of Texas student Mark Kilroy during spring break in the popular Mexican border town. Kilroy's body had been mutilated, along with the others, allegedly in cult rituals by a group of Mexican drug smugglers seeking to obtain supernatural protection for their illegal and high-risk activities (Green

1991). The rituals were orchestrated by Adolpho de Jesus Constanzo, a young, charismatic Cuban-American who selectively culled elements of Afro-Caribbean religions (Santería and Palo Mayombe) and mixed them with indigenous folk beliefs and superstitions. It is not uncommon in Mexico for *brujos* and *curañderos* to visit the villages to cast spells, offer powerful potions and herbs for healing, remove hexes, and sell amulets for good fortune. In this cultural context, Constanzo was hired by the powerful Hernandez family to shield its profitable drug trafficking empire from interlopers and drug enforcement agencies. Constanzo's girlfriend and high priestess, Sara Aldrete Villareal, was reportedly obsessed with the 1987 film *The Believers*, which depicted a group of Santerians in New York practicing ritual human sacrifice in order to derive magical powers (Cartwright 1989). One member of the group, Elio Hernandez Rivera, told authorities he believed bullets would magically bounce off him if he was shot. Villareal later testified in court, however, that only four of the fifteen deceased victims were ever part of any magical or ritual sacrifice. The majority of the victims (eleven) were killed over drug-related disputes ("Death Not Cult-Related, Constanzo Aide Says," *Houston Chronicle*, May 15, 1989). By all indications, Constanzo and Villareal constructed idiosyncratic rituals and ceremonies as part of their efforts to intimidate locals and guard the narcotics operation. Curiously, the print and electronic media framed the stories almost entirely in terms of satanic cult activity while underreporting the drug trafficking angle.

Though the incidents were diffuse, and not peculiar to any region, Victor found that most of the sixty-two reports occurred in small towns and rural areas. Not surprisingly, he determined they were fueled by rumor and unsubstantiated stories. Victor concluded that "In none of these cases was any group found which resembled the stereotype of a Satanic cult, that is, a well-organized group committing crimes and justifying their actions with a 'Satanic' ideology. In a few cases, authorities found groups of juvenile delinquents who had engaged in vandalism and proclaimed themselves 'Satanists' but even that was unusual" (1993:61). He attributed the origins of some of the rumors to "urban legends" prompted by mass media stories, a new genre of horror films, and the growing concern over crime and juvenile violence.

In my own research, I encountered cases of purported satanic cult activity with similar themes and results. In the summer of 1989, for example, I led a team of researchers into a small, rural town in east Texas, following a local satanic cult scare in Sabine County (Wright 1989). According to local news accounts, on April 21, 1989, approximately three hundred students in the Hemphill Independent School District were pulled out of school by frantic parents who descended upon the campus between 9 and 10 A.M. to rescue their children from a rumored satanic cult kidnapping and ritual sacrifice. A rumor had been circulating in the previous days that a satanic cult was planning to abduct two blond, blue-eyed youths for the purpose of a ritual killing. Hysterical parents gathered outside the school told reporters that "the walls of the school were stained in blood, animal organs were discovered in lockers, and teachers were instructing students in satanic activity" (*Sabine County Reporter* April 26, 1989). Some of those interviewed by both newspaper and television stations spoke to reporters as if they had witnessed these things firsthand. Yet an inspection of the buildings by school authorities, accompanied by television cameras, found no evidence of animal organs, blood-stained walls, satanic graffiti, or any other signs of devil worship. The discrepancy between the sensational accounts of panicked parents in the parking lot and the mundane reality inside the school building shown by television cameras was stupefying. Some versions of the narrative depicted students as the source of satanic worship. One woman I interviewed was told by her son that several classmates had discovered decapitated dogs, cats, and chickens in their lockers. It was alleged by some Hemphill residents that the local mortician's son was involved. Another version placed teachers at the center of the plot. Some teachers were reported to be cult leaders infiltrating the school and using their positions of influence to recruit adolescent Satanists. It was later determined by school authorities that the satanic cult scare was started as a ploy by two students attempting to get out of six-week exams. We concluded that the predisposition of the community to accept the satanist stories was due in large part to the proximity of the event to the Matamoros murders that made national headlines in the preceding weeks and that a number of people alluded to during the interviews.

Other sources of satanic subversion in the 1980s arose within small pockets of the mental health community. Psychologists, therapists, and social workers were implicated in legal cases involving charges of implanted memories. Patients who sought clinical help for such problems as eating disorders or depression were diagnosed as victims of satanic ritual abuse, leading to prolonged therapy in search of repressed memories caused by severe trauma. Repression of traumatic experiences during childhood was thought to be producing dissociative disorders that could be recovered only through hypnosis. By putting patients in an altered state of consciousness, some therapists believed they were uncovering repressed memories of ritual abuse, usually involving family members. Some of these patients were confined involuntarily for extended periods of time and heavily sedated by powerful drugs (Smith 1997, 1998a,b). As a result, marriages and families were torn apart, and patients developed a host of other psychological and personal problems. Tragically, patients were victimized by their therapists, suffering unnecessarily from false or implanted memories of incest, murder, cannibalism, and sexual abuse. Scores of patients accused parents of being

Satanists and ritually abusing them in ceremonies of initiation or blood sacrifice. Horrified and befuddled, parents organized national support groups of falsely accused family members both here and abroad. These included the False Memory Syndrome Foundation (FMSF), Casualties of Sexual Allegations (COSA), and the British False Memory Society (BFMS). Where patients eventually realized their memories were implanted, legal actions were taken. Cases of malpractice convictions in civil litigation produced large damage awards. In 1997 a Houston jury awarded a woman, Lynn Carl, $5.8 million for damages she incurred as a result of false memories implanted by therapists at the former Spring Shadows Glen Hospital. Carl was led to believe while in therapy that she had practiced murder, cannibalism, and incest. In November 1997, an Illinois woman, Patricia Burgus, won a $10.6 million settlement in a lawsuit against a leading advocate of satanic ritual abuse therapy, Dr. Bennet Braun, and the Rush-Presbyterian-St. Luke's Hospital in Chicago for emotional and psychological damages. Under treatment by Dr. Braun, Burgus came to believe she was a child molester, the high priestess of a satanic cult, and a cannibal who ate human flesh "meatloaf." She also came to believe through repressed and recovered memories that she possessed three hundred personalities (Smith 1997).

## SATAN AS SYMBOLIC REPRESENTATION

Widespread fears and anxieties about unexplained social disorder and turmoil (crime, violence, drugs, abortion, and suicide) may be expressed as evil and attributed to satanic forces. Western societies are characterized by a dualistic worldview that depicts all reality as consisting of two fundamental modes or opposing principles, one good and the other evil. These two forces are personified in the forms of God and Satan, respectively, and portrayed as warring figures commanding spiritual armies and battling for the souls of humankind. Satan, sometimes referred to as the Evil One, is believed to be the ultimate source of troubles, casting about to subvert human goodness and exploit moral frailty. According to biblical tradition, Satan was once a mighty archangel, Lucifer, who led an army of angels in rebellion against God and was cast out of heaven for his deeds. From that time until now, Satan has sought to take as many human souls as possible to hell with him, wreaking havoc and moral calamity. In popular literature and folklore, the Prince of Darkness is cunning and shrewd, wielding weapons of temptation and seduction to entrap the innocent, and hawking souls to make the Faustian bargain (Russell 1991). The notion that the devil may appear in disguise to the unsuspecting victim is also a common theme. Thus the young are often thought to be particularly vulnerable to the wiles of Satan and in need of special protection and vigilance.

Belief in the devil remains strong, according to polls. A 1998 survey of U.S. adults eighteen or older conducted for *CBS News* found that 64 percent of respondents said they believe in the existence of the devil (Goode 2000:166). Southerners (73 percent), Protestants (72 percent), and African Americans (74 percent) were more likely than other groups to believe in the devil. In a 1995 poll conducted by Princeton Survey Research Associates, researchers sought to determine popular belief in the activity of Satan in the world. Respondents were asked, "Do you think the Devil can make people do evil things they would not do otherwise?" Forty-two percent of those sampled answered yes to this question (Goode 2000:166). With the pervasive belief in Satan in contemporary society, episodes of perceived moral breakdown and discord help to explain why such conditions provoke popular suspicions of subversion in terms of demonic agents.

EXPLAINING THE SATANIC CULT SCARE

The period in which widespread fears of satanic cult conspiracies were believed to be pervasive is aptly explained in terms of moral panic theory (Cohen 1972; Goode and Ben-Yehuda 1994; Jenkins 1992). Moral panic refers to a social condition in which the official reaction to persons or events is significantly disproportionate to any actual threat posed. An exaggerated threat emerges and becomes defined as a danger to societal values, and its nature is presented in stereotypical fashion by interest groups through claims-making activities designed to get the attention of authorities and mass media. The elaboration of threat is spearheaded by "moral entrepreneurs" (Becker 1963) who issue an urgent call to action. Claims by interest groups and moral entrepreneurs defending cherished values may fail initially to arouse authorities or the public because they do not rise to the level of illegality or sufficiently offend the moral order (Jenkins 1992). As such, claims makers then engage in a process of deviance amplification—inflating or exaggerating claims of threat and social harm. Hall et al. (1978) suggest that deviance amplification is more effective when relatively harmless activities are linked to more-threatening ones—a process they call "convergence." Claims of social harm or threat made against suspect groups or practices (for example, new religions, pornography, homosexuality, and abortion), though deviant, are likely to be tolerated in an open democratic society. However, if they can be linked to more serious threats such as satanic ritual abuse, child pornography, sexual predation, or murder, they are more likely to generate official reactions, mobilizing authorities to quell the putative threat. Thus by linking relatively harmless activities to more serious violations, the benign activities are made to appear more menacing and dangerous. The deviant acts are then pushed upward across the threshold of intolerance and illegality, evoking powerful responses. These rhetorical tactics create implicit or explicit parallels, making one activity a necessary outcome of another, thereby stigmatizing the lesser offense and expanding the domain of potential threat. When successful, they culminate in overreaction and panic.

Concomitantly, there is an element of conspiracy imputed to the suspect group whereby through means of rumor and demonization, a "subversion ideology" is developed (Bromley 1991, 1998). From the perspective of cultural opponents, subversive groups embody quintessential evil and are believed to pose a maximum degree of threat to the social order. Subversive groups are said to be formed secretively in order to orchestrate a conspiracy, which is seen as growing rapidly. They may also be portrayed as having gained control over some segment of the conventional social order, which serves as a base of operations. Finally, subversive groups possess a unique power that is destructive to the integrity of normal individuals and groups. Consequently, a crisis is constructed through claims-making activities requiring urgent and dramatic action on the part of authorities. Thus "[w]hen the official reaction to a person, groups of persons or series of events is out of all proportion to the actual threat offered, when 'experts,' in the form of police chiefs, the judiciary, politicians and editors perceive the threat in all but identical terms, and appear to talk with one voice . . . when media representations universally stress 'sudden and dramatic' increases . . . above and beyond that which a sober, realistic appraisal could sustain, then we believe it is appropriate to speak of the beginnings of a moral panic" (Hall et al. 1978:7). Moral panics tend to be episodic and temporary but can lead to officially sanctioned repression of targeted groups—witch-hunts, purges, red scares, and other forms of social control (Goode and Ben-Yehuda 1994).

## SOCIAL FACTORS CONTRIBUTING TO SATANIC CULT SCARE

In the decade before the 1980s, various social conditions converged to give rise to the satanic cult scare. These included the resurgence of Christian Fundamentalism, the emergent anticult movement, the existence of a few real satanic groups, the growth of pornography and the sex industry, feminist efforts to raise awareness of child sexual abuse, and the influx of young mothers into the workforce who placed their children in daycare. These elements were symptomatic of acute social change in the spheres of work, family, and religion. In this period of social upheaval, the construction of a Satanist threat became more salient as an explanation of social problems.

Each of these elements or factors can be shown to contribute to the development of a satanic cult scare.

### Christian Fundamentalism

In the decade of the 1970s, Fundamentalist Christians became a viable political force in American society (Liebman and Wuthnow 1982). With some notable exceptions, Evangelicals and Fundamentalists had kept studiously aloof from American politics through the better half of the twentieth century, concentrating on soul winning and private morality issues (Marsden 1980). But the social activism of liberal and left-wing movements in the 1960s challenged religious conservatives to enter the public arena. Jerry Falwell's Moral Majority mobilized Christian Fundamentalists through direct mail and video programming, mass petition campaigns against abortion, homosexuality and pornography, yellow journalism, and the fiery preaching of Falwell himself in televised services. Falwell's success prompted the formation of other right-wing groups, including the Religious Roundtable, Christian Voice, National Christian Action Coalition, National Right to Life Committee, Concerned Women for America, Christian Family Renewal, Committee for the Survival of a Free Congress, Conservative Caucus, Heritage Foundation, Christian Cause, Christian Coalition for Legislative Action, and Intercessors for America. The range of issues widened to reinstatement of school prayer and Bible reading, greater freedoms for Christian schools and home schooling, as well as opposition to Communism, secular humanism, feminism, ERA, lenient drug laws, gay and lesbian rights, sexual permissiveness, the "liberal media," and other sources of "moral decay" (Diamond 1989).

America's putative decline was trumpeted with great frequency by conservative Christians who were quick to link this decline to biblical and apocalyptic symbolism. Fundamentalists, who have always taken a literalist view of Holy Scriptures and the Bible, predicted the growth and spread of Satan's power in the end time just prior to Christ's return. Millennial and apocalyptic fervor began to build during the 1970s, generated in no small part by the publication of Hal Lindsey's best-selling book *The Late Great Planet Earth* in 1972. Lindsey claimed that biblical prophecy had foretold a number of world events that had recently occurred or were soon to transpire. This message found resonance in the conservative Christian community and was preached from pulpits all over the country. Believers were warned of the coming cataclysm, presaged by the spread of iniquity, wickedness, and corruption. As such, various social problems that appeared to be worsening—crime, violence, drugs, divorce, out-of-wedlock births, pornography, AIDS—were readily seen as evidence of the Last Days and the deepening influence of evil forces at work. Fundamentalist leaders called on the faithful to don spiritual armor, to "fight the good fight," and battle the growing calamity and moral decline. A key figure in end-time biblical prophecy is the Antichrist, an incarnation of the Devil who sets about to rule the world. This final conspiracy is made possible by Satan's minions who manage to deceive worldly authorities and the masses into unwitting collaboration. The specter of covert satanic cult activity in the Last Days, subverting the ignorant and mobilizing the forces of darkness for Satan's reign, was embraced by Fundamentalists as an explanation of social problems.

*Anticultism*
During the 1960s and 1970s, a wave of new religious movements (NRMs) or cults emerged. Many of these were youth movements that drew from the counterculture during a time of heightened social and political experimentation. Youth who joined new religious movements often dropped out of college, quit conventional jobs or career tracks, reduced ties to family and friends, lived communally, and generally rejected mainstream cultural values and lifestyles. In most cases, these choices and actions did not have the enthusiastic support of parents or family of new converts. Some parents became very concerned that sons or daughters were becoming involved in a dangerous or subversive enterprise. Yet the social science research shows that for most converts to NRMs, involvement was short-lived, averaging about two years, and that former members often reported favorable experiences of their involvement (Barker 1984; Galanter 1989; Levine 1984; Lewis 1986; Wright 1984, 1987). Despite sinister characterizations of NRMs as "destructive cults" or unfounded extrapolations from isolated cases of tragedy (for example, Peoples Temple) by news reporters and anticult organizations, the vast majority of new religions have been benign, if not functional (Robbins 1988), and even therapeutic (Galanter 1989; Levine 1984).

The anticult movement (ACM) arose as a coalition of distraught parents, religious leaders, former members, and others, including a few professional therapists and academics. The groups compiled and exchanged information, lobbied legislators, held press conferences, and distributed newsletters condemning new religions for turning members into robots or mental captives. Brainwashing became the prominent metaphor to characterize conversion and justify attacks on so-called cults. To counteract what the ACM called cult "programming," a powerful and extralegal tactic of forcible dissuasion called "deprogramming" was developed. This involved the abduction of members by deprogrammers, usually hired by parents, for purposes of extracting forced recantations of the individual's new faith.

The ACM was successful in disseminating sensationalistic claims and stereotypes about "destructive cults." Surveys revealed widespread public suspicion and distrust aimed at new religions. In Richardson and Van Driel's

(1984) survey of 400 registered voters in Washoe County, Nevada, 35 percent of respondents agreed that "legislation should be passed to control the spread of new religions or cults." A Gallup poll found that 62 percent of adults reported they "would not like to have as neighbors" members of a religious sect or cult (1989), compared with 30 percent in 1981. Another survey found that 26 percent of respondents supported "FBI surveillance of cults" while 37 percent supported laws "restricting solicitation practices of Hare Krishnas" (Bromley and Breschel 1992). The metaphor of brainwashing became an accepted explanation of conversion to cults by a majority of the mass public and significant portions of the media. In the wake of Jonestown, ACM groups effectively propagated the paradigmatic evil cult stereotype that presented the ever-present threat of mass suicide (Hall 1995; Hall, Schuyler, and Trinh 2000).

Beginning in the early 1980s, the ACM exploited the growing attention paid to Satanism. ACM literature consistently reported on satanic cult activities, presenting them as another example of evil cults at work (Bromley 1991). Through annual conferences, newsletters, press releases, media interviews, and other sources, Satanism was incorporated within the larger framework promoted by the ACM.

These efforts eventually penetrated public schools, neighborhood organizations, and churches, providing expedient explanations for any kind of deviant behavior. For example, in March 1990, a series of three teenage suicides sparked intense rumors and parental fears of satanic cult influences in Alberta, Canada. Evidence of black magic was alleged by some residents, as was secret rituals and pacts. The school board chairman announced that as many as one hundred students might be involved in Satanism in the area of Lethbridge. A group of parents stormed the police station, demanding action be taken. Fundamentalist churches in the neighboring province of Calgary organized a public seminar on the dangers of Satanism. Eight teenagers were placed in psychiatric or foster care, though police found no evidence of organized satanic cults (Victor 1993:351).

*Actual Satanist Groups*
Moral panics are best understood as exaggerated perceptions of threat. This assumes the actuality of the phenomenon, though one which poses less threat than is alleged. The existence of a few Satanist groups allowed claims makers to offer up "evidence" of the putative conspiracy. Satanism represented a very small portion of the new religious movements that arose during this time. But because the object of veneration was so sensational, it created a substantial amount of media coverage and attention. Of the several thousand new religious movements that emerged, there were only three organized satanic groups of any size or substance: Anton LaVey's Church of Satan, Michael Aquino's Temple of Set, and The Process.

The Church of Satan, headquartered in San Francisco, received the most attention, partly because of the colorful character of its founder, Anton LaVey. LaVey authored *The Satanic Bible* (1969), which became an occult best-seller and is still in print. The work is largely a promotion of hedonism and self-indulgence. The most succinct summary of the book is found in the Nine Satanic Statements, a diabolical equivalent of the Ten Commandments. It inverts many of the commandments encouraging physical, emotional, and mental gratification. LaVey also edited and published a newsletter, the *Cloven Hoof*, which was disseminated among dues-paying members. He parlayed his notoriety into lucrative consulting work for the entertainment industry. LaVey was a consultant to the producers of the film *Rosemary's Baby* and even appeared briefly in the film as the Devil (Melton 1992:112). A former circus hand and lion trainer for the Barnum and Bailey circus, LaVey was a showman and enjoyed shocking the public. Even at the pinnacle of the church's popularity, the curious far outnumbered the members, and the turnover rate was very high. One researcher who conducted a participant observation of the Church of Satan in the late sixties reported that the church had "only four or five hundred active members" even though it publicly boasted thousands (Alfred 1976:193). The study also found that most of the members were not youth but persons over the age of thirty. Melton estimates that the membership peaked at about one thousand, probably in the early to mid-seventies. Interest in the Church of Satan declined in the late seventies, and by the time LaVey died in 1997, the church was facing bankruptcy. The legacy of LaVey's church far exceeds any measurable impact it had in terms of actual adherents.

The Temple of Set, a schismatic sect led by Michael Aquino, managed a smaller following in Los Angeles. Established in 1975, the group was dedicated to the ancient Egyptian deity believed to have been the model for the Christian Satan. Aquino was thought to be more serious and studious about Satanism than LaVey, who actually did not believe Satan was a literal being. Aquino, on the other hand, claimed to have been visited by Set in a vision and recorded the epiphany in his book, *The Book of Coming Forth by Night* (1975). Aquino was also a lieutenant colonel in the Army and held a Ph.D. in religion. According to Melton (1992:114), the program of the Temple was geared to work with an intellectual elite and required of members formidable in self-discipline and extensive readings. By the end of the seventies, the membership of the Temple grew to about five hundred in North America, with some additional members in Europe (Melton 1992:114).

The Process was a deviant psychotherapy group that emerged in the early sixties. It began as a schism of L. Ron Hubbard's Church of Scientology and evolved from a therapy service to a religious group. The transformation took place when the group sought to "escape civilization" in 1966 and visited a plantation in the Yucatan, experiencing a collective rebirth and forming a religious community and the rudiments of a belief system. Bainbridge (1978) describes in great detail the spiritual journey and evolution of the group in his book, *Satan's Power.* By the late sixties, members of The Process were proselytizing in the streets of large cities in North America and Europe adorned in black robes with red satanic emblems sewn on the chests, accompanied by Alsatian hounds. Though seen as Satanists by outsiders, Bainbridge notes that the group was polytheistic and attributed its own meaning to the gods Lucifer and Satan. The Process was nomadic, sometimes establishing "chapters" in cities but only for a short period of time before closing them down and moving on. In the throes of the Vietnam War in 1970, a Toronto chapter of The Process was started, in part as a Canadian asylum for American conscientious objectors and in part as means to get British members admitted into the U.S. expeditiously and for unlimited periods. The Process encountered massive adverse publicity in the early seventies following the unfounded allegation that the Manson family was connected to them in some way. Bainbridge suggests that the fallout from these rumors contributed to the ultimate demise of the group. The Process experienced a split in 1974, resulting in the attenuation of its more controversial doctrines and eventually became absorbed into the New Age movement. Membership never reached more than a few hundred.

## Growth of Pornography and Sex Industry

Following the 1973 Supreme Court decision in *Miller v. California,* which liberalized the obscenity laws, there was substantial growth in the pornography and sex industry. Adult bookstores, peep shows, erotic magazines and videos, men's clubs, and sex-oriented businesses exploded. What civil libertarians saw as a removal of unconstitutional government restraints on individual liberties, traditionalists decried as an ominous threat to the moral virtues of society. Most Americans occupied the middle-ground on the issue of pornography, preferring to see the private choices of consenting adults left alone by government. Nonetheless, conservatives mounted antiobscenity and antipornography campaigns to mobilize public reactions and challenge the new standards (Zurcher and Kilpatrick 1976). With the election of Ronald Reagan and the emergence of the New Religious Right, conservatives gained enormous political clout and a stronghold in government. The growing pressure of the Religious Right to combat sexual immorality led to the 1986 report of the Meese Pornography Commission, which in turn produced sweeping new law enforcement crackdowns on all manner of sexual materials. The commission's findings were widely criticized by scholars and researchers for its unscientific conclusions (Linz, Penrod, and Donnerstein 1987). The commission was stacked with conservatives and individuals predisposed to attacking explicit sexual images and sex businesses. Equally as important was the development of an increasingly vocal segment of the feminist movement, which became allied with religious conservatives on the issue of sexually oriented expression. Antipornography feminists such as Catherine MacKinnon and Andrea Dworkin argued that pornography should be suppressed because it leads to violence against women. This alliance was highly successful in creating alleged links between pornography and forms of sexual violence against women—rape, incest, pedophilia, harassment, battering, and even murder. So successful was this campaign by allied opponents that it produced what New York University law professor Nadine Strossen later called a "full-fledged sex panic" (1995:20).

*Feminism and Child Sexual Abuse*
In the 1970s, feminists campaigned to expand the public awareness of child battering, wife battering, and sexual victimization. At the forefront of the child-protection movement, feminists mobilized to create "a large child protection apparatus—a network of protective services workers, police officers, and other specialists with a mandate to do something to help child victims. These workers had a vested interest in expanding their organizational turf by discovering and assuming responsibility for new forms of child victimization" (Richardson, Best, and Bromley 1991:10). By the late 1970s, the issues of sexual abuse extended to sexual exploitation linked to child pornography and adolescent prostitution. In the early 1980s, child savers introduced a new form of child victimization—ritual abuse. Incorporating claims of physical and sexual abuse with concerns over missing children, child pornography, and emerging allegations of Satanism, satanic ritual abuse seemed to provide a plausible explanation for the apparent rise in sex abuse cases.

This particular definition of the problem was also largely influenced by the publication of *Michelle Remembers* (Smith and Pazder 1980). The book details the account of a psychiatrist's efforts to help a woman recover childhood memories of trauma when she was reportedly abused and tortured by a satanic cult. This pioneering account was significant because it incorporated virtually all the charges that would become popular among anti-Satanists in the eighties—satanic worship, ritual child abuse, blood sacrifices, murder, cannibalism—and thus effectively shaped the whole occult survivor genre (Jenkins and Maier-Katkin 1991:133). Through hypnosis and treatment covering a period of approximately one year, her therapist, Lawrence Padzer, helped Michelle relive memories of what happened to her when she was five years old. While this account was the first of its kind, by the end of the decade, there were thousands of reported cases by therapists treating satanic ritual abuse victims. However, in none of these cases was there material evidence to support the claims. Anti-Satanists argued that it was a vast conspiracy involving morticians, police, and people strategically placed in positions of authority (Nathan 1991; Nathan and Snedeker 1995).

*Young Working Mothers and Daycare*
In the 1970s, the greatest influx of women into the workforce was among mothers of young children. A generation of women who were raised by stay-at-home mothers were compelled to place their children in the care of strangers during a decade that saw double-digit inflation. Many women experienced apprehensions and anxieties about leaving their children in daycare. The conflict between family economic needs and maternal responsibility for the socialization of children produced understandable tension. Bromley (1991:68) observes that "[t]he individuals making the initial allegations of satanic subversion were family members who entrusted their children to daycare facilities about which they had significant reservations and apprehensions." Accused childcare workers occupied a pivotal point of this tension between the spheres of work and family serving as surrogate parents. The socialization effects on young children in daycare were still largely a matter of public debate and moral conservatives roundly condemned the practice.

In the early eighties, a series of sex abuse scandals at daycare centers centered on claims of Satanism and ritual abuse. Beginning with the *McMartin Preschool* case in suburban Los Angeles in 1983, daycare workers were accused of running an organized operation for child predators and Satanists. Virginia McMartin, her daughter Peggy McMartin Buckey, and her son-in-law Ray Buckey, were tried on fifty-two felony charges after children claimed they were forced to participate in ritualistic sex. In 1990, seven years after the case began, McMartin was acquitted, and the charges against Peggy and Ray Buckey were dropped. Dozens of copycat cases emerged across the country. In El Paso, Texas, in 1985, Gayle Doyle, a popular middle-aged preschool teacher, was charged with sexually molesting both boys and girls, inserting sharp objects into their genitals, threatening children with masks, wild animals, and even vows to kill their parents if they disclosed the crimes. In 1986 in suburban Boston, Violet Amirault, daughter Cheryl Amirault, and son Gerald Amirault were convicted of sexually molesting forty boys and girls aged three to six at their Fells Acres Day School. Their case was overturned in appeal after serving eight years in prison when the judge determined that the evidence was based on false memories implanted by therapists and social workers. In Austin, Texas, a middle-aged couple named Daniel and Frances Keller were also convicted of molesting children and engaging in bizarre sexual acts; they were sentenced to forty-eight years apiece. In Maplewood, New Jersey, Margaret Michaels was convicted of engaging in "nude pileups" with three- to five-year-olds at a daycare center. Michaels was released after five years when a state appeals court overturned her conviction and the New Jersey Supreme Court later criticized investigators for coercive and highly suggestive meth-ods of interviewing the children. In North Carolina in 1993, daycare oper-ator Robert Kelly was convicted on ninety-nine counts of sexual abuse and punished with twelve consecutive life sentences. A PBS *Frontline* documen-tary, "Searching for Satan," covered the incident, revealing that there was no physical evidence of abuse despite thorough medical examinations of the children. The convictions were based solely on child reports garnered by social workers and a female police investigator. Defendants' attorneys asserted that the children were "coached" into confessions.

American ritual-abuse believers also exported their claims to Canada. The first documented charges surfaced in Hamilton, Ontario, in 1985. Al-legations were made against the parents of two young children and the mother's boyfriend. The charges were later dropped for lack of evidence. But in 1992, in the town of Martensville, just north of Saskatoon, nine adults were charged with ritually abusing thirty children at a daycare center. Allegations entailed claims of devil worship, lewd rituals, and an under-ground Satanic network that included police officers. The incident ignited extensive press coverage and was headline news from Montreal to Vancou-ver; it became known as the "Martensville nightmare" (Nathan and Snedecker 1995:230). Rumors of secret covens grew rapidly and extended throughout the community, placing everyone under suspicion. Convic-tions obtained by prosecutors against the adults were later overturned in 1995 on the grounds that investigators improperly questioned the children and tainted their testimonies.

CONCLUSION

Moral panics like the satanic cult scare in North America in the 1980s and early 1990s symbolize the tendency to find or create an enemy to blame for society's ills. Currents of social change introduce new winners and losers in the economy; challenge traditional values; dislodge certain social groups from positions of privilege; rearrange power and status along the lines of race, ethnicity, gender, or age; and create contested terrains of cultural or moral authority as groups vie for social control. The anomic conditions erupting from rapid or acute social change lead to the perception of a crisis threatening the moral order. The threat is embodied in perpetrators or conspirators who become regarded as the "enemy." Stanley Cohen (1972) observes that a process of dichotomization or polarization produces a "we" versus "them" perspective that generates "folk devils." This morality play of good versus evil promotes a scapegoating of targeted groups or individuals in which to assign blame. These targets then become labeled as evil and hence deserving of self-righteous anger, hostility, and punishment. What follows is a predictable social dynamic. Public pressure demands that social control mechanisms be strengthened to protect the innocent from debauchery. Authorities redouble efforts to tighten enforcement of existing laws or push for new ones. Moral entrepreneurs insist that serious steps have to be taken to repair the damage; there must be a crackdown on offenders and purveyors of evil. In the atmosphere of moral panic, those who do not support the crackdown may themselves become suspect. Sympathizers or defenders of targeted groups may be accused as coconspirators through guilt by association. Research on witch-hunts, red scares, and cult scares have demonstrated this pattern of inculpating family, friends, or public supporters of the accused (Bromley and Shupe 1981; Demos 1982; Fried 1996; Karlsen 1987). This appears to explain, in part, why moral panics are not shot down more quickly, as critics may be less inclined to challenge impassioned claims of moral crusaders. Nowhere has this been demonstrated more compellingly than in the red scare of the 1950s driven by the red-baiting senator Joe McCarthy and the House Un-American Activities Committee (HUAC).

Not coincidentally, the satanic cult scare evolved during the same period in which the cold war was winding down, even while the rhetoric aimed at the "evil empire," as Ronald Reagan called it, remained fervent. With the eventual demise of Communism and the diminished threat of a Communist conspiracy, however, Satanists became the new threat, replacing Communists as the designated enemy. Indeed, it appears that the satanic threat increased in direct proportion to the decline of the Communist threat throughout the 1980s. Sociologists have long observed that in situations where external enemies no longer threaten, a society will find groups or individuals within its own ranks that it can construe as threatening (Bergesen 1984; Demos 1982; Durkheim [1895]1960; Erikson, 1966). Social construction of such enemies is particularly important to communities experiencing a crisis in which cherished values are being called into question. According to Bergesen, "A community will commence to ritually persecute imaginary enemies—conduct a witchhunt—to manufacture moral deviants as a means of ritually affirming the group's problematical values and collective purposes" (1984:vii). Deviants come to symbolize threats or changes to the moral order in which a relocation of moral boundaries might be required. In a study of witch-hunts in Puritan New England, Demos (1984) even found that the persecution of witches attenuated during periods of war and reappeared after peace had returned.

Corresponding the rise of the Religious Right and the electoral success of Reagan in the U.S., the country experienced an intensive political, economic, and moral divide (Bennett 1988; Diamond 1989, 1995). Bitter disputes over moral issues (family values, abortion, pornography, and prayer in schools) led to increased polarization and "culture wars." In response to societal disorganization and change, a subversion ideology was formulated by key moral entrepreneurs to explain the perceived crisis and framed in terms of a diabolical plot by an underground satanic cult network (Bromley 1991). Drawing on the scant "evidence" of a few small Satanist groups, occasional confessions of psychopathic serial killers, the growth of macabre horror films about devil worshipers, and other anecdotal proofs, the claim of clandestine satanic activity by a loose coalition of anti-Satanist groups became a proffered explanation of social problems. These claims were buttressed by the emergence of a child-saver movement focusing on sexual abuse of children, stranger abduction, child pornography, and the concomitant rise of "occult survivor" groups. All of this was set in the context of a resurgence of Christian Fundamentalism in local and national politics in which the personification of evil was readily identified in the form of satanic influence. The demonization of "liberalism" as a root cause of social ills and moral decay by conservative politicians allied with the Religious Right was compatible with an emergent belief in a vast underground satanic cult conspiracy.

# The Commodification of Witchcraft

## Tanice G. Foltz

The fascination with witchcraft and magic has a colorful history: one only need look at children's fairytales such as *Snow White and the Seven Dwarfs* or films such as *The Wizard of Oz* to appreciate the enchanting world of witches and magic. Beyond this fantasy, however, lies the religion of Witchcraft, popularly known as Wicca or Paganism.[1] As the religion has grown exponentially since its importation into North America, Witchcraft has become increasingly commodified and marketed to spiritual and material consumers.

Three themes are directly related to Witchcraft's commodification in contemporary North America. The first concerns the numerous manifestations as well as the changing representations of Witchcraft and magic in the media. Prior to the development of this religion in North America, witches were generally portrayed in one of two stereotypical ways. Either they were ugly, old hags who used their powers for evil, or those portrayed as beautiful covertly used their magical powers to "catch" or keep a man or to maintain the peace (as well as traditional gender roles) within their homes. Since the religion's importation, however, which coincides with the women's movement, witches frequently appear in books, films, and television programs, and they are often characterized as attractive, youthful, strong, and independent females who openly use their magical powers to fight against evil for the greater good.

The second theme concerns a potential change in Witchcraft as a religion as a result of its extensive commodification. The tremendous growth of this religion is largely the result of Pagan books, websites, and festivals that attract Pagans and Witches. Furthermore, Witches and other Pagans are consumers of Pagan symbols, such as pentagrams, images of goddesses and gods, statues of fairies, and crystals. Ezzy (2001) contends that as Witchcraft is increasingly influenced by the market, for instance, offering Witchcraft classes online, there could also be a shift in its personal growth orientation to one that is, instead, utilitarian and consumerist. I submit that Pagans' exchange of money for spirituality services such as Wiccan festivals, retreats, and educational programs does not portend a change in the main focus of the religion. In addition, the commercialization of Witch paraphernalia, such as pentacle jewelry or goddess figurines contributes to adherents' ability to define themselves as Witches or Pagans.

The third theme centers on the widespread use of Witchcraft symbols in the mass marketplace—for instance, stars, moons, and spirals, which commonly adorn Wiccan jewelry, clothing, and altar paraphernalia as well as New Age items. For at least a decade, these same spiritual symbols have been appearing extensively in the profane world of common household items. These themes are explored in this chapter.

MANIFESTATIONS AND CHANGING REPRESENTATIONS OF
WITCHCRAFT

*Early Commodification and Commercialization:* Salem, *"Witch City"*
A natural starting point for exploring the manifestations of witchcraft is Salem, Massachusetts, also known as "Witch City." In the early 1690s, long before Wicca became a viable religion in North America, over two hundred people were on trial for practicing witchcraft, and twenty were executed. The Peabody Essex Museum showcases many of the original witch trial documents and renders an authentic and sobering version of the trials. At the same time, it displays a tremendous variety of "witch kitsch" in a hallway filled with posters, postcards, and ceramic witch figurines complete with broomsticks, black cats, and cauldrons. This historical record of Witchcraft's commercialization dates from at least 1862. Leaving the Peabody, one immediately notices multiple store awnings featuring a black-robed pointy-hatted witch with a black cat and the caption "Stop by for a Spell." Salem newspaper dispensers display a witch riding a broom, as do banners hanging from light posts that proudly proclaim "Salem, Haunted Happenings." It appears that every establishment has witch-themed items for sale, including T-shirts, dresses and cloaks, jewelry, ceramics, dolls, dishes, and pictures. The Salem Witch Museum beckons tourists to come in and, for six dollars, see a "show" of the witch trials. At the time of my visit, in October 1999, a special exhibit featured several popular portrayals of witches, from Samantha of *Bewitched,* to *Oz*'s Wicked Witch of the West, to Daniel Day Lewis's character in the television production of Arthur Miller's play, *The Crucible.* In floor-to-ceiling glass casements, a larger-than-life model of a modern-day Pagan woman is in the first display, while a huge stereotypical witch rides a broom in the next. A pictorial time line spanning an entire wall signifies the different beginnings of Pagan and Christian times and depicts the correspondence of significant events, such as the Inquisition's role in the European witch-hunts during the thirteenth through seventeenth centuries. At the end of the time line an American flag covers a wall mural, along with the face of Senator Joseph McCarthy,

who became the symbol of the anti-Communism witch-hunt in the early 1950s.

The highly commercial Salem Witch Museum offers an explanation of the colonial witch hysteria through its tape-recorded show. Its gift shop offers prospective buyers a huge variety of witch kitsch, including post-cards, playing cards, tote bags, coffee mugs, stuffed animals, and flying witch dolls as well as serious books covering the witch trials. Modern-day Salem underscores the entrepreneurial beginnings of the commercialization of Witchcraft in North America, as it profits from the deaths of people killed as witches over 300 years ago. In response to the town's extreme commodification, in 1992 the local Witch Defense League dedicated a memorial to those who were executed as witches.

## WITCHCRAFT AND MAGIC IN POPULAR FILM AND TELEVISION: PRE-WICCA INFLUX

The commmodification of Witchcraft can be explored through its portrayal in popular culture mass media such as film, television dramas, fantasies, and news programs as well as books and the Internet. The world has witnessed tremendous changes in the representation of Witchcraft and magic since it became a recognized religion in North America in the 1970s. This can be seen in a comparative analysis of popular images of Witchcraft in pre- and post-1970s selected films and television programs.

### Early Films

Witches in film have often been portrayed either as ugly, bad, and powerful women or as extremely beautiful and good women. A clear example of this occurs in the film *The Wizard of Oz*, based upon the book by Frank L. Baum, which premiered in 1939 and gained popularity in the 1950s. This is the story of a young girl, Dorothy, who is unhappy with her life on a farm in Kansas when she and her dog, Toto, are swept away in a tornado that takes them to a magical place. Here a pretty blond witch, Glinda the Good Witch of the North, directs Dorothy to magic slippers that can help them, while the ugly Wicked Witch of the West tries to foil their efforts. Throughout the movie the good-bad dichotomy, characterized as white magic versus black magic, is played upon. It seems that the wicked witch is so powerful and devious she is sure to win, until Dorothy remembers Glinda's advice and throws water on the wicked witch, who screeches raucously while she melts into a puddle. The moral of the story is that good magic and believing in oneself can provide the strength needed for tough situations, and it can overcome negative forces, as portrayed by the wicked witch. Viewers are left with stereotypical portrayals of witches and a bal-

ance between good and evil. *The Wizard of Oz* is a classic that mature baby
boomers still enjoy, and the Wicked Witch of the West has gained iconic
status as the epitome of a mean, ugly, powerful old hag.

In 1958, when women were told that their place was in the home as
wives and mothers, a very different, less fantastic type of witch film appeared, targeting adults and starring Jimmy Stewart, Jack Lemon, and Kim
Novak. In *Bell, Book, and Candle* Novak is Gil, a very "hip" pretty blond
beatnik and hereditary witch whose business is an exotic artifact shop. The
audience is told that the Siamese cat is her "familiar" who helps her work
magic spells, such as getting her upstairs neighbor Shep (Stewart) to visit.
Bored, self-centered Gil puts a spell on Shep, who is engaged to another.
He becomes obsessed with Gil and leaves his fiancé. Gil knows she cannot
marry him because she's not human, but when she tells him she's a witch,
he doesn't believe her. When he accepts that she really is one (we are told
that witches cannot cry nor fall in love), he has the spell removed with an
elaborate ceremony and a magic potion. In the final scene, Shep finds an
elegantly dressed Gil in her newly transformed, much less exotic, seashell
shop. While saying good-bye, she cries, whereupon he realizes she is
"human," and they proclaim their love for each other and presumably
marry. This film has more than one moral about women and witches. First,
the film highlights the loneliness of being "different"—a single woman.
Even though the witch lifestyle may seem exciting (holding witch meetings
in beatnik bars with bongos playing), it conflicts with the 1950s gender
roles for women—specifically that women should conform, stay in the
home, and strive for love and marriage rather than independence. Second,
Gil is beautiful, blond, and exotic, and she uses her looks and her magic to
put a spell on her intended lover, even though, as a witch, she does not
have the capacity to love. This irresponsible use of magic reinforces images
of women as deceitful while at the same time challenging the romanticism
built into women's traditional gender roles. Third, she is changed by her
encounter with Shep, who rescues her from her nonhuman qualities, and
her longing for him transforms her capacity to love, cry, and endure emotional pain. In this film, the producers' commodification of witchcraft ultimately sends the message that, while female witches may be beautiful, they
use their power irresponsibly and ultimately must be "saved" by men, on
whom they become dependent and through whom they become responsible mates. These images continued to reign over the next several decades.

*Early Television, 1940s to 1960s*
One of the earliest portrayals of a witch on television occurred in the
*Kukla, Fran, and Ollie* puppet show, which premiered in 1939 on WBKB
in Chicago and continued on NBC for ten years.[2] This early television
program was one of the first to feature a witch, with Buelah Witch playing

one of the core members of the twenty-puppet character cast who comprised the Kuklapolitans. She was stereotypical in her appearance, including a wart on her chin; she cackled and wore a black pointy hat while she buzzed about on her jet-propelled broom. A distinctive feature was that she also studied electronics. Considering the traditional gender norms of the 1940s and 1950s, the image of an unattractive and smart female witch is not entirely surprising. The cast and storyline apparently appealed to a significant audience, judging by the fact that it was profitable enough to air for over a decade, and in the 1970s it played in syndication on CBS.

The first sitcom to showcase the exploits of a "real" woman, also a hereditary witch, was *Bewitched* (1964–72), shown in the U.S. and Canada and still running in syndication. *Bewitched* immediately became a hit, ranking second among all programs in its initial season (Brooks and Marsh 1999). Elizabeth Montgomery played "Sam," the attractive blond housewife-witch who had the ability to do magic by simply twitching her nose. Married to Darrin, a "mere mortal," Sam pledged not to use her powers but always had to break her promise to correct the spells of her eccentric relatives, one of whom was mean spirited, while another was wildly inept.[3] A year later, *I Dream of Jeannie* (1965–70) also still in syndication, emerged, featuring a gorgeous blond genie in a bottle discovered by astronaut Captain Nelson when his space capsule landed on a desert island. Jeannie had the magical quality of invisibility to anyone but her "master," and she served only him. The sitcom's storyline focused on Jeannie getting her master into trouble and then using her magical powers to rescue him from embarrassing situations. In both these sitcoms the women are blond, beautiful, and funny, and their use of magic, however well intended, frustrated the men in their lives. The images of witchcraft and magic are clearly stereotypical: the women wiggle a nose or blink and nod, and poof!— magic happens. These programs arose at the beginning of the second wave of the women's liberation movement, when Witchcraft as a religion had not yet taken hold in North America. The commodification and commercialization of witchcraft was apparently profitable for the network producers, attracting millions of viewers each week and sparking huge residual businesses.[4] Their writers recognized that these magic- and witchcraft-themed programs conveyed relevant gender role messages to women, especially since most women worked within the home and had little power in the larger world. These programs relayed numerous gendered messages, most importantly the following: (1) that beautiful women may use their magical powers, which leads to disorder in their male-female relationships; (2) that men fear women's magic and power and thus impose restrictions on "their" women; (3) and that women will secretly use their magic to restore order and harmony to the threatened relationship. These messages encompass the idea that women cannot be trusted to use their feminine powers wisely and therefore must be restricted by the men in their lives. At the same time, it tells women they must be deceitful to get what they want. While the network producers profited from these comedic, fantasy programs, this commodification of witchcraft conveyed the message that women could be secretly powerful while still maintaining their traditional gender roles of housewife, mother, and girlfriend-servant. As times changed, and the women's liberation movement and the religion of Witchcraft took hold in the 1970s, subsequent television programs witnessed a significant divergence in the characterization and commodification of female witches. Films, however, maintained stereotypical characterizations.

## WITCHCRAFT AND MAGIC IN FILM: POST-WICCA INFLUX

### *The Witches of Eastwick, Practical Magic, The Craft,* and *Blair Witch Project*

Not surprisingly, as Witchcraft has gained recognition as a viable religion in the U.S. and Canada in the 1970s, it has increasingly appeared as the subject matter for films. In addition during this period, a general shift is observed in the portrayal of female witches, from that of being controlled by the Devil to a more positive, morally "good" and increasingly stronger image. However, witches' association with evil proves to be a continuing undercurrent.

One example, adapted from the book *The Witches of Eastwick* (1987), featured Jack Nicholson, portraying the Devil, and Michelle Pfieffer, Susan Sarandon, and Cher as the witch beauties he tempts, seduces, and impregnates as they are uncontrollably attracted to him. When the three women realize the Devil's power over their lives, they take revenge by using the black magic he has taught them. Even though the women hex him and his physical body disappears, his influence remains as witnessed in the final scene in which he peers from multiple television screens at the three women's babies he has sired. The movie blurs notions of witchcraft with Satanism, as the women and the Devil cavort together through most of the movie, until he gains control over them and then treats them mercilessly. The women have unwittingly complied in their own demise, and by the time they recognize their situation and try to change it, it is too late. This example of commodification reinforces the message that while beautiful women can be witches, and they can be harmless, they are ultimately influenced and penetrated by the work of the Devil. The witches' lack of sexual propriety and their willingness to be in a sexual relationship with the same man leads the audience to conclude that when women are given too much sexual freedom, they will be promiscuous and doomed by their actions.

Even more sinister in its premise, *The Craft* appeared in 1996, continuing the witchcraft-as-evil-power theme. In this film three pretty, yet outcast, high school girls discover Witchcraft, begin experimenting with magic, and become obsessed with their newfound powers. In the early parts of the film the rituals seem authentic, derived from the fact that a practicing Witch was a consultant.[5] The majority of the film, however, has the girls using their newly acquired magical skills to deceptively change their physical appearance to control others. In the end the young woman who most egregiously misuses her power is severely punished. This is consonant with Wiccan philosophy concerning the "law of return," that whatever a person sends out shall come back three times over.[6] The film thrives on bits of realism in the rituals and a smattering of Wiccan beliefs thrown in with a vast amount of fantasy. This movie's focus is on good-looking girls who are searching for a sense of belonging, and who turn to magic and witchcraft to gain power and control over others—something the religion itself discourages. Even though the film is based on fantasy, these commercialized images of the Craft reinforce and perpetuate malevolent stereotypes about Wicca.

In 1998, the movie *Practical Magic* arrived on the big screen with an all-star cast. It gave the impression of being a lighthearted, fun film featuring two witch aunts (Stockard Channing and Diane Wiest) and their witch nieces (Sandra Bullock and Nicole Kidman). The strange thing about this family was that all their male partners seemed to be cursed with untimely deaths. As a result of her own husband's demise, the quiet niece, Sally, played by Bullock, avoids using her powers and decides she will never fall in love again. Her sister, Gillian, played by Kidman, leaves town, falls in love with a man who is abusive, and later abandons him and returns home. When the man stalks Gillian, her family conjures up a spell to kill him, and it seemingly works. However, he comes back to life, resulting in their hexing and killing him yet again. Meanwhile, Sally falls in love with the detective who is investigating the case (Aiden Quinn). In the finale, those who contributed to working the spell fly off the rooftop with open umbrellas, looking very much like Mary Poppins's clones. What is the message? Sally, an accomplice to the murder, marries the detective, and the audience is led to believe the women will not face negative sanctions for their actions. This message is contradictory to the religion and its main tenet, the Wiccan Rede, which states, "Harm none and do as thou wilt" as well as the aforementioned law of return. Although intriguing and sometimes amusing chants and spell casting are employed, this film mixes cold-blooded killing alongside lighthearted, semirealistic scenes. In this example of film commercialization, an overriding message is that witches are basically good and, as such, they can kill "bad" people and avoid punishment. These witches are neither frightening nor ugly; rather they are attractive, if slightly eccentric, nice people. The film's portrayal of witches is more positive than negative, as the group is credited with eliminating a dangerous man from the community and bringing the townspeople together. *Practical Magic* interweaves the duality of good witch–bad witch, with the good image winning out. This highly popular film signified a change in the commercialized representations of witches during a time when the religion had gained a considerably firmer hold in North America. While in some ways the commodification of Witchcraft in films became more realistic in the 1990s, in others, it became more fantastically unreal.

*The Blair Witch Project* (1999), for instance, offered a distorted and frightening view of witches. This widely touted low-budget film attracted record audiences, largely because the filmmakers set up an interactive website. The story revolves around three college youth who go off to the woods to find a legendary female witch, using a hand-held video camera to record their experiences. Although they do not believe the witch exists, they lose their course, become anxious, and eerie things begin to happen, especially at night. Soon they are on the edge of sanity, and one of them mysteriously disappears. The other two eventually discover the supposed witch's house, and one of them dies screaming; but the audience is never allowed to view the alleged "witch" or what happened. A highly suspenseful movie, *Blair Witch* sent a frightening message about the "evil" of an imagined witch. Its less popular sequel, *Blair Witch 2: Book of Shadows* (2000), even more appallingly confuses Witchcraft with Satanism when young people are "told" by the Blair Witch to murder campers and place their corpses in the shape of a pentagram. Filled with horrific imagery, the audience is left with the misinformed message that Witchcraft practitioners are really possessed Satanic murderers. The portrayal of witches in these films, who are presented as obsessed with killing, is completely unrelated to the religion of Witchcraft. This type of commodification is representative of the "fantasy, blood, and gore" genre, which harkens back to and perpetuates the "witch as Satanic" motif found in many horror films. While some film portrayals became more authentic in the 1990s, others, such as *Blair Witch,* do not recognize or characterize the Craft as a religion. Witchcraft, as commodifed by this film, serves to perpetuate misleading, negative stereotypes about the religion and its followers. The producers made a fine profit from the first *Blair Witch* film endeavor, and, even though the sequel did not do well at the box office, the proposed prequel was advertised and discussed extensively on the Web even after it had been permanently shelved (www.blair witch3.com).

*Children's Films*

Children's films are particularly illustrative of changing representations of Witchcraft and magic. In contrast to fantasy genre films such as *Oz*, recent children's films have portrayed magic and witchcraft as powers possessed by humans to be used for the benefit of others. The film *Matilda* (1996) is a case in point. Matilda is a child who is "different" because she is extremely bright and has unusual abilities. She teaches herself to read at age three, much to the dismay of her parents who only want her to watch television with them. In fact, they consider her such a bother that they send her away to a school where the female principal loves to torture children by throwing them out the window or locking them in the "chokie," a closet filled with huge spikes. A school teacher, Miss Honey, recognizes Matilda's brilliance and soon befriends her. While the children endure the principal's spite, Matilda discovers she has "powers" to move objects, and ultimately she uses her supernatural resources to foil the nasty principal, convincing her to leave town. Thus, the child's magical abilities enable all her classmates to escape the horrible conditions they were enduring at school. In the end, Matilda finds an agreeable way for Miss Honey to adopt her, and they live happily ever after. In this film, the good-bad dichotomy is apparent, and magic is viewed as a power that even little girls can use to overcome evil. Matilda's character can be compared to Glinda the Good in *Oz*, although Matilda is a child who teaches herself to use these powers. This film's commodification of magic conveys the theme of girls' growing independence in the 1990s as well as themes of self-empowerment and the use of magic for beneficent results.

The positive portrayal of magic and supernatural powers is also apparent in *Harry Potter and the Sorcerer's Stone*, released in 2001 and adapted from J. K. Rowling's book of the same title. This fantastic story about magic and wizardry continues the good-bad, white-black magic dichotomy found in earlier children's stories, but with a twist. Harry is an unwitting wizard who is raised by a mean-spirited foster family, and after enduring their endless abuse, his true caretakers give Harry the opportunity to attend Hogwarts School, where he learns about magic. The film depicts Harry's educational adventures, including his ability to thwart those who use the dark arts. Significantly, one of Harry's female classmates, Hermione, proves to be the brightest, most dependable and resourceful of Harry's friends. The overriding morality message of *Harry Potter* is that the skillful use of magical powers can be positive and can overcome black magic. Extremist Christian groups, however, think that the *Potter* books and films are teaching children black magic, and some have tried to have the books banned from U.S. libraries. These groups have assailed the *Potter* series through a video titled *Harry Potter: Witchcraft Repackaged: Making Evil Look Innocent,* available on the Internet. According to the Lady Liberty League (winter 2001), a Pagan legal defense and referral service, this video is shown at "anti-Potter and anti-Pagan meetings" (www.circlesanctuary.org). This effort is likely in response to the tremendous growth of Wicca as well as to the presence of magic in the *Potter* book and film series.

TELEVISION PROGRAMS, POST-WICCA INFLUX

*Young Adult Situation Comedies and Fantasy Programs*
Much more pervasive than film, television is a popular source of information and images, both real and unreal, true and untrue. According to the Statistical Yearbook of the Economic Commission for Europe 2003, the United States had the highest rate of television receivers in the world in 2000, with 854 receivers per 1000 population (www.unece.org/stats/trend/ch11.htm). This translates into many hundreds of thousands of people who watch television regularly every day. Scholars of mass communication have noted that television sells audiences to advertisers, and audiences tend to accept the values and ideals portrayed by the ads and the programs they watch (Comstock 1999; Kilbourne 1999). Although one may take issue with these views, North Americans are unmistakably curious about Witchcraft and magic, and several fantasy genre programs premiered in the 1990s to satisfy their inquisitiveness. A sampling of programs oriented toward teenagers and young adults includes *Sabrina, the Teenage Witch; Charmed*; and *Buffy, the Vampire Slayer.*[7]

*Sabrina, the Teenage Witch* (1996) is a lighthearted situation comedy originating from a 1972 *Archie* comic book character. The program started with Sabrina as a curvy, blond high school student and witch who has newly discovered powers she wants to keep secret. Because she has not figured out how to harness her magic, she accidentally makes things happen, such as turning a schoolmate into a jigsaw puzzle. Each episode finds her in a predicament, but by the end of the show Sabrina learns from her mistakes. Even though Sabrina has moved out of her witch aunts' home and attends a nearby college, she continues to rely heavily on their advice as well as that of their cat, Salem. Sabrina can be viewed as a youthful descendent of Samantha; in fact, the comic version appeared the same year *Bewitched* stopped production. Although both women are blond and beautiful, Sam generally uses her powers with the best of intentions, while Sabrina's magic is out of control. Like Samantha and Jeannie, Sabrina's powers propel her into trouble; however, unlike her predecessors, she leads a considerably more independent life, due in large part to changes afforded by the women's liberation movement. The shift in television witches' characterization, following the attention given to Wicca in the late 1970s, is fairly straightforward: although this witch is significantly younger and less mature, she is part of a witch family that actually encourages her magical growth. Her sexuality is not subdued like Samantha's but is on display with leather hip huggers and crop top that bare her flat stomach, much like Jeannie's belly-dancing costume. This program highlights Sabrina's adventures as she learns magic through trial and error, and each episode has a morality lesson about using magical powers wisely. She is portrayed as a pretty, powerful, and playful young witch who has much to learn. This comedy program does not present witchcraft as a religion but rather as a collection of magical techniques that result in hilarious situations that must be remedied.

Another witch-themed program, *Charmed* (1998), features the Halliwell sisters who discover they are "charmed ones" and very powerful witches when they work together with "the power of three." Although they try to lead normal lives, each woman exhibits a different magical ability: one can freeze time, another can make objects move (telekinesis), and another can see into the future. They use their powers to protect innocent people who have been attacked or possessed by the demon Source, which in turn tries to eliminate the Witches' powers in order to kill them. The sisters rely on their supernatural resources to accomplish their goals, and in only one episode, when they are transported to the seventeenth century and have no access to these resources, do they learn to work with herbs, similar to many modern-day Witches. The women use incantations and create somewhat realistic magical altars, and yet it is their Hollywood-endowed magic that enables them to vanquish evil and save the day. This program portrays the sister Witches as continually confronting threatening situations that compel them to use their extraordinary powers for good.

Another popular dramatic series, *Buffy, the Vampire Slayer* (1997–present), features a beautiful young woman who, although not a Witch, has magical powers and supernatural strength that she uses to slay vampires, witches, and monsters. Buffy is an ex-cheerleader who relocates to Sunnydale after burning down her vampire-infested high school, only to discover that her new town is full of vampires. She meets the Watcher, a school librarian and vampire expert who guides and protects her on her path of vampire slaying. At the end of the first season, Buffy killed the Master, a six-hundred-year-old vampire, and since then she and her buddies, including Willow (a lesbian Witch), continue to rid Sunnydale of its vampires and demons. In spring 2002, Willow's powers were temporarily put on hold because she was becoming "addicted" to magic and took revenge on those who killed her girlfriend, an unethical act that was very unlike her. In the fall 2002 season, Willow was learning to control her magic and once again, use it for good.

The programs *Charmed* and *Buffy* share several parallel themes. Both depict their lead characters as young, beautiful women who use their considerable powers to counteract evil. Both recognize Witchcraft as a religion and respect the power associated with magic. And both share a gendered message that accompanies the portrayal of Witchcraft and magic in these programs: women can be strong and use their mystical powers for good, even though malevolent beings, often male, try to kill them. These programs can be viewed as a commentary on women gaining greater equality and power in the world as well as men's desire to stop it, enveloped in a

magical context. While these programs do not realistically portray the religion of Witchcraft, the commodified characterizations are not negative,
nor stereotypical, but rather they are overwhelmingly fantastic and positive,
with magic being used to combat pernicious forces. This message is one
that probably does not hurt the religion, although the use of supernatural
powers may concern some audiences, such as the extremist Christian
groups that wish to ban *Harry Potter* books and films.

*Children's Fantasy Television: Specials and Regular Programming*
Children's television differs considerably from programs targeting adult
populations. Producers portray children's subjects as less realistic, more fantastic, and often in the form of fairytales and cartoons. Stereotyped witches
appear in cartoons such as *Scooby Doo and the Witch's Ghost* (2000) as well
as *Tweety* and *Bugs Bunny* cartoons. More serious treatments of Witches
and magic in North America are found in abundance in commercial and
public television for children. A high quality case in point is *The Lion, the
Witch, and the Wardrobe*, based on C. S. Lewis's *Chronicles of Narnia* (1950),
which aired in 1967 and 1988 on PBS. The story follows four British
children who are sent to live with a relative during World War II. While
exploring the house, Lucy, the youngest, discovers a wardrobe that leads to
the magical land of Narnia. While looking for Lucy, her brother Edmund
accidentally meets the White Witch queen, who promises to make him
king if he brings his siblings to her. What he does not know is that she
maintains control over Narnia by turning her foes to stone and killing all
humans. Edmund sets out to retrieve his siblings, but the children realize
their brother is a traitor. With the help of giant beavers, they try to ensure
that Alsan the Lion is restored to his rightful position as the true king of
Narnia. After a battle between Alsan's followers and the queen's thugs,
Alsan sacrifices himself to save the deceitful boy from the White Witch.
After a few grief-stricken moments, the lion is revived by the Deeper
Magic of Narnia. Given C. S. Lewis's conversion to Catholicism, this story
is generally interpreted as a Christian allegory, complete with Resurrection.
Yet it imparts several messages about witches and magic. First, it suggests
that magic, much like prayer, is real and it ensures protection for good
children. Second, the story encourages children to use their imaginations
and to employ magic to fight for justice. The overriding message, however,
is that while witches may seem beautiful and generous on the surface, they
are really dishonest, untrustworthy, power hungry, and ultimately dangerous. This fairytale genre is typical in its portrayal of witches as nasty and
wicked, and yet, at the same time, it characterizes magic as something that
can be positive and can serve the needs of the greater good. Because the
altruistic forces win out, this example of commodification is overwhelmingly positive.

In 2002 the Canadian Broadcasting Corporation aired several regular programs focusing on witchcraft and magic specifically for young children and teens. These included *The Big Book of Spells*, a cartoon; *Worst Witch*, based on books by Jill Murphy; and *The Magician's House*. *Worst Witch* features a female version of Harry Potter, except the lead character is extraordinarily inept and the show focuses on her misadventures in "Miss Cackle's Academy for Witches." Another program, *The Magician's House*, is a children's television series in the tradition of the Chronicles of Narnia, where sorcerers time travel and animals talk. Based on award-winning books by William Corlett, "this fantastical family series is best described as The Lion, the Witch and the Wardrobe with an attitude" (www.telefilm .gc.ca/en/pd/tv/tv00/064.htm).[8] Since many of the programs show magical foibles, Witchcraft is shown as something that is learned and must be mastered, or there will be dire consequences. The positive portrayals of Witchcraft and magic, along with their increasing visibility in regular children's television programs, indicate that these subjects are becoming normalized through their commodification and popularization.

*Adult Drama Episodes Featuring Witchcraft and Magic*

As the religion of Wicca has become more popular in North American culture, it has appeared in select episodes of prime time television shows. As of the late 1990s, Witchcraft as a theme had filtered into prime time, hour-long dramatic television programs such as *JAG*, a program about the navy's judge advocate general system, and *Judging Amy*, a legal drama that focuses on a single mother who is also a juvenile court judge. In April 2000 *JAG* featured a story about a chief petty officer who was also a high priest in a Wiccan coven located on a military base. As the storyline revolves around a man accused of rape by a female coven member, a female undercover agent infiltrates the group. While investigating the case, she learns about the main beliefs of Wicca, the problems of religious discrimination that Wiccans face, and the difference between Witchcraft and Satanism. She also discovers that the accuser engaged in consensual sex but "cried rape" due to her sense of guilt. However, the agent eventually learns that the high priest raped a different woman from the coven, but the victim kept quiet, fearing it would give the religion a bad name. In the end the *JAG* team's case leads to the rapist's conviction. Although the focus of this program is based on an important issue that certain groups are confronting, it may lead viewers to mistakenly generalize this criminal behavior to all Wiccans. Overall, this episode provides the audience with a wealth of accurate information about some beliefs in modern-day Wicca while distorting other dimensions of the religion. The man is portrayed as a rapist *because* he's a Wiccan priest, *not* because he took advantage of his gendered position of power, which occurs throughout the larger society regardless of religious background. This type of commercialization is clearly a double-edged sword for religious tolerance in the sense that it gives insight into a few aspects of the religion's belief system, yet it showcases a highly problematic and stigmatizing incident as the storyline. Although this type of commodification may teach viewers some facts about the religion, it is also misleading, as the audience may be led to believe that sexual abuse is a part of all Wiccan covens, which is not true.

Another popular drama, *Judging Amy*, features juvenile court judge and single mother Amy Gray. In October 1999 an episode featured a Wiccan mother who lost custody of her child to the divorced father because of her adherence to Wicca. Since the possibility of losing child custody is a real and current problem for Wiccan parents, this episode was timely, though it provided a depiction of Wicca that justified the father's case. The mother is portrayed as slovenly and unworthy, and she is referred to as "a bad witch" by an expert witness from the religious defense league. The mother is persuaded, through hate mail and death threats, to give up custody of her child and to leave town. In the end Judge Gray makes a well-intentioned closing statement about intolerance and hatred, but the stereotypes and misleading information about Wiccans as unkempt and contemptible create an overriding negative message that could serve to bolster modern-day witch-hunts.

In another episode a beloved teacher was discovered to be a Witch, and, even though she did not impose her religion on anyone, she was fired for her religious affiliation. The fictional character was shown participating in a ritual in her yard where members of her school viewed the coven, and this led to her eventual suspension. The episode reflects real problems faced by Witches: between 1999 and 2002 at least three teachers were suspended or fired from their teaching positions, and several teens were harassed for their Wiccan beliefs. Additionally, teens were banned from wearing pentacle jewelry in some U.S. high schools in the late 1990s, until lawsuits were threatened. The fact that real cases involving Witchcraft are making debuts on prime time television is a statement about both the significance as well as the penetration of this religion in North American culture. Because viewers appear to be fascinated with Witchcraft, these programs likely draw excellent advertising revenues, regardless of the way in which the subject matter is portrayed. In other words, the commodification of Witchcraft is profitable, and it is probable that these semirealistic portrayals influence viewers' minds. While in some cases the typifications of Witchcraft in these programs are negative stereotypes and perpetuate unrealistic views, in other cases authentic information is relayed that might contribute to a better understanding of Witches. The dilemma is that commodification can result in a greater understanding of the religion as well as one that is distorted and inaccurate.

*Television Specials and News Programs*

Television specials in the 1990s to the present have given the subject of Witchcraft and magic serious treatment on the Discovery Channel, the History Channel, and other cable networks, especially around Halloween, thus making the religion more visible. The Canadian Broadcasting Corporation regularly offers the *Man Alive* series with a "level-headed investigation of the mosaic of religious and spiritual life" that, on occasion, includes Goddess Worship and magic (DuFresne 2002c).

In addition to documentaries and docudramas, television miniseries such as *Joan of Arc, Merlin,* and *The Mists of Avalon* draw wide viewing audiences with large numbers of Pagans, if this can be judged from Pagan list-serv discussions as well as comments on Pagan websites such as "The Witches' Voice" (www.witchvox.com). The miniseries *The Mists of Avalon* was adapted from Marion Zimmer Bradley's tremendously popular book of the same title found on every Pagan booklist. The *Mists of Avalon* (1982) is a fictional account of the Arthurian legends from a feminist point of view, starring Julianna Margolis, Angelica Huston, and Joan Allen, and showcasing sumptuous scenery and beautiful costumes. Margolis plays Morgaine le Fey, Arthur's sister, who is trained in Pagan Avalon and learns to develop magical powers. Her sister-in-law, played by Allen, becomes Christian and turns Morgaine's son against both her and King Arthur. Ultimately the boy kills Arthur. Again, the story is set up as good power versus bad power and, in this case, the Pagans come out looking much better than the bloodthirsty Christians. The Pagan community voiced their approval over the Internet. According to the Lady Liberty League, which tracks all things Pagan, the July 15, 2001, broadcast was "the highest rated show on basic cable for the week of July 9–15 and it was the highest rated mini-series premiere ever on TNT" (www.circlesanctuary.org). It appears that the sale of this mythical story of Paganism was profitable for the sponsors, as it was aired multiple times since the summer 2001 premiere. Whether this television production is indicative of an increased toleration for Paganism is unclear, as the fine actors and actresses, the scenery and period costumes, and the intriguing story all contribute to its popularity.

In addition to specials, commercial television news programs often attempt to interview "a real Witch" around Halloween. These interviews give the audience a sense of Witchcraft and may (or may not) disseminate realistic information about practitioners, depending upon the angle of the producers. For instance, on the Halloween 2000 episode of the CBS *Early Show,* Cheryl Sulyma-Masson, head of the Witches' League for Public Awareness, was interviewed. During the course of the program she was shown at her job in a veterinary clinic, at a Samhain Fair raising money to build a church, and leading a Spiral Dance of sixty people. Apparently, program developers have discovered that Witchcraft themes are both popular and lucrative, as practitioners tune in to see how Witches will be portrayed while non-Wiccans view out of sheer curiosity. This television special was positive in its depiction, focusing on the normalcy of the Witches' everyday existence as well as describing their religious lives. The attempt to discover authentic Witchcraft through media interviews may give viewers a more accurate understanding of Wiccan beliefs and practices.

By the same token, television producers may just as easily distort Witches' messages and mislead audiences, thereby perpetuating derogatory stereotypes. For instance, shortly after the *Early Show* aired, Sulya-Masson and another Witch were interviewed on *E! Talk Soup,* and they were introduced as "bitches" rather than Witches. The program became an opportunity for mockery when the hostess asked to see a photo of a "Witch baby," and then she screamed, "Burn it!" while the television crew laughed. Clearly the producers of *E!* had no interest in presenting an educational show; rather, they approached the subject matter by ridiculing the guests. This program was broadcast to millions, which translates into a highly profitable, albeit disrespectful, commodification of Witchcraft.

*Trade Books and Magazines*

Trade books and magazines have played an important role in spreading information about Witchcraft to the general public, reaching millions, and thus popularizing the religion through their publication. In 1951, after the repeal of England's Witchcraft Act, Britain's Gerald Gardner began discussing his beliefs on the radio and in his books, *Witchcraft Today* (1954) and *The Meaning of Witchcraft* (1959), which inspired a widespread interest in the Witchcraft religion. It was not until the 1970s, however, that Witchcraft began to gain acceptance as part of the religious potpourri of North America. From 1969 through the early 1970s, a huge wave of books on Witchcraft appeared, including Raymond Buckland's *Ancient and Modern Witchcraft* (1970), Stewart Farrar's *What Witches Do* (1971), and Doreen Valiente's *ABC's of Witchcraft* (1972). In this early period of increasing popularity, Craft books and paraphernalia were distributed through specialty shops such as occult, metaphysical, feminist, and holistic health bookstores. In 1979 two benchmark books appeared that held a strong appeal to women: Margot Adler's *Drawing down the Moon* (see also Adler 1997), a compendium of American Pagan and Wiccan groups, and Starhawk's *The Spiral Dance*, a book of rituals and magical exercises. These popular sources marked the dawning of an explosion of print publications on Witchcraft and magic, presumably in response to the demand by practitioners and curiosity seekers. Within a few decades, thousands of books steadily flooded the spirituality, esoteric, religion, New Age, and self-help sections in mainstream bookstores such as Borders and Barnes and Noble. Additionally, these booksellers began to offer an assortment of tarot decks, crystals, divination tools, and other Craft paraphernalia. By the early 1980s Witchcraft had not only arrived in mainstream North America, it also had found a very profitable niche in mainstream commercial culture. And once the World Wide Web took hold in the 1990s, Internet "surfers" curious about Witchcraft began filling their online "shopping carts" at www.Amazon .com and www.barnesandnoble.com.

Books on Witchcraft range from Witches' biographies to how-to books, fundamentals of Wicca, rituals and practices, Wiccan activities for children, Pagan parenting, and spell working for teens.[9] There is even a *Complete Idiot's Guide to Wicca and Witchcraft* (or *Paganism*) as well as *Witchcraft and the Web: Weaving Pagan Traditions Online* by M. Macha NightMare (2001) and *The Virtual Pagan,* a book full of Pagan websites that can be found at www .thevirtualpagan.org (2002). Wiccan ritual ceremonies marking life passages have filtered into the mainstream through self-help books such as *Rituals for Our Times* (Imber-Black and Roberts 1992), *Sacred Circles: A Guide to Creating Your Own Women's Spirituality Group* (Carnes and Craig, 1998), and *The Pagan Book of Living and Dying* (Starhawk and NightMare 1997).

In addition to nonfiction, a vast fiction literature exists, including the already mentioned *Mists of Avalon* and Robert Graves's mythopoetic religious history, *The White Goddess* ([1948] 2001), where he explores the relationship between poetry and the White Goddess, which he believes to be the earliest of European deities. Thousands of fiction and science fiction books address the topics of magic and Witchcraft and, increasingly, teenagers comprise a significant reading audience. A trio of teen Witchcraft fiction books, known as the Sweep Series,[10] chronicles the adventures of a teenaged girl, Morgan, who finds out she's a "blood" (hereditary) Witch. She learns to use her powers with the help of a new classmate, Cal, another blood Witch. The story is fascinating and integrates many authentic rituals wherein the neophytes meet at night in the woods with their new teacher, cast circles, practice magic, and begin to feel like a family. Morgan encounters power plays with her former best friend who lusts after Cal, becomes jealous of Morgan's powers, and begins practicing dark magic. The books are well written and somewhat realistic. However, other trade books trivialize and present false portrayals of Witchcraft and Paganism in the name of making a profit, and Pagans are quick to condemn these publications. The popularity and profitability of realistic as well as unrealistic publications is indicated by the appearance of hundreds of such books on the youth literature shelves in recent years. In fact, Llewellyn Publishing Company, which claims its books focus on self-help and personal transformation, boasts that *Teen Witch* by Silver RavenWolf is their second best seller (www.llewellyn.com 2002). Apparently teens want more control in their lives, and they feel that Wicca can give it to them. Like their baby boomer parents, young people are spiritual consumers, and this translates into the consumption of printed matter.


PAGAN NEWSLETTERS AND WEBSITES

Beyond books and magazines, other major sources of Witchcraft's commercialization include Pagan newsletters and Internet resources. Prior to the development of the Internet, Pagan newsletters catered to seekers and practitioners of Witchcraft and magic by offering relevant information, guidance, and products through the mail. Since the Web's appearance, however, most newsletters are now found on Pagan websites. For instance, *Circle Network News*, begun in 1978 by Selena Fox, founder of Circle Sanctuary, has evolved into the glossy *CIRCLE Magazine* (1999), and its articles are available on the Circle website (www.circlesanctuary.org). *CIRCLE* presents issues of interest to Wiccans and promotes Pagan events and activities such as festivals, conferences, and rituals. The magazine advertises books, jewelry, clothing, and Witchcraft paraphernalia and offers local classes in Witchcraft, herbs, and ritual. Another newsletter, *Of a Like Mind (OALM),* established in 1983, provided a networking resource for lesbian feminists and women who practice Goddess spirituality. Published by the Reformed Congregation of the Goddess, International (RCG-I), a Dianic Wiccan organization with a lesbian separatist and feminist political orientation, *OALM* featured Goddess-oriented articles and publicized local and international Pagan spirituality events with listings distinguished by gender composition. Like Circle Sanctuary, RCG-I's goals are largely educational. Its website advertises a Spirit Sisters study group as well as an Academy of Athena that provides on-site classes. The "Great Goddess Goods" section offers a selection of Wicca books, jewelry, music, and other paraphernalia,[11] while Goddess Travel is available for tours to ancient Goddess sites such as Malta. RCG-I houses the Women's Thealogical Institute and offers the Cella Study Program, a self-directed course of distance learning for women to "discover the inner mysteries of themselves and Goddess religion" using an individualized system of learning (www.rcgi.org/wti/cella.asp 2004).[12] The program requires an initial commitment of one year, including three weekend training sessions at one of its regional meeting bases. To complete the program and become an ordained priestess requires an additional five years of study.

Although *OALM* ceased publication in 2001, at least 100 Pagan newsletters, journals, and online news magazines can be located via the Internet, among them *Sage Woman, Woman of Power,*[13] *Virtual Pomegranate, PanGaia, Free Pagan Press, Pagan Pathways, New Moon Rising,* and, until spring 2002, *Green Egg.* The monthly Online journal *Pagan Review of Books at Pagan*

*Place* reviews Pagan and occult books, divination tools, and music. This plethora of print and electronic media all contribute to the spread of authentic Wicca as well as to its commodification. They offer relevant information about the religion of Witchcraft as well as referring interested readers to other resources, encouraging seekers to become more informed. Although these magazines sell merchandise for the Pagan religion, and therefore commodify Witchcraft and magic, this is not their sole purpose; in fact, their raison d'être is to provide educational and networking information about Paganism and Witchcraft to spiritual seekers and practitioners. This objective stands in contrast to the shallow commercialization of the Craft found in fictional trade books and mail-order catalogs.

While metaphysical, occult, and New Age bookshops cornered the market on books and Witchcraft-related ceremonial paraphernalia during the 1970s and early 1980s, mail-order catalogs such as *Sacred Source, Azure Green* (formerly *Abyss*), and *Pyramid Collection* soon emerged to sell Pagan and New Age supplies and clothing. The advent of the World Wide Web in the early 1990s, however, shifted the concentration of Witchcraft commodification to Internet websites. The Web has become a major resource for the proliferation of Pagan merchandise and information about Witchcraft and magic as well as the building of a Pagan spiritual community (Nightmare 2001).[14] One website, The Witches' Voice (www.witchvox .com) proclaims in its 1997 mission statement: "The Witches' Voice is a proactive educational network dedicated to correcting misinformation about Pagans, Heathens, Witches and Wiccans." This is a noncommercial site that lists nearly 8,000 Pagan links, over 4,000 listings for Pagan merchants, 4,600 local covens and groups as well as over 3,600 world events (June 2004). The site offers such things as information about Wiccan sabbats (holy days), an extensive listing of Witchcraft traditions, and up-to-date news about the world of Wicca. The Google search engine lists well over a million Pagan websites.[15] It is presumed that many of these sites have a commercial aspect: they most likely sell books or magical commodities such as potions, jewelry, crystals, Runes, cauldrons, chalices, candles, smudge sticks, other magical tools, and clothing. For instance, in June 2002, on the noncommercial "WitchVox" site, two young women were shown as having attended a Pagan function, and upon clicking on a photo, a website appeared offering the artist's hand-made ostrich egg chalices, priced from $295 to $650. Other websites offer distance learning classes on such topics as Witchcraft 101, Divination, and Women's Mysteries. In addition, a multitude of chat rooms and list-servs are available to curiosity seekers and practitioners. Together these Internet offerings not only help to advance the diffusion of the religion through educational resources but also contribute to its commercialization. For example, in May 2004, WitchVox.com received nearly three million page hits, with 792,226 unique Internet provider addresses (Jung 2004). Although the Witches' Voice website is noncommercial, its nearly 800,000 visitors *could* click onto links for commercial Pagan websites, thereby participating in and becoming potential consumers of Witchcraft's commodification on the Web. Pagans purchase items to "mark" themselves as Pagans and to affirm their spiritual identity. Preferred items include such things as crystals and goddesses, chalices and *athames,* exotic robes, and jewelry adorned with pentacles, moons, spirals, or snakes.

## WITCHCRAFT AND MAGIC IN MUSIC

Music is an important medium where Witchcraft and magic have historically been extolled as forbidden and alluring, mysterious and sexy, and more recently they are rendered as celebratory, nature oriented, life affirming, and sexual. Witchcraft and magic have long been commodified in music as well as in film, television, and printed matter. Prior to the 1970s, many popular song lyrics contained the words "magic," "spell" and variants on the word "witch." For instance, the theme song from the *Wizard of Oz* proclaimed, "Ding Dong, the Witch Is Dead," and Screamin' Jay Hawkins (1949) sang the very sensual blues song "I Put a Spell on You." Somewhat later, American Bandstand spun the (mostly gibberish) hit record "My Friend, the Witch Doctor," much to the delight of the younger set. Frank Sinatra and others crooned to "That Old Black Magic," "Witchcraft," and "Bewitched, Bothered, and Bewildered." After the 1970s, teenagers danced to the pop song "Love Potion Number Nine," while the Eagles chanted "Whoo-who, Witchy Woman." Fleetwood Mac had a *Black Magic Woman* album (1971), and Santana mesmerized hippies with the hit "She's a Black Magic Woman," while flower child Donovan whiningly intoned "Must Be the Season of the Witch." The songs about witchcraft and magic are too many to recount here, but it is clear that the lyrics portray Witchcraft and magic as something that is mysterious, perhaps deceptive, and definitely sexy.

Songs about Witchcraft have qualitatively changed along with the increasing growth of Wicca. Pagan vocal artists are writing and singing songs that extol their spirituality, much as Christian musicians do for their religion. For instance, Pagan audiotapes and CDs can be found on a myriad of websites, including Serpentine Music, which features links to Pagan Internet radio sites, such as the "Pagan Chant of the Month" page, Pagan rock bands on the web, and the Music of Witchcraft, a Witches' Voice website (2004). The Pagan Music website (www.Paganmusic.com) features links to "Wiccan/Pagan" websites and pages such as online Wiccan/Pagan stores, online Wiccan/Pagan "Friendly" stores, Wiccan/Pagan music, and

Wiccan/Pagan radio stations. MP3 stations abound and feature all types of Pagan music. For instance, Above a Star Earth Spirit Best MP3 World Music Mix includes folk ("Mother of the World" by Sharon Knight), Celtic ("The Druid Tree" by The Druid Tree), world fusion ("Moon Daughter" by Inannamusic), mood music ("Season of Mist" by The Changelings), pop ("Cool to Be a Witch-Pagan/Wiccan" by Alexian), and Goth ("Pagan Queen" by John McNair). There's also spiritual rock ("The Wheel" by Kari Tauring), Native American, and many more. MP3 listeners are enticed to click onto the Magickal Musickal Surfin Site where listeners can surf for new music while listening to Pagan music. A sampling of other "streaming music stations" include All Magickal Musickal MP3 Women, Best Earth Spirit Instrumentals ("Goth to African and Native American drumming to meditation music"), Book of Shadows ("more radical music focusing on the Wiccan faiths and lots of ritual music"), and Celtic Cauldron of Magickal Music (2002). Ladyslipper Records features women's spirituality and Goddess music groups such as Libana, Kiva, and Lisa Thiel. CDs and MP3 websites provide listeners with a multitude of choices that can further their interest in Wicca and Paganism or another spiritual path.

The explosion of Pagan music titles and lyrics in the last decade is indicative of a receptive and developing market that corresponds to the growth of the religion. Pagan practitioners and music enthusiasts readily purchase music that reflects their theology and connects them to fellow believers. Thus, the development of Pagan musical options has contributed to the commodification of the religion by providing CDs and audiotapes for a profit while at the same time helping to establish musical traditions that like-minded people can relate to and share, and which contribute to Pagans' spiritual identity.

## COMMODIFICATION AND THE EXCHANGE RELATIONSHIP

For those who wish to pursue Witchcraft, Wiccan websites can be invaluable resources of information about the religion as well as sites for new forms of spiritual community (see Dawson 2005; Hellend 2002). Ezzy (2001), however, warns that the consumerism inspired by some of these websites may change the religion of Witchcraft itself. He is most concerned about the possible suppression of Witchcraft's original objectives of personal development and self-responsibility and their replacement by the profit motive. Ezzy defines commodified Witchcraft as "a set of products inscribed with beliefs and practices broadly consistent with the religion of Witchcraft, but for which the dominant institutional goal is profit" (2001:34). He draws upon Carrier's (1991) analytical distinction between gifts and commodities to discuss the types of relationships involved in each;

for instance, with a gift there is a link between the "gift giver" and recipient, which engenders a sense of mutual trust and moral obligation. To the contrary, "commodity transactors are self-interested, independent individuals who exchange with people with whom they have no enduring links or obligations" (Carrier 1991:122). Thus, the *structure* of the exchange relationship reflects the meaning attached to it. In his examination of Witch websites, Ezzy contrasts varying degrees of the commodification of Witchcraft. A key part of his analysis relates to whether the website visitor is encouraged to seek out further information or to rely upon the website as the "expert authority." He further explains that the commodification of Witchcraft can promote consumption as a short-term Hedonistic way to deal with loneliness and isolation, devoid of the search for spiritual knowledge. For instance, a person surfing Wiccan websites might be enticed to purchase a book of spells to bring him or her love and then decide that the book alone is not enough and something else must be purchased to perform the magical spell. This exemplifies consumerism, which, according to Ezzy, "doesn't aim to satisfy needs. Rather, it aims to stimulate desire, but to never fully satisfy that desire" (2001: 38). Thus commodified Wicca stands in distinction to the personal growth goals of Witchcraft as well as the structure through which it has traditionally been transmitted, in a face-to-face relationship with an experienced teacher whose guidance is paramount to one's learning. In his conclusion Ezzy cautions, "the stronger the influence of the market on Witchcraft, the greater likelihood that it will loose [*sic*] its critical political edge, and that it will tend to become instrumental and materialistic, rather than transformative and encouraging of self-discovery" (2001:43).

Whether this development in the religion is inevitable remains to be seen and may depend entirely upon the exchange context. While materialistic instrumentalism may be an overriding feature for most business conducted over the Internet, through the mail, or in bookstores, it is doubtful that paying a fee for activities and events such as Witch Camps, Mystery Schools, Pagan festivals, and Women's Music Festivals will create less of a personal and invested exchange for participants. Rather, participants may experience a greater degree of personal investment and spiritual commitment when they engage in a weekend, week-long, or year(s)-long program for which they pay. Put differently, even though money is exchanged and someone is making a profit by providing Witchcraft training, this is not the commodification that Ezzy describes. Instead, unlike Carrier's "commodity transactors" who impersonally purchase products, attendees engage in face-to-face interaction with Witch Camp owners and teachers, distinguishing their exchange relationship from that of commodification. Thus, the fear that the religion will significantly change its focus is not likely to be realized in contexts where people are exchanging money to further their religious-spiritual training and where interpersonal contact plays a role. Clearly, those who offer such services are in business to make a profit, yet profit seems not to be their "dominant institutional goal"; rather, they are responding to the very real market that Witches and Pagans comprise.

## WITCH CAMPS, MYSTERY SCHOOLS, PAGAN FESTIVALS, AND WOMEN'S MUSIC FESTIVALS

### Witch Camps and Mystery Schools

Witch Camps provide fee-based training for Witches, Pagans, and other seekers. Organized around the beliefs of the Craft, the activities are led by qualified Witches who help participants to explore their psyches, to realize their connection with others and the natural world, and to live responsibly. One such camp, facilitated by the Reclaiming Collective, is held at a variety of geographical sites throughout the year in North America. Diana's Grove in southern Missouri hosts an annual Reclaiming Witch Camp led by American and Canadian facilitators. The Grove offers gourmet food, drumming and dancing, and a ritual every night that culminates in a grand finale ritual at the end of the week. The heart of the teaching is known as "path work" and involves psychospiritual training accompanied by small-group "processing" (debriefing and reflection) each day. The nearly one hundred people who go through this week-long "work" may experience intense personal changes that extend into their interpersonal relations. Participants range in age from teens to seventies, while most are between the ages of twenty and sixty, and many return year after year.

While week-long Witch Camps are not free and are therefore commercial, the ones I attended focused on personal transformation. The type of relationship involved in paying for Witch Camp is very different from purchasing an impersonal commodity through a bookstore or over the Internet; the spiritual seeker pays for an experience with expert guides with whom a relationship is established. In other words, the structure of the relationship becomes that of seeker, who is a gift giver (purchaser) to the gift recipient (the business), with the seeker changing places with the Witch Camp owners as gift giver and recipient. To illustrate, the spiritual seeker pays the Witch Camp owners, the owners provide expert facilitators who guide and "gift" the seeker with insight and spiritual experiences, and, generally, a relational bond is formed.[16]

This is not to say that participants are uninvolved in commercial exchanges while at the camp. Naturally induced altered states of consciousness are common, and participants are often inspired to buy Pagan goods such as CDs, books, tarot decks, unusual clothing, and even drums. The structure of the monetary exchange is uncommon in the sense that vendors leave their cash boxes open while they are away, with a note asking that buyers write down what they purchased and that they deposit the correct amount. All participants are asked to keep track of their Grove purchases and pay before leaving the premises at the end of the week. Even the commercial aspects of Witch Camp and the Grove can be characterized as similar to a gift giver–recipient exchange, and this type of relationship is found in other Wiccan activities and training such as Mystery Schools.

*Mystery School at Diana's Grove*
Although Diana's Grove is the physical site of the Witch Camp, that is not its primary focus. Co-owners Patricia and Cynthia offer year-round Mystery School and leadership training and spirituality events on their more than one hundred acres of land as well as online Mystery School training for those who can't afford the time or money to regularly travel to this remote location. The year-long on-site training includes several weekends and week-long sessions, or participants can choose to receive monthly packets in the comfort of their homes, using the Internet for discussions.[17] The Grove owners are trained in psychology and have created a sustainable alternative community based on myths, Gods and Goddesses, astrology, tarot, drumming, and sacred theater. Their 2002 Mystery School brochure states: "Through myth we can restore ourselves. We can restore our relationship with the world and each other. That is what Mystery School is all about." The 2004 brochure describes Mystery School succinctly as "a year of self-discovery and mystical thinking."

The Grove's raison d'être is to provide an "off-the-grid back-to-the-land sanctuary" where skilled training fosters the development of responsible spiritual community. The number of Mystery School participants has grown steadily, from 15 in 1996 to 280 in their tenth year of existence (Canyonhawk 2004). A significant number volunteer their time and talents, and many financially support the Grove's work. Some individuals have even built homes on the land. Participants do not see the Grove as a commercial venture based on profit; rather, they have established a committed reciprocal relationship with Cynthia and Patricia, they make contributions to the Grove as one would to a favored charity, and they receive spiritual nourishment in return for their membership in this spiritual community.

## REFORMED CONGREGATION OF THE GODDESS, INTERNATIONAL

Samantha Jade River is cofounder of the Re-formed Congregation of the Goddess, International (RCG-I), a tax-exempt religious organization that caters to Goddess women. RCG-I sponsors a summer retreat and offers the

Cella Priestess training program. The Goddess–Witch Camp is a weekend gathering of Dianic Witches and potential recruits in a wooded setting, complete with workshops on Dianic beliefs, practices, and ethics. A small number of vendors sell runes, crystals, clothing, books, and other magical paraphernalia. When I attended the camp in the early 1990s, the weekend included opening and closing rituals, and workshops on topics such as homosexuality and bisexuality, recovery from abuse, divination, and Goddesses. I later interviewed several women I met there, and as a result of their positive camp experience, they began using Dianic Wicca as a complement to their Alcoholics Anonymous recovery program (see Foltz 2000). This weekend camp is a small part of RCG-I; it also offers a one- or six-year priestess training called Cella. Participants are expected to co-create their program of study involving distance learning and face-to-face contact with an advisor for three weekends annually over a period of six years.[18] Establishing a personal relationship between trainee-initiate and advisor is an indispensable part of the Cella training, and therefore, like the Grove's Mystery School training, it differs from Ezzy's version of commodified Witchcraft. The primary goal of the Cella training is to guide the participants in their search for inner growth and personal transformation rather than to simply stimulate a desire to purchase commodities. The interpersonal interaction and spiritual nurturance fostered in these trainings comprise an important component, and they distinguish these learning relationships from simple commodity transactions. This is not to say that women and men who engage in these programs do not consume Pagan commodities—they do. Many believe in "walking the talk" and spending money on Pagan artifacts, clothing and jewelry, which are often one of a kind and hand-made by Pagan artisans.

*Pagan Festivals and Renaissance Fairs*
Pagan festivals and Renaissance fairs provide far-reaching resources for Pagan and non-Pagan artists and craftspersons to reach a wide consumer market. Hundreds of Pagan festivals take place in North America throughout the year (about one-tenth of these are in Canada) with most occurring during the warmer months. A prime example, the Pagan Spirit Gathering (PSG), is sponsored by Circle Sanctuary, one of the longest-running and most respected Pagan establishments in the U.S. Co-owners Selena Fox and Dennis Carpenter host seasonal celebrations on their Wisconsin land, but PSG, Circle's major annual event, is held in Ohio for a week of camping and community building over the summer solstice. Here people are encouraged to be part of a spiritual community by offering workshops, attending rituals and activities, and donating work shifts to the festival. Selena and Dennis, Pagan psychologists, have made PSG unique among such festivals by providing a space for Pagan scholars to network and share

their research.[19] In addition to Native American sweat lodges and other earth-based rituals, myriad workshops are offered such as astronomy, astrology, weather witchery, drumming, belly dancing, and body painting. Nightly bonfire drumming and dancing is a staple, and a costume ball is held near the end of the week. On the final Saturday night everyone contributes food to a shared ritual feast followed by a talent show that entertains attendees before the festival comes to a close.

The nearly one thousand PSG participants pay a nominal fee[20] to attend the festival and camp. Although inside the festival grounds attendees may choose not to spend their money, Merchants' Row serves as a popular hangout and networking area for potential customers, spiritual seekers, and Pagan practitioners. Vendors sell a variety of specialty merchandise such as cauldrons, crystal balls, chalices, ankle bracelets, toe rings, chain-mail outfits, elaborate cloaks, clothing, and ceremonial knives, and they donate a percentage of their proceeds to the festival coordinators. Here, Pagans can purchase a wide range of unique material goods that allow them to visibly present themselves as Pagans. Renaissance fairs can be viewed as natural extensions of Pagan festivals: the main difference is the focus on medieval times. Celtic and belly dancers, face painters, actors, and jousters provide some of the attractions, and patrons are encouraged to make entertainment donations. Pagan and non-Pagan vendors sell similar types of clothing, jewelry, and folk art found at Pagan festivals. These fairs often attract thousands of people each day, and vendors can make a considerable profit while satisfying consumers' desires.

*Women's Music Festivals*
A variety of women's music festivals attract similar vendors as the Pagan celebrations and Renaissance fairs. Two such Midwestern festivals are the National Women's Music Festival (NWMF) held in July at the Ohio State University campus in Columbus, Ohio,[21] and the Michigan Womyn's Music Festival (Michigan Fest), a week-long August campout event held in the woods in Western Michigan. The former is a weekend event attracting about three thousand attendees, while the Michigan Fest draws about five thousand to eight thousand women, including a significant Canadian representation. Although these festivals differ in length, location, and attendance, each offers a number of women's spirituality workshops that have been led by well-known Witches Margot Adler, Ruth Barrett, Zsuzsanna Budapest, Jade River, and Diane Stein. Music festivals have featured drummers Ubaka Hill and Layne Redmond, and both teach drum workshops that incorporate Goddess imagery and feminist spirituality.[22] In fact, drumming has become associated with Pagan spirituality, as both Pagan and women's festivals offer group drumming as a major activity, and, as a result, many drums are sold in these venues. Craftswomen, artists, and other ven-

dors (not necessarily Pagan) display their wares in the huge festival market-place. Vendors sell a wide assortment of jewelry made with Wiccan and New Age symbols such as Goddesses, pentacles, spirals, spiders and laby-rinths as well as handmade and specialty clothing, pillows, ceramics, fresh herbal remedies, smudge sticks, crystals, geodes, and other ceremonial paraphernalia. Because of the exposure to thousands of potential buyers, women's music festivals are highly profitable for vendors: the festival mar-ketplaces literally swarm with women who voraciously consume and dis-play their woman-made goods during the festivals.

Prior to the appearance of Pagan websites, festivals were one of the main places, besides occult bookstores, where people could shop for Wiccan wares and magical paraphernalia. Today, vendors work a circuit of these music festivals, Renaissance fairs, and Pagan spirituality events, and their websites give them the opportunity to reach customers the year round. Thus, vendors can participate in the Pagan community experience while at the same time meeting consumer demands for Pagan supplies and accessor-ies. Although the primary goal is to sell their wares, vendors engage in a face-to-face exchange relationship with potential buyers. The consumers, in turn, may experience a sense of camaraderie during their interactions and transactions with vendors. A shared worldview may be implied by things said and done during the transaction or through the type of item offered. Even though the vendor is there to make a profit, the patron may feel engaged in a more personalized relationship than found in a depart-ment store, particularly if the commodity is handcrafted or is somehow unique. Thus, the entrepreneurialism offered by festival vendors is qualita-tively different from the mass marketing of witchcraft found in mainstream society, and the word-of-mouth advertising they receive from satisfied cus-tomers increases their market (Pagan and non-Pagan) considerably.

## APPROPRIATING WITCHCRAFT SYMBOLISM IN MAINSTREAM ADVERTISING

Witchcraft and its symbols have a considerable history of appropriation by mainstream businesses; in fact, Halloween has long been one of the most celebrated and profitable holidays in North America, second only to Christmas. In both the U.S. and Canada, well before October, witch and wizard costumes, brooms, pointy hats, and warty-nosed green masks beckon to children from store shelves, along with stuffed witch figurines, banners and windsocks, talking witch heads, witch dolls, cups, sweatshirts, and puppets. Adults are cajoled by advertisers to join in the spirit of Hal-loween, not only by outfitting their children and their home's interiors but by purchasing multitudes of outdoor decorations such as pumpkin lights to hang from decks and fences, huge day-glow skeletons, ghosts, and witches for windows and trees, and giant spider webs to cover the shrubbery. Halloween is a tremendously successful commercial venture that persuades people to masquerade as stereotypical witches, Casper the Ghost, or Harry Potter characters while encouraging hosts to purchase party items embellished with witches, ghosts, and black cats.

The extreme commercialization of Halloween and witches is insulting to many Pagans in their religious observance of Samhain, or Hallowmas, their spiritual new year. Samhain marks summer's end and the beginning of the "dark time" of the year, the time when the "veil between the worlds" is said to be very thin. Thus it marks a reverent occasion of communicating with beloved, deceased ancestors and encourages Pagans to re-examine their lives and to nurture future projects. This holy day stands in contrast to the commodified image of ugly witch hags raucously flying about on their brooms. To defuse this portrayal, many Pagans give media interviews. This is not to negate the fact, however, that many Pagans and Witches engage in the rampant consumerism of witch kitsch that is emblematic of this time of year. Pagans buy six-foot doll witches on brooms to hang from their trees or decks, while some purchase sock witches-in-a-cup for their workplace desks, and others buy "witchy" lights for their homes and yards. Others make it a point to attend Samhain rituals in full stereotypical witch dress, complete with black wig, long flowing robe, a pointy hat, and face painted for the occasion. Whether one chooses to identify as a Witch, make fun of stereotypical images, or simply join in the freedom-to-be-anything that Halloween permits, Witches comprise a significant portion of the Halloween market.

Although stereotyped images of witches abound during the fall months, symbols of Witchcraft pervade mainstream material culture regardless of the season. Such symbols include the moon, associated with the cycles of women and nature; Goddess figures, representing the female divine; the five-pointed star, or pentacle, representing the human body along with its spiritual connection; spirals, related to the shape of DNA; snakes, connoting spiritual wisdom and regeneration; and spiders, representing the Web of Life (see Lozano and Foltz 1990). The most popular symbols are the moon and stars, celestial motifs that are also present in the New Age movement.

Perhaps the most obvious commodity appropriating Witchcraft symbolism is jewelry, as most major department stores and catalogs carry moon and star pins, rings, bracelets, pendants, earrings, and even toe rings. Beyond jewelry, the numbers and kinds of objects bedecked with Wiccan symbols is awe inspiring. Mail-order catalogs, television ads, and Sunday newspaper advertisement sections sell moon and stars socks, slippers, robes, linens, comforters, towels, shower curtains, and window dressings. Select shoe stores carry moon and stars tennis shoes, and pet stores sell purple star-studded dog sweaters. The *Wireless* catalog offers a white star-shaped baby bunting complete with gold tassel sprouting from the top point and a shiny gold star forming the front closure. Other catalogs offer items such as a sun and moon birdhouse, a "Fishing Goddess" sweatshirt, and a "Night Stars" nightstand covered in glow-in-the-dark stars and moons on a blue background. *Frontgate,* an upscale outdoor furniture catalog, advertises a "Sun and Moon Fire Pit," a huge cauldron-shaped device with crescent moons cut into its metal sides, for "years of open pit barbecue feasts and blazing bonfires," for $399. While feasts and bonfires are commonplace in Pagan ceremonies, in this ad Witchcraft symbolism is aimed to appeal to the financially comfortable. In 2002, Pontiac named its new model car the Solstice. Unlike the Bronco, Lynx, and Mustang models, which connote fast, powerful animals, solstices refer to holy days in the Witches' year. Since Wiccan motifs and language have become a part of profitable North American mass marketing, I concur with Donovan that it "must be the season of the Witch."

## DISCUSSION AND IMPLICATIONS

A growing commodification of Wicca has been observed since the religion has taken hold and expanded in North America. Wicca has become an increasingly popular subject matter in television, films, and books, and the representation of witches has been significantly transformed over time. Televised portrayals of witch roles have changed considerably from the 1960s when Samantha of *Bewitched* played the good wife and mother who used her magic surreptitiously to set things right within her family's world. This domesticated role stands in contrast to the 1990s roles of television witches in *Sabrina, Charmed,* and *Buffy,* all of whom are young, vibrant, and endowed with magical powers. Although Sabrina shares some characteristics with her earlier incarnations—she is blond, beautiful, and makes magical mistakes—she differs in others as a single, independent college student who unabashedly experiments with magic. Sabrina's television contemporaries, the Halliwell sisters and Buffy, represent more serious, stronger characters who are rendered as young, sexy, and capable and who use their powers to destroy malevolent beings. Generally, the forces of evil are characterized as male, mirroring the male backlash that has accompanied women's advances. The contrast in the representation of witches, pre- and post-Witchcraft influx, is compelling: whereas they were once depicted as ugly old hags who were powerful and mean or as beautiful creatures who used their powers to catch or keep a man (such as Gil, Sam, and Jeannie), since the influx of Witchcraft, they are overwhelmingly portrayed as beautiful, youthful, and independent women who use their magical powers for the greater good, even if it means killing the enemy. To illustrate this point, in the 2004 *Buffy* finale, Willow the Witch cast a spell that gave every girl the option to be a Slayer and to fight evil.[23] The contemporary commodified characterizations of Witches emphasizing respect for the strong, wise female protector figure, is reflective of the Wiccan religion as well as of women's greater access to equality and power in the world.

The fact that dramatic television shows are featuring Witchcraft as a theme indicates significant audience interest in this subject and profitability for producers. The Witch-themed episodes focus on realistic problems arising in the Wiccan community, such as child custody issues or losing a job because of one's religion. Although the depictions incorporate some realistic aspects of the Craft, they negatively skew others, giving an overall representation that is often misleading and inaccurate. This commodification of Witchcraft has dual results: while it informs large audiences about some of the Craft's religious beliefs and practices, at the same time, it may characterize the religion and its practitioners in a distorted manner, thereby reinforcing stereotyped notions.

In contrast to television programs, films tend to send the message that (women) witches are either good or bad. For instance, *The Blair Witch Project* treats the imagined Blair witch as a bloodthirsty female killer, and *The Craft* depicts the teenaged witches as power-hungry maniacs who use magic to gain total control over others' lives. Yet films such as *Witches of Eastwick* and *Practical Magic* depict witches as having human qualities and using their powers to eliminate destructive males, sometimes with no negative consequences. The message seems to be that if witches (read: women) acquire too much power, they will try to take over, no one will be able to stop them, and worse yet, they will not be held responsible for their actions. Thus, while the commodification of Witchcraft in television and film offers North Americans some familiarization with the Craft, its characterization of women and the religion itself is often negatively biased and disingenuous.

Nonfiction books on Wicca have increased tremendously along with the growth of the religion, and this type of commodification has, in many cases, served to transmit more accurate information about the Craft. The effect of these publications and thousands of Wicca-based websites featuring information, products, music, and classes cannot be underestimated in the vast penetration of Witchcraft into North American culture.

Finally, it is clear that the marketplace has found a gold mine in Wiccan and celestial symbols such as moons, stars, and goddesses, widely available in mass-marketed jewelry, clothing, home fashions, and other merchandise. The act of visibly wearing a Goddess or pentacle pendant can be a statement about Wiccans' spirituality, similar to Catholics who wear a gold cross to proclaim their beliefs, with the important exception that the Pagan symbol challenges mainstream religion. While Pagan jewelry may hold profound spiritual meaning for Wiccan practitioners and even New Age adherents, for others, Wicca and its accoutrements have simply become fashion statements. For instance, among teenagers and the Goth subculture, wearing these items may hold no religious or spiritual connotation, similar to the hippie "wannabe" consumerists in the 1960s who wore love beads and leather fringed vests without embracing a countercultural political ideology.

Further, symbols of Witchcraft have been thoroughly co-opted and trivialized through mass advertising. For instance, in a Gillette television advertisement, the Schick Venus shaver is accompanied by the music "I'm your Venus, I'm your fire, at your desire," as if buying the razor will turn the user into a goddess of love. In contrast, Whirlpool appliance ads portray women as washing machine and refrigerator goddesses, leading one to wonder if washing clothes and preparing food are part of a goddess's "essential nature." Wealthy parents can purchase Bob Mackie's Moon Goddess Barbie ($198) for their little girls, or Mattel's Secret Spells Barbie trio[24] complete with magical accessories, while the women's clothing catalog *Junonia,* aimed at "majestic-sized" women, claims that it "takes its name from the goddess Juno—the protectress of the well-being of women." On a more utilitarian note, DuFresne (2002b) suggests that the symbol of the Paleolithic Goddess with huge pendulous breasts and giant thighs has reached iconic status as a logo in a "Big Is Beautiful" electronic discussion group and in a medical discussion website on bulimia and anorexia.[25] Here, Pagan Goddess symbolism is used to promote self-acceptance and to affirm women's inner beauty in a world where youthfulness and slimness are extolled as moral virtues. Clearly, Witchcraft and magic have been commodified in the extreme, with Pagan holy symbols co-opted, popularized, and sold to the masses. By the same token, Witches and Pagans comprise a significant market in their own right as they purchase ritual paraphernalia and jewelry, moon and stars shower curtains, and witch kitsch dolls, all the while creating and reifying their spiritual identity.

As Wicca's symbols penetrate North American culture through the media, and the spiritual community provided by Witch Camps, festivals, and the Internet grows, one would expect a parallel rise in tolerance for and acceptance of the religion. However, the conservative political climate in the United States in the early twenty-first century has elucidated fear and fanaticism about the subject of Witchcraft. Even if this is not replicated in Canada, the religion is also marginalized there. U.S. Religious Right leaders, including Rev. Jerry Falwell, have actively cautioned their congregations to avoid learning about Witchcraft while, at the same time they equate it with "Satanism," "evil" and "the work of the devil." A case in point occurred on the eve of the release of the film *Harry Potter and the*

*Chamber of Secrets* when a Maine minister tore up a *Harry Potter* book in front of his followers. Having claimed the *Potter* books were full of Witch-craft and Pagan religion, he stated, "You get involved in this, it's gonna make you dirty" (*Post-Tribune* 2002). This attitude has not permeated the entire society, as the popularity of the *Harry Potter* books and movies bear witness to. Recently my African-born physician commented that his eleven-year-old daughter identifies as a witch, because "in Harry Potter there are good witches." And thus, the moral duality of Witchcraft as dark or light, good or evil continues through the commodification of Witchcraft and magic. This duality is not uniquely applied to Wicca but can be seen as permeating North American culture.[26]

Since the 1970s North American culture has witnessed a huge growth in Pagan goods and services as well as increasing appearances of Witches in the mass media. The producers are the big "winners" in this development, as they have found a tremendously profitable overlapping market of Pagan and non-Pagan consumers. Although the past few decades have witnessed a burgeoning commodification of Witchcraft and magic, the net effect is not the religion's "normalization" but rather its trivialization, distortion, and a perpetuation of negative stereotypes that could prove dangerous to Wiccan practitioners.

# Notes

## INTRODUCTION

1. Throughout this text all the authors capitalize *Witch*, *Witchcraft*, *Pagan*, and *Paganism* when referring to the contemporary religion and leave the words lowercased when describing mythical, historical, or cross-cultural practices that are referred to by those names.

## CHAPTER I. NEW AGE AND MAGIC

1. For American Spiritualism, see Brandon 1983; Brown 1970; Hardinge [1869] 1970; Kerr 1973; Moore 1977; Nelson 1969; and Stemman 1976.
2. On the history and development of Theosophy, refer to B. Campbell 1980; Godwin 1994; Gertrude Marvin Williams 1946; Nethercot 1960 and 1963; Fuller 1988; C. Ryan 1975; and A. Taylor 1992.
3. For Gnosticism, see Bloom 1992; Couliano 1992; Jonas 1963; and Segal 1995. Originally an identifiable group of Jewish, Christian, and nominally pagan movements that became condemned by the Christian Church as heretical, Gnosticism assumes a radically transcendental interpretation of reality and the godhead. The means to salvation consists in the acquisition of *gnosis* ('knowledge') rather than through christological redemption.
4. Studies on New Thought include Dresser 1919; Melton 1990; and Parker 1973. As a loosely structured movement, New Thought emerged in the United States during the latter parts of the nineteenth century. It holds that true reality is spiritual, the material is mental error, and that the human essence or soul is a part of the Mind of God
5. Emphasis added.
6. Alice and Foster Bailey founded the Lucis Trust in 1922 to publish Alice's books as well as the journal *The Beacon*. The following year they established the Arcane School as an organization dedicated to unfolding the plans of the spiritual hierarchy known as the Great White Brotherhood. The Arcane School in turn sponsors such enterprises as World Goodwill, dedicated to service and humanitarian causes, and the Triangles Program, which operates through groups of three people dedicated to daily mediation. See York 1995b:63–66 and Melton et al. 1990:26–28.
7. Following historical convention, I have retained designating *paganism* in lower case for two reasons. First, I follow this custom elsewhere (e.g., York 2003) to stress the distinction of paganism as the root of religion and to differentiate it from the world's other religions. In many respects, I wish to re-appropriate the term in

much the same way as the customarily disparaging term *witch* has been reclaimed by modern adherents to designate a special religiosity in today's world. Second, *paganism* in lower case stresses the term as a generic rather than a specific religion. The term Neopagan, however, I do capitalize precisely because it may be recognized as a bona fide religion with specifically identifiable features.

8. MacLaine 1987:173–75; York 1995b:78.

9. For discussions on the history of magic, some recommendations include Cavendish 1989; Colquhoun 1975; Davis 1998; King 1990; McIntosh 1972; and Thorndike 1958. See also Greenwood 2000—especially for an understanding of magic as it affects the contemporary spiritual arena.

10. Boyer 2001; Sagan 1995.

11. Emphasis added.

12. I am here indebted to Sian Reid (Carleton University, Department of Sociology), who kindly allowed me to consult her unpublished dissertation, "Disorganized Religion: An Exploration of the Neopagan Craft in Canada."

## CHAPTER 2. WITCHCRAFT AND NEOPAGANISM

1. The 2000 U.S. census listed the population as 281,421,906.

2. Only one out of every five Canadian households was asked to complete the long survey that included question about religious affiliation (Reid 2001). The number of individuals who actually chose Pagan when completing the census was, therefore, 1,106.

3. Hutton (1999) attributes the term to a nineteenth-century Englishman, W. F. Barry, who used it disparagingly.

4. Murray wrote the introduction to *Witchcraft Today* (Gardner 1954).

5. Salomonsen (2002) claims the collective was formed in 1979, and NightMare with Willow (2002), one of the early members, contends that the collective began in 1980.

## CHAPTER 3. WEBS OF WOMEN

I am indebted to Robin Buyers, Lucie DuFresne, Chris Klassen, M. J. Patterson, Kate Slater, Johanna Stuckey, and Ghislaine Yergeau for their help with information on Canada.

1. That section within the AAR still flourishes today.

2. In the 1980s there was a community on an island off Vancouver made up of older lesbian women who had all taken the surname *Crone*. They published a magazine called *Web of Crones* for older lesbians and Wiccan women (Marron 1989).

3. When doing ethnographic research on a coven of feminist Witches in the late 1980s, I was early to a sabbat ritual and present when one of the women read aloud selections from Daly's book *Gyn/Ecology* and cried. Reading Daly's works was required for the coven's apprentices.

4. "a woman who Dares to counter the patriarchal deadly sin of deception: Coura-

geous Truth-sayer" (Daly 1987:165). Tracing the etymology of the word *wicked*, Daly claims that her *Wickedary* is a dictionary for Witches.

5. The night of April 30th is the ancient Walpurgis Eve in German folklore, when witches were said to hold celebrations to scare away the Christians who were trying to convert them. The date is also Beltane Eve, a sacred Wiccan festival that falls exactly between the equinox and the solstice.

6. Alternate ways of spelling the word *women*, such as womon, wimmin, womyn, were intended to indicate the separatist nature of the group. Men were even excluded from the word.

7. This book was republished in 1980, largely unchanged, as Budapest's *The Holy Book of Women's Mysteries*, vol. 1, revised ed. (Oakland, Calif.: Susan B. Anthony Coven No. 1).

8. There is also a form of feminist Witchcraft begun by Morgan McFarland in Texas in the early 1970s that called itself Dianic and included men. Its stated purpose was to train high priestesses, and although it never grew to the extent that Budapest's Dianic Craft did, it is still in existence and is currently known as the McFarland Dianic tradition.

9. This book's title is a play on the traditional Wiccan *Book of Shadows*.

10. This saying has also been attributed to the late Faery priest Gwydion Penderwen.

11. Patriarchy itself may be hexed as well, and I have often been in circles where I will hear "May Patriarchy fall for the good of all!"

12. At rituals where I have seen the hexing of an individual or a specific type of individual, it is done with the words "Change or die," thus presumably providing the rapist or child molester with a way of escaping the hex and, at the same time, putting the responsibility for it on him.

13. Bachofen's book was listed under "outstanding reference books" in *The Feminist Book of Light and Shadows*, along with those written by Leland and Graves.

14. Budapest et al. (1979:105) list it as an "outstanding reference book," and it was popular in Canada as well.

15. Technically, it was never about a matriarchy, the flip side of patriarchy, but about a more egalitarian, matrifocal or matricentric culture. However there were (and are) those who seem to believe that if men do not rule women, then women must rule men.

16. See, for example, *The Pomegranate: A New Journal of Neopagan Thought*, issues number 6, November 1998, and number 7, February 1999.

17. This was published in Canada the same year as *The Paradise Papers*.

18. Vol. 17, no. 1, 1983.

19. The women's spirituality movement has often been accused of addressing the concerns primarily of white women, so the approach taken by *Women and Power* was especially noteworthy.

20. Thanks to Johanna Stuckey (2002) for this insight.

21. I was told that Canadian Witches do make "a big fuss" over the return of the sun and that candles in a snow-filled forest are a lovely special treat. One Christian website from an island off British Columbia announces that the solstice celebrations are better attended there than the local church is (http://www.christianity online.com/ct/9tDD/9TD054.html, accessed January 19, 1999).

22. Some evangelical feminists struggled with language of the Bible; as the "word of God," it is supposed to be inviolate. But by couching radical ideas in fairly traditional terms, the Evangelical and Ecumenical Women's Caucus was able to de-sex the Divine. "We believe in God the Father Almighty, and in Jesus Christ his Son" became "We believe that God, the Creator and Ruler of All, has been self-renewed as the Trinity" (Coleman 1993:105–26).

23. For an excellent annotated bibliography, see Carson 1992.

24. I found this on several web pages as well. On one, created by a pastor of the Armenian Apostolic Church, there was also a "frowny" face and in large, bold type the word "yukkkk!"

25. Although this was said several months before the Re-Imaging Conference, reportedly 234 attendees at the conference were Roman Catholic (Cloud 2001).

26. I attended a funeral service for a young Jewish man in 2000 where the Reform rabbi said, "When we cry, the Shekhinah sheds tears with us."

## CHAPTER 4. SHAMANISM AND MAGIC

1. See also Jeanne Achterberg in Nicholson 1987:113. Rutherford (1986:15) mentions Diószegi's consideration of a derivation from an Indo-European root *sa-* 'to know' that suggests the shaman as 'one who knows.'

2. *Psychonaut* is a term that is used to describe a person who engages in exploration of consciousness using such Shamanic means as meditation, sleep-deprivation, fasting, psychotropic ingestion, and/or other forms of physical austerity.

3. The classical works on Shamanism are Shirokogoroff 1923 and 1980 as well as Eliade's *Le Chamanisme et les techniques de l'extase* (1951)—English version: Eliade 1964. Combining the Siberian focus with Finno-Ugrian forms of Shamanism, there is Casanowicz 1924; Czaplicka [1914] 1969; Diószegi 1968; Diószegi and Hoppál 1978; Hajdú 1975; Hatto 1970; Hoppál 1984 and 2001; Lehtinen 1986; Pentikäinen 2001; and Siikala 1978. Pentikäinen 2001 retains the same focus but extends it to include Hungarian, Greek, and modern, nontraditional invented forms.

    Some other key works on Shamanism in general include Blacker [1975] 1992 (on Japanese shamanism); Heissig 1980 (on Mongolian shamanic religion), Lewis 1971 (on ecstatic religion), and Rasmussen 1930 (on Iglulik Inuits).

4. See, in particular, Hoppál in Nicholson 1987 (82–93).

5. On the history of confrontation between Siberian shamanism and the Russian state, see Elena Glavatskaya in Pentikäinen 2001 (237–47).

6. For coverage of North American Amerindian forms of Shamanic practices, recommended works include Aberle 1966; Bean 1976; Brown 1953; Hovens 1981; Jilek 1982; LaBarre 1938 and 1972; and Park 1938. Among the works by self-proclaimed Native American spiritual leaders are Andrews 1981; Black Elk 1932; Medicine Eagle 2000; Sun Bear 1984; and Teish 1985.

7. See LaBarre 1972; Miller 1985; Mooney 1973; and Thornton 1986.

8. Harner's Center for Shamanic Studies was founded in Norwalk, Connecticut.

9. The classic exposition on soul-duality is Hultkrantz 1953. See also York 1999a or, on distinguishing the spirit from the soul, Rutherford 1986:81.
10. There are countless works that have appeared and are appearing on the parameters of psychonautic Shamanism. Two of the more popular contributions in North America are McKenna 1992 and Ott 1996.
11. Typical of the kind of popular book on urban shamanism, albeit of a more New Age inclination, are S. King 1990 and Telesco 2000.
12. See also Derrida 1987 as well as York [1996] 1999 61 and passim).
13. On 'complexity theory, see Eve et al. 1997 and Waldrop 1992.
14. These ideas are discussed further in Eve et al. 1997; Pirsig 1991; and Waldrop 1992. See also York 1999b.

CHAPTER 5. LUCUMÍ

1. Lucumí is also a dialect of the Yoruba language.
2. There is documentation of *cabildos* established as early as 1568.
3. The spirits of the dead.
4. As a rule in Afro-Caribbean cultures it is common to have allegiance to more than one religion.
5. The word *regla* is used in the same sense as the religious rules of the Catholic Church.
6. The concept of the Deus Otiose cannot describe the concept about God for this culture. Even though creation is under the management of the diverse Orichas/ Santos, God remains a force to be reckoned with. He is invoked at the beginning of every significant act in the religious tradition through his praise names, *Olofi, Olorun, Olodumare*.
7. Pataki is a sacred account. The corpus of stories contains the wisdom of the culture, and priests use it in divination to assert and diagnose problems.
8. The particle *olo* in God's praise names signals His absolute ownership.
9. The noun *santo* refers in popular Spanish to any object able to house supernatural energy and exercise its own volition. In that sense Lucumí culture makes a distinction between Catholic santos (those of the church) and African santos.
10. I will follow Lucumí spelling for the purpose of this work. Since Spanish lacks the sound *sh* it became *ch*. Hence all Yoruba words and names in Lucumí are spelled with *ch*. Some scholars favor the *sh* especially when writing in English. I believe, as a member of the culture that this is an imposition that misrepresents the Lucumí and accomplishes nothing.
11. *Palos* refers to trees and also to dry sticks used for magic and religious purposes.
12. Despite his role as the male counterpart of the earth, Oricha Oko is not considered the universal father that role belongs to Obatalá, the creator spirit
13. *Hacer santo*, or to make santo, refers to the consecration of an individual as a priest or priestess.
14. For information about deities not discussed in the chapter, see Bascom 1978, 1991; Thompson 1983; Murphy 1993; and Flores-Peña 1994.
15. These issues also encountered by the rest of the African Diaspora in the Western

Hemisphere manifested itself in different ways depending on historical and political conditions. The Spanish-speaking world still faces many of the same problems created by a society that considers Western culture as the measure for civilization.

16. Loosely translated as "son-of-a-bitch."

17. Orisha-Voodoo attempted to amalgamate both of the most powerful cultures of the Caribbean; Orisha, from Afro-Cuban tradition, and Voodoo (vodoun) from Haiti. The idea was to worship both pantheons as needed by the initiate.

18. Examples of this are the Orisha Temple in Puerto Rico founded in 1982 and the Church of the Lucumi Babalu Aye in Florida.

19. Similar groups exist in other countries.

20. There are other variants of Espiritismo such as Espiritismo Cruzado, which mixes Lucumí and Congo practices and pantheons.

21. This is also true in Florida among Haitian immigrants. The establishments that supply magico-religious services in these communities are also using the Spanish designation *botánica*.

### CHAPTER 7. THE COMMODIFICATION OF WITCHCRAFT

1. Although the terms *Wicca* and *Witchcraft* imply different types of training and mean different things to those who identify with each, the terms are used interchangeably with *Paganism* as a more reader-friendly device for the purposes of this chapter.

2. PBS showed *Kukla, Fran and Ollie* from 1969 to 1971, and CBS aired it from 1971 to 1979. ABC also ran the program for a short time (Brooks and Marsh 1999).

3. Although *Bewitched* ceased production in 1972, it currently airs several times a week on Nickelodeon. In 2002, the "Funtasia Bewitched Website" offered a *Bewitched* T.V. Tin bank, Samantha-on-a-broom sweatshirt, *Bewitched* black cat pumps, salt and pepper shakers, a *Bewitched* decal mug, and videos. The Barbie 2002 Collector Edition offers a "Barbie as Samantha from Bewitched," complete with the clothing worn by the animated Sam in the opening credits.

4. Jeannie websites sell online greeting cards, games, wallpaper, trivia, collectibles, rare photos, bottles, coffee mugs, and more. On January 11, 2002, Jeannie made a guest appearance on *Sabrina, the Teenage Witch*.

5. A member of the coven with whom I conducted participant observation in the late 1980s was a consultant for this film. She was extremely disappointed with the plot, over which she had no control.

6. The number three has magical connotations in Witchcraft and Paganism.

7. These programs, along with many Hollywood films, are available in English-speaking Canada. *Bewitched* is one of the few television programs translated into French, titled "Ma Sorciére Preferée" (DuFresne 2002d, personal communication).

8. Other programs, although not specifically focused on magic and Witchcraft, target Canadian adolescents. For instance, *Are You Afraid of the Dark?* features scary stories told by a group of teens around a campfire in the woods. Another hit is *Big Wolf on Campus*, where a high school football player is bitten by a werewolf, turns into one, and has to hide it from all but one friend who is "into" the occult.

9. In a local Barnes and Noble, I happened upon *Spells for Teenaged Witches: Get Your Way with Magical Powers* (Baker 2000) in the New Age/magical arts section. The back jacket claims to have an "anti-cramp spell," as well as spells for a "fantastic party" and "bully freeze." In a scan of the contents, I found a non-sensationalized, positive spiritual approach.

10. The series includes *The Book of Shadows*, *The Coven*, and *Blood Witch*, by Cate Tiernan (New York: Penguin Putnam Books, 2001).

11. Witchcraft paraphernalia include Goddess candleholders and candles, kitchen magnets, Witch patches, stamps, and bumper stickers with sayings like "Life is a Witch, and then you fly!"

12. The annual cost is based on a sliding scale, averaging about $380 per year (2002).

13. In May 2004, women at a Goddess gathering were bemoaning the cessation of Woman of Power.

14. Scholars of religion are addressing this issue; see Berger and Ezzy 2004; Dawson and Cowan 2004; Griffin 2004; Dawson 2005; Hellend 2002.

15. In June 2004, upon entering the term *Witch* into the google.com search engine, 4,650,000 sites were found, while the term *Witch website* brought only 803,000 sites, and the term *Witch websites* (plural) yielded 166,000 sites. The number of "Goddess" sites were 3,870,000, 712,000, and 177,000, respectively; and for "Pagan," 3,180,000, 460,000, and 128,000. The terms *witchcraft, feminist spirituality,* and *women's spirituality* produce fewer sites. It is difficult to assess what these numbers really mean, as websites are duplicated. Nonetheless, in tracking these websites between 2002 and 2004, there has been a significant two- to eight-fold increase.

16. Many spiritual teachers say that their protégés should pay for teachings, as well as charge for their own teaching time and talents, in order to fully value their talents or gifts.

17. In 2004 Diana's Grove weeklong intensives were $450; the weekends, $175; and the four-day or guest weekend, $195. Registration fees cover the cost of gourmet vegetarian and non-vegetarian food and beverages. Tenting is free, and there is a nominal charge for cabin space. Each program requires different combinations of week-long and weekend events. In 2002, web-based monthly study packets were $240 for the first person, and less if a family or small group wished to study together.

18. According to the RCG-I website (2002), the Cella training fees, with two years per cycle, or 18 weekends overall, are these: Cycle I = $355–$560; Cycle II = $340–$540; Cycle III = $265–$385 and the intensives are not included. The Cella weekend program is offered in eight different regions in the United States, with one near the Canadian border in Bellingham, Washington.

19. In May 2004 for the first time, RCG-I invited a group of Goddess scholars to meet and share research in a pre-gathering symposium prior to the annual weekend Goddess gathering and priestess ordination. These scholars are creating a university-sponsored Goddess scholars website.

20. The sliding scale was $150–$170 for adults in 2002; the late registration fee was $250 for the week in 2004.

21. Although the National Women's Music Festival was originally held at Indiana University's Bloomington campus for many years, it moved to Muncie and in

2003 to the Ohio State University campus in Columbus. In 2004 NWMF is celebrating its thirtieth anniversary; the Michigan festival is also nearly three decades old.

22. See Foltz 2003, 2004, and forthcoming for essays on spirituality and drumming. Ubaka Hill's CDs are titled *ShapeShifters* and *Dance the Spiral Dance*, while Layne Redmond's CDs include *Since the Beginning* with the Mob of Angels, *Being in Rhythm, Chanting the Chakras: The Roots of Awakening, Trance Union* (with Tommy Brunjes), and *Invoking the Muse* and her videos are *Ritual Drumming* and *Rhythmic Wisdom*. These artists have taught at Goddess-oriented venues, with Ubaka teaching weeklong intensives at Diana's Grove, the Michigan Womyn's Music Festival, and in British Columbia. Ubaka co-sponsors a weeklong women's drumming event ("The Happen'n' ") in upstate New York and founded the DrumSong Institute Museum and Archive of Women's Drumming Traditions. Layne Redmond has performed solo at the National Women's Festival while she and Tommy Brunjes have taught weekend workshops at Diana's Grove, as well as six-month intensives in Michigan, California, New York, North Carolina, and Florida.

23. Thanks to Wendy Griffin for this information.

24. Mattel Toys released Secret Spells Barbie "charm" dolls (Barbie, Kayla, and Christie) in late fall 2003. They come complete with magic potions, a magic mixing pot, and a magic pet. Average price on E-bay as of June 2004 is about $16 plus $7 shipping and handling per doll.

25. DuFresne reported that she located over 200 items featuring the Paleolithic Goddess figurine, including "jewelry, candles, altar tools, t-shirts, book covers, divination tools, corporate and NGO logos, trademarks, political banners, bumper stickers, tattoos (both permanent and temporary), stencils for wall painting, quilts, the Gillette Venus razor, garden statuary, landscaping, etc." within a week's time (DuFresne 2002b).

26. A good example of this duality is U.S. president George W. Bush, who publicly proclaims that he views the world's nations and people in black and white, as good or evil. He freely admits to calling upon his conservative Christian religion to guide his political decisions. See, for example, *Frontline*, "The Jesus Factor" April 29, 2004.

# Works Cited

Aberle, David F. 1966. *The Peyote Religion among the Navaho.* New York: Wenner-Glen Foundation for Anthropological Research.

Adler, Margot. 1979. *Drawing Down the Moon: Witches, Druids, Goddess-Worshippers, and Other Pagans in America Today.* Boston: Beacon Press.

———. 1986. *Drawing down the Moon: Witches, Druids, Goddess-Worshippers, and Other Pagans in America Today.* Revised and expanded ed. Boston: Beacon Press.

———. 1997. *Drawing down the Moon.* Revised and expanded ed. New York: Penguin/Arkana.

Alexander, Jane. 1989. "The Selling of the New Age." *i-D Magazine* 75 (November): 20–3.

Alfred, Randall. 1976. "The Church of Satan." In *The New Religious Consciousness,* ed. Robert N. Bellah and Charles Glock, 183–98. Berkeley and Los Angeles: University of California Press.

Anderson, Victor. 1996. "Interview." In *Being a Pagan: Druids, Wiccans, and Witches Today,* ed. Ellen Evert Hopman and Lawrence Bond, 76–88. Rochester, Vt.: Destiny Books.

Andrews, Lynn V. 1981. *Medicine Woman.* New York: Perennial Library.

Aquino, Michael A. 1975. *The Book of Coming Forth by Night: Analysis and Commentary.* Los Angeles: Temple of Set.

Attorney General's Commision on Pornography. 1986. *Final Report.* U.S. Department of Justice. Washington, D.C.: U.S. Government Printing Office, 1986.

Bainbridge, William Sims. 1978. *Satan's Power: A Deviant Psychotherapy Cult.* Berkeley and Los Angeles: University of California Press.

———. 1997. *The Sociology of Religious Movements.* New York: Routledge.

Baker, Marina. 2000. *Spells for Teenage Witches: Get Your Way with Magical Powers.* London: Kyle Cathie Ltd.

Barker, Eileen. 1984. *The Making of a Moonie: Choice or Brainwashing?* London: Blackwell.

Barker, Eileen, and Margit Warburg, eds. 1998. *New Religions and New Religiosity.* Aarhus: University Press.

Bascom, William. 1978. *Sixteen Cowries: Yoruba Divination from Africa to the New World.* Bloomington: Indiana University Press.

———. 1991. *Ifa Divination: Communication between Gods and Men in West Africa.* Bloomington: Indiana University Press.

Basil, Robert, ed. 1988. *Not Necessarily the New Age: Critical Essays.* New York: Prometheus.

Bean, Lowell John. 1976. "California Indian Shamanism and Folk Curing." In *American Folk Medicine,* ed. Warren D. Hand, 109–23. Berkeley and Los Angeles: University of California Press.

Becker, Howard. 1963. *The Outsiders.* New York: Free Press.

Beckford, James. 1984. "Holistic Imagery and Ethics in New Religious and Healing Movements." *Social Compass* 31:259–72.

———. 1992. "Religion and Modernity, Post-Modernity. In *Religion: Contemporary Issues,* ed. Bryan Wilson, 11–23. London: Bellew.

Bednarowski, Mary Farrell. 1992. "The New Age Movement and Feminist Spirituality: Overlapping Conversations at the End of the Century." In *Perspectives on the New Age,* ed. James Lewis and Gordon Melton, 167–78. Albany: State University of New York Press.

———. 1999. *The Religious Imagination of American Women.* Bloomington: Indiana University Press.

Benjamin, Gwen. 1998. *Re-Imagining Conference Minneapolis USA 1993 and Re-Imagining Follow Up in 1998.* Episcopalian/Anglican Women's Ministries. *http://ecusa.anglican.org/women/reimage.html.* Available February 4, 2002.

Bennett, David. 1988. *The Party of Fear: From Nativist Movements to the New Right in American History.* New York: Vintage Press.

Berger, Helen A. 1994. "Witches and Scientists." *Sociological Viewpoints* 10 (fall): 56–65.

Berger, Helen A. 1999. *A Community of Witches: Contemporary Neo-Paganism and Witchcraft in the United States.* Columbia: University of South Carolina Press.

Berger, Helen A., and Douglas Ezzy. 2004. "The Internet as Virtual Spiritual Community: Teen Witches in the United States and Australia." In *Religion Online: Finding Faith on the Internet,* ed. Lorne L. Dawson and Douglas E. Cowan, 175–88. New York: Routledge.

Berger, Helen A., Evan A. Leach, and Leigh S. Shaffer. 2003. *Voices from the Pagan Census: A National Survey of Witches and Neo-Pagans in the United States.* Columbia: University of South Carolina Press.

Berger, Peter L. 1954–55. "Sociological Study of Sectarianism." *Social Research* 21.4 (winter): 467–85.

Bergesen, Albert. 1984. *The Sacred and the Subversive: Political Witch-Hunts as National Rituals.* Washington, D.C.: Society for the Scientific Study of Religion.

Best, Joel. 1990. *Threatened Children: Rhetoric and Concern about Child-Victims.* Chicago: University of Chicago Press.

Bibby, Reginald. 1993. *Unknown Gods: The Ongoing Story of Religion in Canada.* Toronto: Stoddart.

Black Elk. 1932. *Black Elk Speaks.* New York: W. Morrow.

Blacker, Carmen. [1975] 1992. *The Catalpa Bow: A Study of Shamanistic Practices in Japan.* London: Mandala.

Bloch, Jon. 1998. *New Spirituality, Self, and Belonging: How New Agers and Neo-Pagans Talk about Themselves.* Westport, Conn.: Praeger.

Bloom, Harold. 1992. *The American Religion.* New York: Simon & Schuster.

———. 1996. *Omens of Millennium: The Gnosis of Angels, Dreams, and Resurrection.* London: Fourth Estate; New York: G. P. Putnam's Sons.

Bolívar Aróstegui, Natalia. 1990. *Los Orichas en Cuba.* Havana: Ediciones unión, Unión de Escritores y Artistas de Cuba.

Bonewits, Isaac. [1983] 2001. "The Original Open Letter from Isaac Bonewits." www.neopagan.net/originsadf.html

———. 1989. *Real Magic.* York Beach, Maine: Samuel Weisner.

———. 1996. "The Druid Revival in Modern America." In *The Druid Renaissance,* ed. Philip Carr-Gomm, 73–88. London: Thorsons.

Boyer, Pascal. 2001. *Religion Explained: The Human Instincts That Fashion Gods, Spirits and Ancestors.* London: Heinemann.

Brandon, Ruth. 1983. *The Spiritualists.* New York: Knopf.

Bromley, David G. 1991. "Satanism: The New Cult Scare." In *The Satanism Scare,* ed. James T. Richardson, Joel Best, and David G. Bromley, 49–72. New York: Aldine de Gruyter.

———. 1998. *The Politics of Religious Apostasy: The Role of Apostates in the Transformation of Religious Movements.* New York: Praeger.

Bromley, David G., and Edward F. Breschel. 1992. "General Population and Institutional Elite Support for Social Control of New Religious Movements: Evidence from National Survey Data." *Behavioral Sciences & the Law* 10.1:39–52.

Bromley, David G., Joel Best, and James T. Richardson. 1992. *The Satanism Scare.* New York: Aldine de Gruyter.

Bromley, David G., and Anson D. Shupe. 1981. *Strange Gods: The Great American Cult Scare.* Boston: Beacon Press.

Broner, Esther M. 1993. *The Telling.* San Francisco: HarperCollins.

Brooks, Tim, and Earle Marsh. 1999. *The Complete Directory to Prime Time Network and Cable TV Shows, 1946–Present.* Completely revised and updated. New York: Ballantine Books.

Brown, Joseph Epes, ed. 1953. *The Sacred Pipe: Black Elk's Account of the Seven Rites of the Oglala Sioux.* Norman: University of Oklahoma Press.

Brown, Slater. 1970. *The Heyday of Spiritualism.* New York: Hawthorn Books.

Budapest, Zsuzsanna. 1991. Videotaped interview by author, June 17.

Budapest, Zsuzsanna, Janet Roslund, Helen Hancken, Ann Doczi, Nina, Anna Kria, Tannie Braziel, Mildred Schmidtt, Miki Jackson, and Joya. 1979. *The Feminist Book of Lights and Shadows*. Oakland, Calif.: Susan B. Anthony Coven No. 1.

Buyers, Robin. 2002. Personal communication, February 4. Used with permission.

Campbell, Bruce F. 1980. *Ancient Wisdom Revived: A History of the Theosophical Movement*. Berkeley and Los Angeles: University of California Press.

Campbell, Colin B. 1972. "The Cult, the Cultic Milieu and Secularisation." In *A Sociological Yearbook of Religion in Britain 5,* ed. Michael Hill, 119–36. London: SCM Press.

Campion, Nicholas. 2000. "The Beginning of the Age of Aquarius." *Correlation* 19.1 (summer): 7–16.

Canadian Security Intelligence Service. 1999. "Doomsday Cults." Religious Tolerance. www.religioustolerance.org.

Capra, Fritjof. 1984. *The Tao of Physics*. Toronto: Bantam Books.

Caron, Charlotte. 1992. *To Make and Make Again: Feminist Ritual Thealogy*. New York: Crossroad.

Carrier, J. 1991. "Gifts, Commodities, and Social Relations: A Maussian View of Exchange." *Sociological Forum* 6: 119–36.

Carson, Anne. 1992. *Goddesses and Wise Women: The Literature of Feminist Spirituality 1980–1992*. Freedom, Calif.: Crossing Press.

Cartwright, Gary L. 1989. "The Work of the Devil." *Texas Monthly* 17 (June): 78–82, 152–56, 163.

Casanowicz, Immanuel Moses. 1924. *Shamanism of the Natives of Siberia*. Annual report. Washington, D.C.: Smithsonian Institution.

Castaneda, Carlos. 1968. *The Teachings of Don Juan: A Yaqui Way of Knowledge*. Berkeley and Los Angeles: University of California Press.

Castellanos, Jorge and Isabel Castellanos. 1992. *Cultura afrocubana: Las religiones y las lenguas*. Vol. 3. Miami: Ediciones Universal.

Cavendish, Richard. 1989. *The Encyclopedia of the Unexplained: Magic, Occultism, and Parapsychology*. London: Arkana.

Christ, Carol. 1982. "Why Women Need the Goddess: Phenomenological, Psychological, and Political Reflections." In *The Politics of Women's Spirituality*, ed. Charlene Spretnak, 71–86. Garden City, N.Y.: Anchor Press.

Christ, Carol, and Judith Plaskow. 1979. *Womenspirit Rising: A Feminist Reader in Religion*. San Francisco: Harper & Row.

Cloud, David W. 2001. *WCC Conference Honors Sophia Goddess, Gives Ovation to Lesbians*. Way of Life Literature's Fundamental Baptist Information Service. *http://www.wayoflife.org/fbns/reimaging.htm*. Available February 4, 2002.

Cohen, Stanley. 1972. *Folk Devils and Moral Panics*. Oxford: Blackwell.

Coleman, Lee. 1989. "Medical Examination for Sexual Abuse: Have We Been Misled?" *Issues in Child Abuse Accusations* 1.3: 1–9.

Coleman, Lee, and Patrick E. Clancy. 1990. "False Allegations of Child Sexual Abuse." *Criminal Justice* fall: 14–20, 43–47.

Coleman, Linda. 1993. "Ritual Creedal Language and the Statement of Faith of the Evangelical Women's Caucus. In *Women and Religious Ritual*, ed. Leslie Northup. Washington, D.C.: Pastoral Press.

Colquhoun, Ithell. 1975. *Sword of Wisdom: MacGregor Mathers and "The Golden Dawn."* New York: Putnam.

*Common Ground*. 1999. 100 (summer).

Comstock, George, and Erica Scharrer. 1999. *Television: What's on, Who's Watching, and What It Means*. San Diego: Academic Press.

Couliano, Ioan. 1992. *The Tree of Gnosis*. New York: Harper Collins.

Cowell, Alan. 1993. "Pope Issues Censure of 'Nature Worship' by Some Feminists." *New York Times*, July 5, 1:6.

Crowley, Vivianne. 1996. Reprint. *Wicca: The Old Religion in the New Millennium*. London: Thorsons/Harper Collins. Original edition, *Wicca: The Old Religion in the New Age*. Wellingborough: Aquarian Press, 1989.

———. 2000a. *First Directions*. London: Thorsons.

———. 2000b. "Healing in Wicca." In *Daughters of the Goddess: Studies of Healing, Identity, and Empowerment*, ed. Wendy Griffin, 151–65. Walnut Creek, Calif.: AltaMira Press.

Cunningham, Scott. 1988. *Wicca: A Guide for the Solitary Practitioner*. St. Paul, Minn.: Llewellyn Publications.

———. 1994. *Living Wicca: A Further Guide for the Solitary Practitioner*. St. Paul, Minn.: Llewellyn Publications.

Curott, Phyllis. 1998. *Book of Shadows: A Modern Woman's Journey into the Wisdom of Witchcraft and the Magic of the Goddess*. New York: Broadway Books.

Czaplicka, Marie Antoinette. [1914] / 1969. *Aboriginal Siberia: A Study in Social Anthropology*. Oxford: Clarendon Press.

Daly, Mary. 1992. *Outercourse*. San Francisco: Harper SanFrancisco.

Daly, Mary (with Jane Caputi). 1987. *Websters' First New Intergalactic Wickedary of the English Language*. Boston: Beacon Press.

Dart, John. 1985. *Los Angeles Times*, September 14, pt. II, p. 17.

Davis, Erik. 1998. *TechGnosis: Myth, Magic and Mysticism in the Age of Information*. New York: Harmony Books/Crown.

Dawson, Lorne. 2005. "Religion and the Internet: Presence, Problems, and Prospects." In *New Approaches to the Study of Religion*, ed. Peter

Antes, Armin Geertz, and Randi Warne. Berlin: Walter de Gruyter, forthcoming.

Dawson, Lorne, and Douglas E. Cowan, eds. 2004. *Religion Online: Finding Faith on the Internet.* New York: Routledge.

Demos, John Putnam. 1982. *Entertaining Satan: Witchcraft and the Cult of Early New England.* New York: Oxford University Press.

Derrida, Jacques. 1987. *Psyché: Inventions de l'autre.* Paris: Galilée.

Diamond, Sara. 1989. *Spiritual Warfare: The Resurgence of the Christian Right.* Boston: Sound End Press.

————. 1995. *Roads to Dominion.* New York: Guilford Press.

Diószegi, Vilmos. 1968. *Tracing Shamans in Siberia: The Story of an Ethnographical Research Expedition.* Oosterhout: Anthropological Publications.

Diószegi, Vilmos and Mihály Hoppál, eds. 1978. *Shamanism in Siberia.* Budapest: Akadémiai Kiadó.

Dresser, Horatio. 1919. *History of the New Thought Movement.* New York: T. Y. Crowell.

Drury, Nevill. 1989. *The Elements of Human Potential.* Shaftesbury: Element.

DuFresne, Lucie 2002a. Personal communication, March 5 and June 10. Used with permission.

————. 2002b. Personal communication, April 24.

————. 2002c. Personal communication, February.

————. 2002d. Personal communication, February 15.

Durkheim, Emile. [1895]. 1960. *The Division of Labor in Society.* Trans. George Simpson. New York: Free Press.

————. 1965. *The Elementary Form of Religious Life.* New York: Free Press.

Ehrenreich, Barbara, and Deirdre English. 1973. *Witches, Midwives, and Nurses: A history of women healers.* Old Westbury, N.Y.: Feminist Press.

Eliade, Mircea. 1964. *Shamanism: Archaic Techniques of Ecstasy.* Trans. W. R. Trask. Princeton, N.J.: Princeton University Press.

Eller, Cynthia. 1984. *Feminist Spirituality and Social Transformation.* M.A. thesis, University of Southern California.

————. 1993. *Living in the Lap of the Goddess: The Feminist Spirituality Movement in America.* New York: Crossroad Press.

Eve, Raymond A., Sara Horsfall, and Mary E. Lee, eds. 1997. *Chaos, Complexity, and Sociology: Myths, Models, and Theories.* Thousand Oaks, Calif.: Sage Publications.

Ezzy, Douglas. 2001. "The Commodification of Witchcraft." *Australian Religion Studies Review* 14.1: 31–44.

Ezzy, Douglas, and Helen A. Berger. 2003. "Ritual Technologies of Self-Transformation: Teenage Witchcraft in Australia and the United States." Presented at Heidelberg University, June.

Faber, M. D. 1996. *New Age Thinking: A Psychoanalytic Critique.* Ottawa: University of Ottawa Press.

FBI. 1999. *Project Megiddo.* CENSUR, www.cesnur.org.

Ferguson, Marilyn. 1987. *The Aquarian Conspiracy: Personal and Social Transformation in Our Time.* Los Angeles: J. P. Tarcher.

Finley, Nancy. 1991. "Political Activism and Feminist Spirituality." *Sociological Analysis* 52.4: 349–62.

Flores-Peña, Ysamur. 1994. *The Garments and Altar of Santeria: Speaking Without Voice.* Jackson: University Press of Mississippi.

Foltz, Tanice. 2000. "Thriving, Not Simply Surviving: Goddess Spirituality and Recovery from Alcoholism." In Daughters of the Goddess, ed. W. Griffin, 119–35. Walnut Creek, Calif.: Alta Mira Press.

———. 2003. "Women, Drumming and Community." *Journal of the Indiana Academy of the Social Sciences* 7: 100–109.

———. 2004. "Women's Spirituality, Drumming and Healing." Paper presented at the annual meeting of the Association for the Sociology of Religion, San Francisco, August 13–15.

———. Forthcoming. "Drumming and Re-enchantment: Creating Spiritual Community." In *Popular Spiritualities: The Politics of Contemporary Enchantment,* ed. L. Hume and K. McPhillips. Aldershot: Ashgate Publishing.

Fox, Matthew. 1999. "On the Path." *Common Ground 100,* summer: 127–56.

Fried, Albert. 1997. *McCarthyism: The Great American Red Scare.* New York: Oxford University Press.

Fuller, Jean Overton. 1988. *Blavatsky and Her Teachers: An Investigative Biography.* London: East-West Publications.

Gage, Matilda Joselyn. [1893] 1980. *Woman, Church, and State.* Watertown, Mass.: Persephone Press.

Galanter, Marc. 1989. *Cults: Faith, Healing and Coercion.* New York: Oxford University Press.

Galdman, Sharon Mae. 1988. *Harbingers and Healers: A Study of Contemporary Goddess Worshippers.* M.A. thesis, University of Calgary.

Gallup Organization. 1987. "Opinion Round-up." *Public Opinion,* July/August: 23.

Gardell, Mattias. 2001. "The New Romantics." *Intelligence Report of the Southern Poverty Law Center,* spring: 10.

Gardner, Gerald. 1954. *Witchcraft Today.* London: Rider.

———. [1954]. 1973. *Witchcraft Today.* Secaucus, N.J.: Citadel Press.

———. 1959. *The Meaning of Witchcraft.* London: Aquarian Press.

Gibbons, Jenny. 1998. "Recent Developments in the Study of the Great European Witch Hunt." *The Pomegranate,* issue 5 (August): 2–17.

Gimbatus, Marija. 1989. *The Language of the Goddess*. San Francisco: Harper & Row.

———. 1974. *The Gods and Goddesses of Old Europe, 7000 to 3500 BC: Myths, Legends and Cult Images*. Berkley and Los Angeles: University of California Press.

Godwin, Joscelyn. 1994. *The Theosophical Enlightenment* Albany: State University of New York Press.

Goldenberg, Naomi. 1979. *Changing of the Gods: Feminism and the End of Traditional Religion*. Boston: Beacon Press.

Goode, Erich. 2000. *Paranormal Beliefs: A Sociological Introduction*. Prospect Heights, Ill.: Waveland Press.

Goode, Erich, and Nachman Ben Yehuda. 1994. *Moral Panics: The Social Construction of Deviance*. London: Blackwell.

Graves, Robert. [1948] 2001. *The White Goddess*. Newe York: Farrar, Straus, and Giroux.

Green, Thomas A. 1991. "Accusations of Satanism and Racial Tensions in the Matamoros Cult Murders." In *The Satanism Scare,* ed. James T. Richardson, Joel Best, and David G. Bromley, 221–36. New York: Aldine de Gruyter.

Greenwood, Susan. 2000. *Magic, Witchcraft and the Otherworld: An Anthropology*. New York: Berg.

Griffin, Wendy. 1995. "The Embodied Goddess: Feminist Witchcraft and Female Divinity." *Sociology of Religion* 56.1 (spring): 35–48.

———, ed. 2000. *Daughters of the Goddess: Studies of Healing, Identity and Empowerment*. Walnut Creek, Calif.: AltaMira Press.

———. 2002a. "Goddess Spirituality and Wicca." In *Her Voice, Her Faith: Women Speak on World Religions*, ed. Arvind Sharma and Katherine Young. Boulder, Colo.: Westview Press.

———. 2002b. "Weaving the Web: Witches On-Line." Presented at the Association for the Sociology of Religion meetings in Annaheim, Calif.

———. 2004. "The Goddess Net." In *Religion Online: Finding Faith on the Internet,* ed. L. L. Dawson and D. E. Cowan, 189–203. New York: Routledge.

Griffin, Lozano, Wendy, and Tanice G. Foltz. 2001. "Into the Darkness: An Ethnographic Study of Witchcraft and Death." In *Extreme Methods,* ed. J. M. Miller and R. Tewksbury, 155–67. Needham Heights, Mass.: Allyn and Bacon. Originally published in *Qualitative Sociology* 13.3 (1990): 211–34.

Gross, Rita. 1996. *Feminism and Religion*. Boston: Beacon Press.

Hajdú, Péter, ed. 1975. *Ancient Cultures of the Uralian Peoples*. Budapest: Corvina.

Hall, John. 1995. "Public Narratives and the Apocalyptic Sect." In *Arma-*

*geddon in Waco: Critical Perspectives on the Branch Davidian Conflict,* ed. Stuart A. Wright, 201–35. Chicago: University of Chicago Press.

Hall, John, Philip Schuyler, and Sylvia Trinh. 2000. *Apocalypse Observed: Religion and Violence in Japan, Europe and North America.* New York: Routledge.

Hall, Stuart, Chris Critter, Tony Jefferson, John Clarke, and Brian Roberts. 1978. *Policing the Crisis: Mugging, the State, and Law and Order.* London: Macmillan.

Hanegraaff, Wouter J. 1996. *New Age Religion and Western Culture: Esotericism in the Mirror of Secular Thought.* Leiden: Brill.

Hardinge, Emma. [1869] 1970. *Modern American Spiritualism.* Hyde Park, N.Y.: University Books.

Harner, Michael J. 1982. *The Way of the Shaman: A Guide to Power and Healing.* New York: Bantam. Original edition, San Francisco: Harper & Row, 1980.

————, ed. 1973. *Hallucinogens and Shamanism.* New York: Oxford University Press.

Harvey, Graham. 1997. *Contemporary Paganism: Listening People, Speaking Earth.* New York: New York University Press.

Hatto, Arthur T. 1970. *Shamanism and Epic Poetry in Northern Asia.* London: University of London.

Heelas, Paul. 1996. *The New Age Movement: The Celebration of the Self and the Sacralization of Modernity.* Oxford: Blackwell.

Hellend, Christopher. 2002. "Surfing for Salvation." *Religion* 32.4: 293–302. Available online at www.idealibrary.com and www.academicpress.com/religion.

Heissige, Walther. 1980. *The Religions of Mongolia.* Berkeley: University of California Press.

Heyward, Carter. 1989. *Touching Our Strength: The Erotic as Power and the Love of God.* San Francisco: Harper & Row.

Hoppál, Mihály. 2001. *The Book of Shamans: Shamanism in Eurasia.* Luzern: Motovun.

————, ed. 1984. *Shamanism in Eurasia.* Gottingen: Edition Herodot.

Hovens, Pieter, ed. 1981. *North American Indian Studies.* Gottingen: Edition Herodot.

Huizinga, Johan. 1950. *Homo Ludens: A Study of the Play Element in Culture.* Boston: Beacon Press.

Hultkrantz, Ake. 1953. *Conceptions of the Soul among North American Indians: A Study in Religious Ethnology.* Stockholm: Statens Etnografiska Museum.

Hurtak, James Jacob. 1987. *The Book of Knowledge: The Keys of Enoch.* 3rd ed. Los Gatos: Academy for Future Science.

Hutton, Ronald. 1997. "The Neolithic Great Goddess: A Study in Modern

Tradition." *The Pomegranite: A New Journal of Neopagan Thought.* 2 (August): 22–35.

———. 1999. *The Triumph of the Moon: A History of Modern Pagan Witchcraft.* New York: Oxford University Press.

Jacobs, Calude F., and Andrew J. Kaslow. 1991. *The Spiritual Churches of New Orleans: Origins, Beliefs, and Rituals of an African-American Religion.* Knoxville: University of Tennessee Press.

Jacobs, Janet L. 1990. "Women-Centered Healing Rites: A Study of Alienation and Reintegration." In *In Gods We Trust: New Patterns of Religious Pluralism in America,* 2nd ed., edition, ed. Thomas Robbins and Dick Anthony, 373–83. New Brunswick, N.J.: Transaction Publishers.

Jenkins, Philip. 1992. *Intimate Enemies: Moral Panics in Contemporary Britain.* New York: Aldine de Gruyter.

Jenkins, Philip, and Daniel Maier-Katkin. 1991. "Occult Survivors: The Making of a Myth." In *The Satanism Scare,* ed. James T. Richardson, Joel Best, and David G. Bromley, 127–44. New York: Aldine de Gruyter.

Jilek, Wolfgang G. 1982. *Indian Healing: Shamanic Ceremonialism in the Pacific Northwest Today.* Blaine, Wash.: Hancock House.

Jonas, Hans. 1963. *The Gnostic Religion.* Boston: Beacon Press.

Jorgensen, Danny L., and Scott E. Russell. 1999. "American Neo-Paganism: The Participants' Social Identities." *Journal for the Scientific Study of Religion* 38.3 (September) 325–38.

Judah, J. Stillson. 1967 *The History and Philosophy of the Metaphysical Movements in America.* Philadelphia: Westminster.

Jung, Fritz. 2004. WitchVox Webcrafter. Personal communication.

Kaplan, Jeffrey. 1996. "The Reconstruction of the Asatru and Odinist Traditions." In *Magical Religion and Modern Witchcraft,* ed. James R. Lewis, 193–236. Albany: State University of New York Press.

———. 1997. *Radical Religion in America: Millenarian Movements from the Far Right to the Children of Noah.* Syracuse, N.Y.: Syracuse University Press.

Karlsen, Carol F. 1987. *The Devil in the Shape of a Woman.* New York: Vintage.

Kelly, Aidan A. 1991. *Crafting the Art of Magic: Book I.* St. Paul, Minn.: LLewellyn Publications.

Kelly, Russel. 1984. "The WITCHINESS of Women." *Globe & Mail,* April 14. *http://www.raperliefshelter.ba.ca/herstory/with.html.* Accessed February 2, 2002.

Kerr, Howard. 1973. *Mediums, and Spirit-Rappers, and Roaring Radicals.* Urbana: University of Illinois Press.

Kilbourne, Jean. 1999. *Deadly Persuasion.* New York: Free Press.

King, Francis. 1990. *Modern Ritual Magic: The Rise of Western Occultism.* Bridport, Dorset: Prism and Unity Press.

King, Serge Kahili. 1990. *Urban Shamanism: A Handbook for Personal and Planetary Transformation Based on the Hawaiian Way of the Adventurer.* New York: Fireside/Simon & Schuster.

King, Ursula. 1993. *Women and Spirituality: Voices of Protest and Promise.* 2nd ed. London: Macmillan.

Klassen, Chris. 2002. Personal communication, January 13. Used with permission.

Korn, Anna. 1996. "Interview." In *Being a Pagan: Druids, Wiccans, and Witches Today,* ed. Ellen Evert Hopman and Lawrence Bond, 62–68. Rochester, Vt.: Destiny Books.

LaBarre, Weston. 1938. *The Peyote Cult.* New Haven, Conn.: Yale University Press.

———. 1972. *The Ghost Dance* New York: Dell.

Lafaye, Jacques. 1990. "La sociedad de castas en la Nueva España." *Artes de Mexico* 8:25–35.

Lanning. Kenneth. 1989. "Satanic, Occult, and Ritualistic Crime: A Law Enforcement Perspective." *The Police Chief,* October: 62–83.

Lehtinen, Ildikó, ed. 1986. *Traces of Central Asian Culture in the North.* Helsinki: Finno-Ugric Society.

Levine, Saul. 1984. *Radical Departures: Desperate Detours to Growing Up.* New York: Harcourt, Brace & Jovanovich.

Lewis, I. M. 1971. *Ecstatic Religion: An Anthropological Study of Spirit Possession and Shamanism.* Harmondsworth and Baltimore: Penguin Books.

Lewis, James R. 1986. "Reconstructing the 'Cult' Experience." *Sociological Analysis* 47.2: 151–59.

Liebman, Robert, and Robert Wuthnow. 1982. *The New Christian Right.* New York: Aldine Press.

Linz, Daniel, Steven D. Penrod, and Edward Donnerstein. 1987. "The Attorney General's Commission on Pornography: The Gaps Between 'Findings' and Facts." *American Bar Foundation Research Journal* 4 (fall): 713–36.

Liston, Mary Kay. 1985. "Reclaiming the Body: Essential Element of Revelation in Feminist Spirituality." D.Min. thesis, Pacific School of Religion.

Lozano, Wendy G., and Tanice Foltz. 1990. "Into the Darkness: An Ethnographic Study of Witchcraft and Death." *Qualitative Sociology* 13.3 (fall): 211–34.

Ludeke, Joan Carole. 1989. "Wicca as a Revitalization Movement among Post-Industrial, Urban, American Women." Ph.D. thesis, Iliff School of Theology and the University of Denver.

Luhrmann, Tanya M. 1989. *Persuasions of the Witch's Craft: Ritual Magic in Contemporary England*. Cambridge, Mass.: Harvard University Press.


MacLaine, Shirley. 1987. *It's All in the Playing*. New York: Bantam.

Malinowski, B. 1954. *Magic, Science and Religion and Other Essays*. Garden City, N.Y.: Dover.

Mandelbaum, David G. 1979. *The Plains Cree: An Ethnographic, Historical, and Comparative Study*. Regina: University of Regina, Canadian Plains Research Center.

Manning, Christel. 1996. "Embracing Jesus and the Goddess: Towards a Reconceptualization of Conversion to Syncretistic Religion. In *Magical Religion and Modern Witchcraft*, ed. James R. Lewis, 299–326 Albany: State University of New York Press.

Marron, Kevin. 1989. *Witches, Pagans, and Magic in the New Age*. Toronto: Seal Books.

Marsden, George. 1980. *Fundamentalism and American Culture*. New York: Oxford University Press.

Martin, Bill. 1992. *Matrix and Line: Derrida and the Possibilities of Postmodern Social Theory*. Albany: State University of New York Press.

McFague, Sallie. 1987. *Models of God: Theology for an Ecological, Nuclear Age*. Philadelphia: Fortress Press.

McIntosh, Christopher. 1972. *Eliphas Lévi and the French Occult Revival*. London: Rider.

McKenna, Terrence. 1992. *Food of the Gods: The Search for the Original Tree of Knowledge: A Radical History of Plants, Drugs, and Human Evolution*. New York: Bantam.

Medicine Eagle, Brook. 2000. *The Last Ghost Dance: A Guide for Earth Mages*. New York: Ballantine Wellspring.

Melton, J. Gordon. 1978. *The Encyclopedia of American Religions*. Wilmington, N.C.: McGrath.

———. 1986. *Encyclopedic Handbook of Cults in America*. New York: Garland.

———. 1990. *New Thought: A Reader*. Santa Barbara, Calif.: ISAR.

Melton, J. Gordon, Jerome Clark, and Aidan A. Kelly. 1990. *New Age Encyclopedia*. Detroit: Gale Research.

Miller, David Humphreys. 1985. *Ghost Dance*. Lincoln: University of Nebraska Press.

Miller, Jay, and Carol M. Eastman, 1984. *The Tsimshian and Their Neighbors of the North Pacific Coast*. Seattle: University of Washington Press.

*Minneapolis Star Tribune*. 1993. "Re-Imagining Conference," November 3.

Moody, Edward. 1974. "Magical Therapy: Contemporary Satanism." In *Religious Movements in Contemporary America*, ed. Irving I. Zaretsky and Mark P. Leone, 355–84. Princeton, N.J.: Princeton University Press.

Mooney, James. 1973. *The Ghost Dance Religion and Wounded Knee*. New York: Dover.

Moore, R. Laurence. 1977. *In Search of White Crows*. New York: Oxford University Press.

Morgan, Robin, ed. 1970. *Sisterhood Is Powerful*. New York: Vintage Books.

Murphy, Joseph. 1993. *Santería: African Spirits in America*. Boston: Beacon Press.

Murray, Margaret A. [1921] 1971. *The Witch-Cult in Western Europe*. Oxford: Clarendon Press.


Nathan, Debbie. 1991. "Satanism and Child Molestation: Constructing the Ritual Abuse Scare." In *The Satanism Scare,* ed. James T. Richardson, Joel Best, and David G. Bromley, 75–94. New York: Aldine de Gruyter.

Nathan, Debbie, and Michael Snedeker. 1995. *Satan's Silence: Ritual Abuse and the Making of a Modern Witch Hunt*. New York: Basic Books.

Neitz, Mary Jo. 1990. "In Goddess We Trust." In *In Gods We Trust: New Patterns of Religious Pluralism in America,* 2nd ed., ed. Thomas Robbins and Dick Anthony, 353–72. New Brunswick, N.J.: Transaction Publishers.

Nelson, Geoffrey L. 1969. *Spiritualism and Society*. New York: Schocken Books.

Nethercot, Arthur H. 1960. *The First Five Lives of Annie Besant*. Chicago: University of Chicago Press.

———. 1963. *The Last Four Lives of Annie Besant*. Chicago: University of Chicago Press.

Nicholson, Shirley, comp. 1987. *Shamanism: An Expanded View of Reality*. Wheaton, Ill.: Theosophical Publishing House.

NightMare, M. Macha. 2001. *Witchcraft and the Web: Weaving Pagan Traditions Online*. Toronto: ECW Press.

NightMare, M. Macha, with Vibra Willow. 2002. "Reclaiming-Tradition Witchcraft." *Reclaiming Quarterly: The Magazine for Witchcraft and Magical Activism* 88 (autumn): 19–20, 53–58.

Niven, Ann. 2002. Personal correspondence, January 22. Used with permission.

Noll, Richard. 1983. "Shamanism and Schizophrenia: A State-Specific Approach to the 'Schizophrenia Metaphor' of Shamanic States." *American Ethnologist* 10: 443–59.

Northup, Leslie. 1993. "Expanding the X-Axis: Women, Religious Ritual and Culture." In *Women and Religious Ritual,* ed. Leslie Northup, 141–54 Washington, D.C.: Pastoral Press.

Olmos Fernández, Marguerite, and Lizabeth Paravisini, eds. 2000. *Sacred Possessions: Vodou, Santería, Obeah, and the Caribbean.* New Brunswick, N.J.: Rutgers University Press.

Orion, Loretta. 1995. *Never Again the Burning Times: Paganism Revived.* Prospect Heights, Ill.: Waveland Press.

Ostling, Richard N. 1983. "O God Our [Mother and] Father; New Translations Seek to Rid Bible of 'Male Bias.'" *Time Magazine,* October 24, 56–57.

Ott, Jonathan. 1996. *Pharmacotheon: Entheogenic Drugs, Their Plant Sources and History.* 2nd ed. Kennewick, Wash.: Natural Products Co.

Otto, Rudolf. 1928. *The Idea of the Holy.* Trans. John W. Harvey. London: Oxford University Press.


Park, Willard Z. 1938. *Shamanism in Western North America: A Study in Cultural Relationships.* Evanston, Ill.: Northwestern University Press.

Parker, Gail T. 1973. *Mind Cure in New England.* Hanover, N.H.: University Press of New England.

PAR-L. 2002. *Milestones in Canadian Women's History: The 1970's.* A CanadianElectronic Feminist Network/Un réseau électronique féministe canadien. *http://www.unb.ca/PAR*-L/milestones2.htm. Available March 3, 2002.

Parry, J. H., ed. 1991. *A Short History of the West Indies.* New York: St. Martin's Press.

Pentikäinen, Juha, ed. 1997. *Shamanism and Culture.* Helsinki: Etnika & Co.

———, ed. 2001. *Shamanhood: Symbolism and Epic.* Budapest: Akadémiai Kiado.

Pike, Sarah, M. 2001. *Earthly Bodies, Magical Selves: Contemporary Pagans and the Search for Community.* Berkeley and Los Angeles: The University of California Press.

Pirsig, Robert M. 1991. *Lila: An Inquiry into Morals.* New York: Bantam.

Plaskow, Judith. [1983] 1995. "The Right Question Is Theological." In *On Being a Jewish Feminist,* ed. Susannah Heschel, 223–33. New York: Schocken.

———. 1991. "Feminist Anti-Judaism and the Christian God." *Journal of Feminist Studies in Religion* 7.2: 99–108.


Rabinovitz, Shelly, and James Lewis, eds. 2002. *The Encyclopedia of Modern Witchcraft and Neo-Paganism.* New York: Citadel Press.

Ranck, Shirley Ann. 1986. *Cakes for the Queen of Heaven.* Boston: Unitarian Universalist Association.

Raphael, Melissa. 1996. "Models of God." In *An A to Z of Feminist Theol-*

*ogy*, ed. Lisa Isherwood and Dorothea McEwan, 146–49. Sheffield: Sheffield Academic Press.

Rasmussen, Knud. 1930. *Intellectual Culture of the Iglulik Eskimos.* Trans. William Worster. Copenhagen: Report of the Fifth Thule Expedition 7.1.

Reid, Sian. 2001. "Disorganized Religion: An Exploration of the Neopagan Craft in Canada." Ph.D. diss. Carleton University, Ottawa, Canada.

*Religious Freedom Alert.* 1989. "Missouri Police Waste Time, Money on False Rumors of Satanic Activity," May: 9.

Reuther, Rosemary Radford. 1983. Sexism and God–Talk: Towards a Feminist Theology. Boston: Beacon Press.

Richardson, James T., and Baren van Driel. 1984. "Public Support for Anti-Cult Legislation." *Journal for the Scientific Study of Religion* 23: 412–18.

Richardson, James T., Joel Best, and David G. Bromley. 1991. *The Satanism Scare.* New York: Aldine de Gruyter.

Robbins, Thomas. 1988. *Cults, Converts and Charisma: The Sociology of New Religious Movements.* London: Sage.

Rodríguez Reyes, Andrés, and Ileana Reyes Herrera. 1993. "Los Santos Parados o Santos de Manigua." *Del Caribe* 21: 28–34.

Roihl, Janis. 2002. *Re: Funeral of Rev. Sue Hiatt.* June 18. Online posting. Institute for Feminism and Religion. Used with permission.

Rose, Wendy. 1992. "The Great Pretenders: Further Reflections on White Shamanism." In *The State of Native America,* ed. Annette M. Jaimes. Boston: South End Press.

Ross, A. S. 1994. "Blame it on the Devil." *Redbook,* June, 88.

Rothstein, Mikael, ed. 2001. *New Age Religion and Globalization.* Aarhus: University Press.

Russell, Jeffrey. 1988. *The Prince of Darkness: Radical Evil and the Power of Good.* Ithaca, N.Y.: Cornell University Press.

Rutherford, Ward. 1986. *Shamanism: The Foundations of Magic.* Wellingborough: Aquarian Press/Thorsons.

Ryan, Barbara. 1992. *Feminism and the Women's Movement.* New York: Routledge

Ryan, Charles J. 1975. *H. P. Blavatsky and the Theosophical Movement.* Pasadena, Calif.: Theosophical University Press.

Sagan, Carl. 1995. *The Demon-Haunted World: Science as a Candle in the Dark.* Durham, N.C.: Duke University Press.

Salomonsen, Jone. 2002. *Enchanted Feminism: The Reclaiming Witches of San Francisco.* New York: Routledge Press.

Sasso, Sandy. 1993. "Unwrapping the Gift." In *Women and Religious Ritual,* ed. Leslie Northup, ix–xvi. Washington, D.C.: Pastoral Press.

Schafer, Shernie. 1993. "Return to the Dance: The Power of Ritual in Ordinary Lives." In *Women and Religious Ritual*, ed. Leslie Northup, 77–86. Washington, D.C.: Pastoral Press.

Segal, Robert, ed. 1995. *The Allure of Gnosticism*. Chicago: Open Court.

Shallcrass, Philip. 1996. "The Bardic Tradition and the Song of the Land." In *The Druid Renaissance,* ed. Philip Carr-Gomm, 52–67. London: Thorsons.

Shirokogoroff, Sergei Mikhailovich. 1923. "General Theory of Shamanism among the Tungus." *Journal of the Royal Asiatic Society, North-China Branch Shanghai* 54: 246–49.

———. 1980. *Psychomental Complex of the Tungus*. London: Routledge & Kegan Paul. Original edition, New York: AMS, 1935.

Siikala, Anna-Leena. 1978. *The Rite of the Siberian Shaman*. Folklore Follows' communications, 220.

Sjoo, Monica. 1989. "Some Thoughts about the New Age Movement." *Wood and Water* 2 (summer): 28.

Slater, Kate. 2002. Personal correspondence, January 17. Used with permission.

Smart, Ninian. 1989. *The World's Religions*. Cambridge: Cambridge University Press.

———. 1996. *Dimensions of the Sacred: An Anatomy of the World's Beliefs*. Berkeley and Los Angeles: University of California Press.

Smith, Alexa. 1998. *Re-Imagining Revival Marks the End of the Ecumenical Decade of Churches in Solidarity with Women*. Episcopalian/Anglican Women's Ministries. *http://ecusa.anglican.org/women/reimage.html*. Available February 4, 2002.

Smith, Mark. 1997. "Jury Awards $5.8 Million in Satanic Memories Case." *Houston Chronicle*, August 16, 1A.

———. 1998a. "Woman Sues over False Memories." *Houston Chronicle*, April 21, p.1A.

———. 1998b. "Criminal Trial Begins in False Memory Case." *Houston Chronicle*, September 10, 1A.

Smith, Michelle, and Lawrence Pazder. 1980. *Michelle Remembers*. New York: Congdon & Lattes.

Spink, Peter, 1996. *Beyond Belief: How to Develop Mystical Consciousness and Discover the God Within*. London: Piatkus.

Spretnak, Charlene. 1978. *Lost Goddess of Early Greece*. Berkley: Moon Books.

———. 1990. "Ecofeminism: Our Roots and Flowering." In *Reweaving the World*, ed.Irene Diamond and Gloria Orenstein, 3–14. San Francisco: Sierra Club Books.

Starhawk (Simos, Miriam). 1979. *The Spiral Dance: A Rebirth of the Ancient Religion of the Great Goddess*. San Francisco: Harper & Row.

————. 1982. *Dreaming the Dark*. Boston: Beacon Press.

Starhawk and M. Macha NightMare. 1997. *The Pagan Book of Living and Dying: Practical Rituals, Prayers, Blessings, and Meditations on Crossing Over.* San Francisco: Harper Collins.

Stemman, Roy. 1976. *Spirits and Spirit Worlds*. Garden City, N.Y.: Doubleday.

Stone, Merlin. 1976. *When God Was a Woman*. New York: Harcourt Brace Jovanovich.

————. 1979. *Ancient Mirrors of Womanhood*. Boston: Beacon Press.

Stratford, Lauren.1988. *Satan's Underground*. Eugene, Ore.: Harvest House.

Streiker, Lowell D. 1990. *New Age Comes to Main Street: What Worried Christians Must Know*. Nashville, Tenn.: Abingdon.

Strossen, Nadine. 1995. *Defending Pornography: Free Speech, Sex and the Fight for Women's Rights*. New York: Anchor Books.

Stuckey, Johanna. 1998. *Feminist Spirituality*. Toronto: York Centre for Feminist Research.

————. 2002. Personal communication, January 20. Used with permission.

Sun Bear. 1984. *Sun Bear, the Path of Power: As Told to Wabun and to Barry Weinstock*. Spokane, Wash.: Bear Tribe Publications.

Taylor, Anne. 1992. *Annie Besant: A Biography*. Oxford: Oxford University Press.

Taylor, Sarah McFarland. 2001. "Green Nuns." Paper presented at the Association for the Sociology of Religion, Anaheim, Calif. August 17–19.

Taylor, Tony, and Sable Taylor.1996. "Interview." In *Being a Pagan: Druids, Wiccans, and Witches Today,* ed. Ellen Evert Hopman and Lawrence Bond, 14–21. Rochester, Vt.: Destiny Books.

Teish, Lusiah. 1985. *Jambalaya: The Natural Woman's Book of Personal Charms and Practical Rituals*. San Francisco: Harper-San Francisco.

Telesco, Patricia. 2000. *Shaman in a 9 to 5 World*. Freedom, Calif.: Crossing Press.

Thompson, Robert Farris. 1983. *Flash of the Spirit: African and Afro-American Art and Philosophy*. New York: Vintage Books.

Thorndike, Lynn. 1958. *A History of Magic and Experimental Science*. New York: Columbia University Press.

Thornton, Russell. 1986. *We Shall Live Again: The 1870 and 1890 Ghost Dance Movements as Demographic Revitalization*. New York: Cambridge University Press.

Thunderstorm, Eclecta. 2002. Personal correspondence, February 17. Used with permission.

Valgard, Murray. 1999. "Response to the *Megiddo* Report. CENSUR. www.censur.org.

Valiente, Doreen. 1973. *The ABC's of Witchcraft, Past and Present.* Custer, Wash.: Phoenix Publishers.

———. 1978. *Witchcraft for Tomorrow.* Custer, Wash.: Phoenix Publishers.

Vega, Marta. 2000. *The Altar of My Soul: The Living Tradition of Santería.* New York: Ballantine Publishing Group.

Victor, Jeffrey. 1993. *Satanic Panic: The Creation of a Contemporary Myth.* Chicago: Open Court.

———. 1995. *Satanic Panic: The Creation of a Contemporary Legend.* New York: Open Court.

Vitebsky, Piers. 1995a. "From Cosmology to Environmentalism: Shamanism as Local Knowledge in a Global Setting." In *Counterworks: Managing the Diversity of Knowledge,* ed. Richard. Fardon, 182–203. London: Routledge.

———. 1995b. *The Shaman: Voyages of the Soul: Trance, Ecstacy and Healing from Siberia to the Amazon.* London: Macmillan.


Wakefield, Hollida, and Ralph Underwager. 1992. "Assessing the Credibility of Children's Testimony in Ritual Sexual Abuse Allegations." *Issues in Child Abuse Accusations* 4: 32–44.

Waldrop, M. Mitchell. 1992. *Complexity: The Emerging Science at the Edge of Order and Chaos.* New York: Touchstone.

Wallis, Roy. 1984. *The Elementary Forms of the New Religious Life.* London: Routledge and Kegan Paul.

Watkins, Calvert. 1969. "Indo-European roots." In *The American Heritage Dictionary of the English Language,* ed. William Morris, 1505–50. Boston: Houghton Mifflin.

Wehmeyer, Stephen Connor. 2002. "'Indian' Spirits and the Sacred Landscapes: American Spiritualism." Diss., University of California Los Angeles.

Wessinger, Catherine. 1997. "Millennialism with and without the Mayhem." In *Millennium, Messiahs, and Mayhem: Contemporary Apocalyptic Movements,* ed. Thomas Robbins and Susan J. Palmer, 47–59. New York & London: Routledge.

———. 2000. *How the Millennium Comes Violently: From Jonestown to Heaven's Gate.* New York: Seven Bridges.

Williams, Delores. 1993. "Sin, Nature and Black Women's Bodies." In *Ecofeminism and the Sacred,* ed. Carol J. Adams, 24–30. New York: Continuum.

Williams, Gertrude Marvin. 1946. *Priestess of the Occult: Madame Blavatsky.* New York: Knopf.

Wilson, Bryan R. 1959. "An Analysis of Sect Development." *American Sociological Review* 24.1 (February): 3–15.

———. 1969. "A Typology of Sects." In *Sociology of Religion: Selected Readings,* ed. Roland Robertson, 361–83. Harmondsworth: Penguin.

————. 1973. *Magic and the Millennium*. London: Heinemann.

Winter, Miriam Therese, Adair Lummis, and Allison Stokes. 1994. *Defecting in Place: Women Claiming Responsibility for Their Own Spiritual Lives*. New York: Crossroad.

Wright, Stuart A. 1984. "Post-Involvement Attitudes of Voluntary Defectors from Controversial New Religious Movements." *Journal for the Scientific Study of Religion* 23.2: 172–82.

————. 1987. *Leaving Cults: The Dynamics of Defection*. Washington, D.C.: Society for the Scientific Study of Religion.

————. 1989. "Satanic Cults, Kidnapping and Ritual Sacrifice: A Study of Moral Panic in Rural Texas." Paper presented at the annual meetings of the Society for the Scientific Study of Religion, Washington, D.C., November 6–8.

York, Michael. 1994. "The World Parliament of Religions, Chicago, 1993." *Religion Today: A Journal of Contemporary Religions* 9.2 (Spring): 17–20.

————. 1995a. "The Church Universal and Triumphant." *Journal of Contemporary Religion* 10.1: 71–82.

————. 1995b. *The Emerging Network: A Sociology of the New Age and Neopagan Movements*. Lanham, Md.: Rowman & Littlefield.

————. [1996] 1999. "Postmodernity, Architecture, Society and Religion: 'A Heap of Broken Images' or 'A Change of Heart.'" In *Postmodernity, Sociology and Religion,* ed. Kieran Flanagan and Peter C. Jupp, 48–63. New York: St. Martin's Press.

————. 1997. "New Age and the Late Twentieth Century: A Review Article." *Journal of Contemporary Religion* 12.3 (October): 401–19.

————. 1999a. "Review of Peter Novak's *The Division of Consciousness.*" In *The Journal of Contemporary Religion* 14.1 (January): 169–72.

————. 1999b. "Emergentism and Some Post-Big Bang Perspectives." *Journal of Contemporary Religion* 14.2 (May): 291–97.

————. 2003. *Pagan Theology: Paganism as a World Religion*. New York: New York University Press.

Zelman, Patricia. 1982 *Women, Work and National Policy: The Kennedy-Johnson Years*. Ann Arbor, Mich.: UMI Research Press.

Zurcher, Louis, and Roger J. Kilpatrick. 1976. *Citizens for Decency: Anti-Pornography Campaigns as Status Defense*. Austin: University of Texas Press.

# Contributors

HELEN A. BERGER, professor of sociology at West Chester University, is author of *A Community of Witches: Contemporary Neo-Pagans and Witches in the United States* (University of South Carolina Press, 1999) and coauthor of *Voices from the Pagan Census: A National Survey of Neo-Pagans and Witches in the United States* (University of South Carolina Press, 2003). She is currently working on a book about teenage Witches in the United States, England, and Australia.

YSAMUR M. FLORES-PEÑA, adjunct professor at Otis College of Art and Design, is author of *Santería Garments and Altars: Speaking without a Voice* (University of Mississippi Press, 1994) and scholarly essays on Latino spirituality, folklore, and ritual.

TANICE G. FOLTZ, associate professor of sociology, Indiana University Northwest, is author of *Kahuna Healer: Learning to See with Ki* (Garland Publishing, 1994) and over twenty articles and book chapters on a variety of topics, including alternative healing, deviance, drumming, Goddess Spirituality, and feminist Witchcraft. She is currently working on a book on drumming, spirituality, and community.

WENDY GRIFFIN, professor of women's studies at California State University, Long Beach, is the editor of *Daughters of the Goddess: Studies of Healing, Identity and Empowerment* (AltaMira Press, 2000), author of nine scholarly chapters and articles on Goddess Spirituality, and coeditor of AltaMira's series in Pagan studies. She is currently working on a book on women's Goddess rituals.

STUART A. WRIGHT is assistant dean of graduate studies and research and professor of sociology at Lamar University. He is the author of *Leaving Cults* (Society for the Scientific Study of Religion, 1987) and editor of *Armageddon in Waco* (University of Chicago Press, 1995) and has over thirty journal and book chapter publications in scholarly venues.

MICHAEL YORK, Bath Spa University College professor of cultural astronomy and astrology, is author of *The Roman Festival Calendar of Numa*

*Pompilius* (Peter Lang, 1986), *The Emerging Network: A Sociology of the New Age and Neopagan Movements* (Rowman and Littlefield, 1995), *The Divine Versus the Asurian: An Interpretation of Indo-European Cult and Myth* (Rowman and Littlefield, 1995), and *Pagan Theology: Paganism as a World Religion* (New York University Press, 2003). His research areas include paganism, new religious movements, cultural astronomy, Indo-European studies, and modern-postmodern cultural change.

# Index

*ABC's of Witchcraft* (Valiente), 152
Adefumi, Oba Ofuntola Osejiman Adelabu, 110–11
Adler, Margot, 29, 39, 42, 45, 47, 74–75, 80, 152, 162
African Americans, 110–11, 112, 119
Afro-Caribbean religions: Curanderismo as, 3, 112, 118–19; as magical, 7; Neopaganism and, 4; Orisha-Voodoo as, 111, 174n17; Palo as, 3, 112, 117–18; roots of, 6–7; spirituality of, 114–17; Voodoo as, 3; Yoruba as, 3, 103–5
Age of Aquarius, 8, 10, 14–15, 24
Age of Aries, 14
Age of Information, 18
Age of Pisces, 14, 15
alchemy, 25
American Academy of Religion, section on women, 59
American Gnosticism. *See* Gnosticism
American New Thought movement, 10
American Spiritualism, 10, 115
Amirault, Cheryl, 133
Amirault, Gerald, 133
Amirault, Violet, 133
*Ancient and Modern Witchcraft* (Buckland), 152
"Ancient Wisdom Tradition," 11, 18
Anderson, Cora, 67
Anderson, Victor, 48–49, 67
angels, 1, 12
Anglo-American Theosophical movements, 10
animal magnetism, 10
anticult movement (ACM), 128–29
apocalyptic millennialism, 16

*The Aquarian Conspiracy* (Ferguson), 16
Aquino, Michael, 129, 130
*Aradia* (Leland), 61, 63
Arcane School, 10, 17
ÀrnDraíocht Féin (ADF), 42, 43
Aryan Pagans, 46
Ásatrú, 46
Ásatrú Free Assembly, 47
Ascended Masterhood, 21
Association for Research and Enlightenment, 10
Astara Foundation, 10
astronomy, New Age and, 14–15
axis mundi, 85

Bailey, Alice, 10, 17
Bainbridge, William Sims, 19, 26, 131
Bantu: in Cuba, 117; Lucumí relating to, 103
Barrett, Ruth Rhiannion, 70, 162
Baum, Frank L., 138
Bednarowski, Mary Farrell, 75, 77–78
*The Believers*, 122
*Bell, Book, and Candle*, 140
*The Beltane Papers: A Journal of Women's Mysteries*, 71, 171n19
Berger, Peter, 13, 39, 47
*Bewitched*, 141, 146, 165, 174n3
*Beyond God the Father: Toward a Philosophy of Women's Liberation* (Daly), 59
*The Big Book of Spells*, 149
*Blair Witch Project*, 142, 144, 166
Blavatsky, Helena Petrowna, 11
Bloom, Harold, 11, 12, 18, 19, 20
Bolen, Jean Shinoda, 71
Bonewits, Isaac, 42–44

*The Book of Coming Forth by Night* (Aquino), 130

Book of Revelation, 14

books. *See* Witchcraft, commodification of

botánicas, 4, 111–13, 118, 174n21

Bradley, Marion Zimmer, 71, 151

*Brain/Mind Bulletin*, 16

Braun, Dr. Bennet, 124

British Traditional Witches, 39

British Wiccans, 68

Buckland, Raymond, 36, 56, 152

Buckland, Rosemary, 36, 56

Budapest, Zsuzsanna, 38, 48, 55, 60–64, 67–70, 162

Buddhism, 11, 21, 24

Buddhist missionaries, 86

*Buffy, the Vampire Slayer*, 146, 147, 165–66

*Bugs Bunny*, 148

Burgus, Patricia, 124

Burning Times, 66, 80

*The Burning Times*, 72

Byrd, James, Jr., 45

cabildos, 104–5, 111, 174n18

*Cakes for the Queen of Heaven: A Seminar in Feminist Thealogy*, 70–71

Campion, Nicholas, 15

Canada: Druid groves, 42; feminist spirituality in, 57–60, 69–70, 72; globalization relating to, 9–10; Lucumí in, 113–14, 119; Pagans counted in census, 26, 28–29; Witchcraft in, 37, 72, 171n21

Canadian Security Intelligence Service, 45

*Canadian Women's Studies*, 70

Carl, Lynn, 124

Carpenter, Dennis, 51, 161

Castaneda, Carlos, 90, 99

Catholic Church, 103, 109

Cayce, Edgar, 10, 16

Cella Priestess training program, 161

Celtic: Druids/Druidism as, 43; Odinists/Odinism as, 47

*The Chalice and the Blade* (Eisler), 72

Chaney, Earlyne, 10

*Charmed*, 40, 146, 147, 165

child sexual abuse, 132–33

Chinese immigrants, 105

Chopra, Deepak, 16

Christ. *See* Jesus

Christian feminists, 55, 72–74, 78, 79

Christian Fundamentalism, 127–28, 136

Christianity, 11, 19, 41, 55, 88

Christian missionaries, 86

Christian Science movement, 10, 12

Christian wing, of New Age, 15–16

*The Chronicles of Narnia* (Lewis), 148

*The Church and the Second Sex* (Daly), 58, 59

The Church of All Worlds (CAW), 50, 51

The Church of Satan, 4, 129–30

The Church of Scientology, 130

Church Universal and Triumphant, 14

*CIRCLE*, 154

*Circle Network News*, 154

Circle of Aradia, 70

Circle Sanctuary, 51, 52, 154

Circumpolar Woman's Conference, 89

Civil Rights Act, 56

Civil Rights movement, 109, 173n15

*The Cloven Hoof*, 130

*Colección de Oraciones Escogidas* (Kardek), 116

Commission on the Status of Women, 56

*Complete Idiot's Guide to Wicca and Witchcraft*, 153

Congregationalist Witchcraft Association, 51

consciousness raising (CR), 58, 60

Constanzo, Adolpho de Jesus, 122

Contemporary Witchcraft: background of, 28; demographics of, 28–29, 170n2; Neopaganism and, 28–54; Wicca as, 28–33

Corlett, William, 149

cosmology, of Druids/Druidism, 44

The Covenant of the Goddess (CoG), 51, 70

covens, 31–32, 34, 37, 38, 60

*The Craft*, 142, 166, 174n5

crone, 59, 170n2

*The Cross of Changes*, 93

Crowley, Vivianne, 22, 33–34, 35

*The Crucible* (Miller), 138

Cuba, 117

Cuban Revolution, 108–9

Curanderismo, 3, 112, 118–19

Curott, Phyllis, 34, 35

Curtis Hopkins, Emma, 12, 13

Daly, Mary, 58–60

Davis, Elizabeth Gold, 65

daycare, 133–34

de Fiore, Joachim, 14

deities: Lucumí beliefs relating to, 107, 173n14; of Odinists/Odinism, 46

Dharmic theology, 11, 21

Dianic Witches/Witchcraft, 55, 61–64, 67, 70, 75, 79; magic, 63–64; men excluded from, 62, 170n8; Neopaganism and, 28; training, 70; Triple Goddess, 61–62

"Doomsday Religious Movements," 45

Doyle, Gayle, 133

*Drawing Down the Moon* (Adler), 45, 74, 152

Druids/Druidism, 39, 40, 41–45; background of, 41; as Celtics, 43; cosmology of, 44; groves of, 44; Neopaganism and, 2; organizations of, 42–43; as polytheistic, 43

DuFresne, Lucie, 69, 89, 167, 175n25

Dworkin, Andrea, 132

*E! Talk Soup*, 152

*Early Show*, 151, 152

EarthSpirit Community, 51–52

Eddy, Mary Baker, 10, 12

Eisler, Riane, 72

Elf Lore Family, 52

Eliade, Mircea, 82, 86, 90, 96, 99

Eller, Cynthia, 57, 75–76

El Madamo Jo, 117

Equal Employment Opportunity Commission, 56

Equal Pay Act, 56

Esalen Center of Big Sur, California, 10

Espiritismo, 112; American Spiritism as, 10,

115; Kardecian Spiritism as, 115, 174n20; Puerto Rican migration relating to, 116–17; trance possession in, 115–16

Espiritismo Científico, 115

Espiritismo Cruzado, 117, 174n20

*Evangelio Según el Espiritismo* (Kardek), 116

Ezzy, Douglas, 137, 157–58, 161

Faery Tradition, 38, 48–49, 67

Falwell, Jerry, 127, 167

Farrar, Stewart, 152

Federal Bureau of Investigation (FBI), 4–5, 45, 121, 129

*The Feminine Mystique* (Friedan), 56

feminism, 132–33

*The Feminist Book of Light and Shadows* (Budapest), 63

feminist Christians, 55, 72–74, 78, 79

feminist Jews, 72–74, 78

feminist spirituality: during 1980s, 68–74; during 1990s, 74–77; in Canada, 57–60, 69–70, 72; conferences on, 66–67; family of, 55–56; matriarchy's importance in, 64–74; reemergence of, 56–60; streams of, 76; teaching of, 58–60, 62, 170n3; tradition and rituals of, 77–80; Web of Life and, 35, 80, 164

Feminist Wicca, 62

feminist Witchcraft, 2, 38, 60–64, 68, 70, 171n6

Ferguson, Marilyn, 16, 17

festivals: of music, 162–63; of Neopaganism, 52–54; of Paganism, 68–69, 161–62, 167

films. *See* Witchcraft, commodification of

*The First Sex* (Davis), 65

Ford, Arthur, 10

Foundation for Shamanic Studies, 91, 95

Fox, Matthew, 16, 17

Fox, Selena, 51, 154, 161

Frazer, Sir James, 65

Freemasonry, 19, 25, 41

Friedan, Betty, 56

*Full Circle*, 72

Gardner, Gerald, 31–33, 36, 39, 152
Gardnerian Wicca, 61
Gardnerian Witchcraft: rituals of, 31–33,
    41; scourge used in, 32; skyclad used in,
    32
Gimbutas, Marija, 65–66, 72
globalization: Canada relating to, 9–10;
    New Age Movement relating to, 9–10,
    19; North America relating to, 9
glocalization, 9
Gnosticism, 11–13, 18, 20, 23, 169n3
God, 12, 73, 172n22; Lucumí beliefs in,
    105–6, 173n6; Satan versus, 124
*The Goddesses and Gods of Old Empire* (Gim-
    butas), 65–66, 171n15
*Goddesses in Every Woman* (Bolen), 71
*The Goddess Remembered*, 72
Goddess Spirituality, 60, 65, 67, 70, 72, 74,
    78
*Goddess Within*, 67
Goddess Worship, 1, 2, 7, 28–31, 36, 49,
    55, 67; Dianic Triple Goddess in, 61–62;
    Great Mother Goddess in, 65, 75
Goldenberg, Naomi, 67, 72
*The Golden Bough* (Frazer), 65
Graves, Robert, 61, 65, 153
Great Mother Goddess, 75; as Creatrix, 65;
    as Destroyer, 65
*Green Egg*, 50
Gross, Rita, 78–79

*Hair*, 8, 14
Halloween, 151, 164
Hanegraaff, Wouter, 10, 21
Hare Krishnas, 129
Harner, Michael, 91, 92, 96, 99
*Harry Potter* books, 6, 40, 148, 168; *Harry
    Potter and the Chamber of Secrets* (Row-
    ling), 167–68; *Harry Potter and the Sorcer-
    er's Stone* (Rowling), 145
*Harry Potter: Witchcraft Repackaged: Making
    Evil Look Innocent*, 145
Harvey, Graham, studies of, 41

healing: in Lucumí, 111–13; Witches' pow-
    ers of, 35–36; in Yoruba, 1
*Hecate's Loom: A Journal of Magical Arts*, 71
Hedonism, 46
Heinlein, Robert A., 50
Hendge of Keltria, 43
herbal remedies, 1, 7, 36
hermeticism, 18
Hexes, 64, 171n11–12
Hinduism, 11, 21, 34, 86
*Holy Book of Women's Mysteries* (Budapest),
    69
"Homenaje a la Madama," 116
Hoppál, Mihály, 82, 89–90
House Un-American Activities Committee
    (HUAC), 135
Hubbard, L. Ron, 130
Human Potential Movement, 10, 13, 16,
    22, 23, 95, 100
Hurtak, James Jacob, 21
Hutton, Ronald, 31, 64, 65
Huxley, Aldous, 18

*I Dream of Jeannie*, 141, 146, 174n4
Illuminism, 25
indigenous practices, 81
indigenous Shamanism, traditional, 83–86,
    90, 101
International Asatru/Odinic Alliance
    (IAOA), 45
Introvigne, Masimo, 8, 15, 25
Iron and Pearl Pentacles, 49

Jade River, Samantha, 160, 162
*JAG*, 149
Jesus, 10, 12, 13, 78, 79, 127
Jewish feminists, 72–74, 78
*Joan of Arc*, 151
John Paul, 77
Judah, J. Stillson, 10
Judaism, 41, 55
*Judging Amy*, 149, 150

kabbalah, 18, 25, 26
Kaplan, Jeffrey, 45, 46, 47

Kardecian Spiritism, 115
Kardek, Allan, 115, 116
Keller, Daniel, 133
Keller, Frances, 133
Kelly, Robert, 134
*Keys of Enoch* (Hurtak), 21
Kilroy, Mark, 121
King, William, 45
*Kukla, Fran, and Ollie*, 140–41

Lady Liberty League, 145, 151
Lafaye, Jacques, 109
Lakota, 18–19
*The Late Great Planet Earth* (Lindsey), 127
LaVey, Anton, 129–30
law of equal exchange, 22, 24
*Leading Edge Bulletin*, 16
Leland, Charles, 61, 63
lesbians/lesbianism, 69, 79
Lewis, C.S., 148
Lindsey, Hal, 127
*The Lion, the Witch, and the Wardrobe*, 148, 149
love magic, 24
Lucifer, 5, 124
Lucis Trust, 17, 169n6
Lucumí: Bantu relating to, 103; botánicas in, 111–13, 118, 174n21; cabildos used by, 104–5, 111, 174n18; in Canada, 113–14, 119; Catholic Church's role in, 103; Chinese immigrants relating to, 105; healing in, 111–13; New Age and, 103; religious culture of, 103–5; royalty in, 104; slavery's role in, 103; Yoruba relating to, 103–5, 115
Lucumí, beliefs of: deities relating to, 107, 173n14; one God as, 105–6, 173n6; Orichas relating to, 106–7, 173n12; Pataki relating to, 106–7, 173n7; santos relating to, 106–8, 173n9, 173n13
Lucumí diaspora, 108–11; African Americans relating to, 110–11, 112, 119; botánicas relating to, 111–13, 118, 174n21; Civil Rights movement relating to, 109,

173n15; Cuban Revolution relating to, 108–9; factions of, 110–11; mestizaje relating to, 109; Spain relating to, 110
Luhrmann, Tanya, 22, 34, 35, 39

MacKinnon, Catherine, 132
MacLaine, Shirley, 16, 21–22
Madamas, 116–17
magazines. *See* Witchcraft, commodification of
magic, 3; consequences of, 24; definition of, 1; Dianic, 63–64; love, 24; Neopaganism and, 33–36; New Age and, 8, 22–27; Paganism and, 22–27; religion versus, 1; Shamans/Shamanism and, 81, 92, 97–98; spell casting as, 63–64; Wicca/Wiccans and, 34–36; Witchcraft and, 33–36, 54, 156–57
magical religions: Afro-Caribbean, 7; contemporary, 6–7; non-Afro-Caribbean, 7; roots of, 6–7
*The Magician's House*, 149
Maharishi Mahesh Yogi, 16, 17
*Man Alive*, 151
*Matilda*, 144–45
McCarthy, Joseph, 135, 138
McFarland, Morgan, 66–67
McFarland Dianic Witches, 67
McMartin Preschool case, 133
*The Meaning of Witchcraft* (Gardner), 152
mediumistic possession, 11
mediums, Shamans versus, 85
Meese Pornography Commission, 131
Megiddo Report, 5, 45
Melton, Gordon, 8, 9, 10, 130
*Merlin*, 151
Mesmer, Anton, 10, 12
mestizaje, 109
Michaels, Margaret, 133–34
Michelet, Jules, 57
*Michelle Remembers* (Smith and Pazder), 132
Michigan Womyn's Music Festival, 162
millenarianism, 87–88
Miller, Arthur, 138

*Miller v. California*, 131
miracles, 1
*The Mists of Avalon* (Bradley), 71, 151, 153
Montgomery, Elizabeth, 141
Montgomery, Ruth, 16
Moral Majority, 127
moral panic, 125–26, 135
*Ms.*, 62
Murphy, Jill, 149
music festivals, 162–63
music/magic, 156–57

National Action Committee on the Status of Women, 58
National Council of Churches, 73
National Organization for Women (NOW), 56, 58
National Women's Music Festival (NWMF), 162, 175n21
Native Americans, 18–19; practices of, 82, 88–89, 99
nature, 3
Nazi racism, 5
Neo-Nazi Neopagans, 5, 45–47
Neo-Nazi Pagans, 5
Neo-Nazis, 4–5, 45–47
Neopaganism: Afro-Caribbean religions and, 4; Dianics as form of, 28; Druidism as form of, 2; feminist Witchcraft as form of, 2; festivals of, 52–54; as legitimate religion, 5; magic and, 33–36; nature celebrated in, 3; Neo-Nazi relating to, 5, 45–47; New Age and, 19–20, 25–26; Odinism as form of, 2; organizations of, 50–52; spirituality of, 29–30, 40–41; Witchcraft and, 28–54
New Age, 1; as Age of Information, 18; astronomy and, 14–15; Christian wing of, 15–16; consciousness and, 12; criticisms of, 17–19; expectations of, 15–17; Gnosticism and, 12, 23; Lucumí and, 103; magic and, 8, 22–27; Neopaganism and, 19–20, 25–26; New Thought and, 12–13, 19–20, 169n4; Paganism versus, 19–

20, 26; Satanism and, 4; Shamans/Shamanism and, 89–94, 97, 99, 101; techniques of, 3; theology of, 19–22; Theosophy and, 12–13, 19–20, 23
New Age Movement: American New Thought movement as part of, 10; Anglo-American Theosophical movement as part of, 10; commercialism of, 8–10; demise of, 8–10; fundamentals of, 21; globalization relating to, 9–10, 19; as occult, 2, 19; paranormal relating to, 9, 11, 23; Spiritualism and, 11
New England Transcendentalism, 10, 12
New Reformed Druids of North America (NRDNA), 42
new religious movements (NRMs), 128
New Thought, 19–20
New York Radical Women, 56
NightMare, M. Macha, 30, 153
Noel, Daniel, 90, 91
Norse mythology, 46–47
North America: globalization and, 9; Shamans/Shamanism and, 86–89, 100, 101, 172n6; Wicca influenced by, 36–40

Obeah, 113, 117–18
occult: definition of, 2; New Age Movement as, 19
Odinists/Odinism, 41; Ásatrú as, 46; as Celtic, 47; deities of, 46; Heathen as, 46; Neo-Nazis relating to, 45–47; Neopaganism and, 2; Norse mythology and, 46–47; as polytheistic, 46; spirituality of, 47
*Of a Like Mind (OALM)*, 154
Order of Bards, Ovates, and Druids, 41–42
Orichas, 106–7, 173n12
Orisha-Voodoo, 111, 174n17
Orthodox Christianity, 11

Padzer, Lawrence, 132
*Pagan*, 51
*The Pagan Book of Living and Dying*, 153
Paganism: ceremonial aspects of, 19; cycle of, 20–21; festivals of, 68–69, 161–62,

167; magic and, 22–27; New Age versus, 19–20, 26; Western, 19, 22, 26; Witchcraft as, 137. *See also* Neopaganism

Pagans: Aryan, 46; Neo-Nazi, 5; newsletters for, 154–56

Pagan Shamans, 94–97, 101

Pagan Spirit Gathering (PSG), 161–62

Palestine Liberation Organization, 26

Palo, 3, 112, 117–18

paranormal, 9, 11, 23

Parliament of World Organizations, 5, 50

Parliament of World Religions, 52, 88; Chicago Parliament of World Religions, 19

Pataki, 106–7, 173n7

Patriarchy, 63, 72

Peabody Essex Museum, 138

Perls, Fritz, 10

Plotinus, 21

*The Politics of Women's Spirituality* (Spretnak), 71

polytheism, 43, 46

pornography/sex industry, 131–32

positive reality, 13

positive thinking, 13

*Practical Magic*, 142, 143, 144, 166

precession of the equinoxes, 14, 15

The Process, 129, 130–31

Protestant Christian Feminists, 55

Puerto Rican migration, 116–17

Pythagoras, 21

quantum leap, 15, 24

Quimby, Phineas Parkhurst, 12

Ram Dass, Baba, 16, 17

RavenWolf, Silver, 40, 153

RCG-I (Re-formed Congregation of the Goddess, International), 70, 154, 160–61

*Real Magic* (Bonewits), 44

Reclaiming Collective, 47–48, 68–69, 159

Reclaiming Tradition, 37, 41, 47–50, 79; classes relating to, 48–50, 68

Redstockings, 57

Re-formed Congregation of the Goddess (RCG), 70

Re-formed Congregation of the Goddess, International. *See* RCG-I

Reformed Druids of North America (RDNA), 42–43

Re-Imagining Conference, 76, 77

Reincarnation, 33

religion: magical components of, 1–2; magic versus, 1; miracles/angels in, 1; worship/prayer in, 1. *See also* Afro-Caribbean religions; magical religions; Witchcraft

Religious Right, 131, 135, 136, 167

Reyes, Rodríguez, 103, 104

right-wing groups, 127

*Rituals for Our Times*, 153

Rivail, Hippolyte. *See* Kardek, Allan

Rivera, Elio Hernandez, 122

Roman Empire, schools of, 25

*Rosemary's Baby*, 130

Rosicrucianism, 19, 25

Rowling, J. K., 145

royalty, in Lucumí, 104

*Sabrina, the Teenage Witch*, 40, 146, 165

*Sacred Circles: A Guide to Creating Your Own Women's Spirituality Group*, 153

*Sacred Possessions* (Olmos), 117

*SageWoman*, 71

Saint-Germain, Comte de, 14

Salem, Massachusetts, 6, 138–39

Salem Witch Museum, 138, 139

Samhain, 164

Santería. *See* Lucumí

santos, 106–8, 173n9, 173n13

Sappho Witch Camp, 69

*The Satanic Bible* (LaVey), 130

Satanic cults, 120–36; allegations of, 120–24; moral panic and, 125–26, 135; Satan and, 124–25; support groups and, 124

Satanic cult scares, 134–36; actual Satanist groups and, 129–31; anticultism and, 128–29; child sexual abuse and, 132–33; Christian Fundamentalism and, 127–28,

Satanic cult scares (*continued*)
136; daycare and, 133–34; feminism and, 132–33; pornography/sex industry and, 131–32; right-wing groups and, 127
Satan/Satanism, 88, 124–25; definition of, 4; God versus, 124; Lucifer and, 124; Neo-Nazis and, 4–5; underground of, 5
*Satan's Power* (Bainbridge), 131
*Satan's Underground* (Stratford), 121
*Scooby Doo*, 148
scourge, 32
"Searching for Satan," 134
Second Coming of Christ, 16
sex industry/pornography, 131–32
sexual abuse, of children, 132–33
Shamans/Shamanism, 1, 3, 39; core, 91–92; courses for, 91–92; indigenous practices of, 81; magic and, 81, 92, 97–98; mediums versus, 85; Native American practices and, 82, 88–89, 99; Neo-Shamanism, 99–100; New Age, 89–94, 97, 99, 101; Pagan, 94–97, 101; paradigms of, 82, 172n2; traditional indigenous, 83–86, 90, 101; traditional North American, 86–89, 100, 101, 172n6; urban, 97; Western, 83, 90, 94, 95, 96, 101
Shiite Sufism, 18
Shirokogoroff, Sergei, 82, 86, 99
Simos, Miriam. *See* Starhawk
*Sister*, 55
*Sixth and Seventh Books of Moses*, 113
skyclad, 32
slavery, 103
Smart, Ninian, 82, 83
*Snow White and the Seven Dwarfs*, 137
Sophia, 76–77, 172n24
*La Sorcière* (Michelet), 57
Southern Poverty Law Center (SPLC), 45–46
Spain, 110
spell casting, 63–64
*The Spiral Dance* (Starhawk), 20, 29, 37, 67, 68, 69, 152

Spiritual Frontiers Fellowship, 10
spiritualism, 7; American, 10; mission of, 11; New Age Movement and, 8, 11, 18, 19, 23
spirituality: of Afro-Caribbean religions, 114–17; of Goddess, 60, 65, 67, 70, 72, 74, 78; of Neopaganism, 29–30, 40–41; of Odinists/Odinism, 47. *See also* Espiritismo; feminist spirituality
Spretnak, Charlene, 71, 74
Starhawk, 20, 22, 29, 37–38, 41, 47–50, 67–70, 152
Stein, Diane, 162
Stone, Merlin, 66
*Stranger in a Strange Land* (Heinlein), 50
Stratford, Lauren, 121
Sulyma-Masson, Cheryl, 151, 152
Susan B. Anthony Coven Number 1, 61
swansk. *See* Shamans/Shamanism
Swedenborg, Emanuel, 10, 25
*Sweep Series*, 153

*The Tao of Physics* (Capra), 2
*The Teachings of Don Juan* (Castaneda), 90
techno-shamanic practices, 96–97
*Teen Witch* (RavenWolf), 153
television. *See* Witchcraft, commodification of
Temple of Set, 129, 130
"thealogy," 38, 67
theology: Dharmic, 11, 21; New Age, 19–22
Theosophy, 7; New Age and, 12–13, 19–20, 23; roots of, 10–11
"Three Ages of History" (de Fiore), 14
training: of Cella Priestess, 161; of Dianics, 70; of Witches, 30–31, 34–35, 70
trance possession, 115–16
Transcendentalism, 10, 12
Trismegistus, Hermes, 11
*Tweety*, 148

Unitarian Universalist Church, 70
urban Shamanism, 97

Valiente, Doreen, 32, 152
Villareal, Sara Aldrete, 122
*The Virtual Pagan*, 153
vision quest, 85, 92
Vitebsky, Piers, 86, 89
*Voices from the Pagan Census*, 47
Voodoo: as Afro-Caribbean religions, 3; Orisha-Voodoo as form of, 111, 174n17; Satanism and, 4

Walker, Barbara, 71
*The Way of the Shaman: A Guide to Power and Healing* (Harner), 91
Web of Life, 35, 80, 164
websites. *See* Witchcraft, commodification of
Western Paganism, 19, 22, 26
Western Shamanism, 83, 90, 94, 95, 96, 101
*What Witches Do* (Farrar), 152
*When God Was a Woman* (Stone), 66
*The White Goddess* (Graves), 65, 153
Wiccan Rede, 36, 63, 143
Wicca/Wiccans, 22, 26; British, 68; as Contemporary Witches, 28–33; Feminist, 62; Gardnerian, 61; magic and, 34–36; in North America, 36–40; resources for, 37–40; spread of, 37, 56, 57, 61; Witchcraft as, 137, 174n1
Wilson, Bryan, 13, 17
WITCH, 57–60, 61, 67
Witch Camps, 48, 68–70, 72, 159–60, 167
"Witch City." *See* Salem, Massachusetts
Witchcraft, 1, 26; background of, 2; in Canada, 37, 72, 171n21; commercialism of, 5–6; evil associated with, 4; feminist, 2, 38, 60–64, 68, 70, 171n6; Gardnerian, 31–33, 41; as legitimate religion, 5; magic and, 33–36, 54; nature celebrated in, 3; Neopaganism and, 2, 28–54; as Paganism, 137; resources for, 37–40; as Wicca, 137, 174n1. *See also* Contemporary Witchcraft
*Witchcraft and the Web: Weaving Pagan Traditions Online* (NightMare), 153
Witchcraft, commodification of, 165–68;

adult television drama in, 149–50; books and magazines in, 152–54, 175n9; children's fantasy television in, 148–49, 174n8; children's films in, 144–46; early films in, 139–40; early television in, 140–42; exchange relationship in, 157–59; films in, 142–44; mail-order catalogs in, 155, 164, 165; music festivals in, 162–63; music/magic in, 156–57; mystery schools in, 160, 175n17; pagan festivals/fairs in, 68–69, 161–62, 167; pagan newsletters in, 154–56; RCG-I relating to, 160–61; Salem ("Witch City") and, 138–39; symbolism in, 163–65; television specials/news in, 151–52; themes relating to, 137–38; websites in, 154–56, 175n15; Witch Camps in, 159–60, 167; young adult television in, 146–48
*Witchcraft Today* (Gardner), 31, 152
Witch Defense League, 139
Witches, 3–4; British Traditional, 39; definition of, 59–60, 170n4; Dianic, 55, 61–64, 67, 70, 75, 79; etheric energy of, 34; healing powers of, 35–36; Satanists and, 4; symbol of, 60, 171n5, 172n25; training of, 30–31, 34–35, 70
Witches' League for Public Awareness, 151
*The Witches of Eastwick*, 142, 166
*Witch's Ghost*, 148
"Witch wars," 30
*The Wizard of Oz*, 137, 139, 144
Woman-Church, 55
*WomanSpirit*, 58, 66, 71
*Women and Power*, 71
Women's Bureau, 56
*The Women's Encyclopedia of Myths and Secrets* (Walker), 71
World Council of Churches, 76
World Goodwill, 17
*Worst Witch*, 149

Yoruba: elements of, 3–4; healing within, 1; Lucumí relating to, 103–5, 115; Satanism and, 4